Ultimate Excel with Power Query and ChatGPT

Master MS Excel's Dynamic Lookup Functions, Generative AI, and Power Query to Navigate Data, Solve Complex Tasks and Optimize Productivity

Crispo Mwangi (MVP)

www.orangeava.com

Copyright © 2023, Orange Education Pvt Ltd, AVA™

All rights reserved. No part of this book may be reproduced, stored in a retrieval system, or transmitted in any form or by any means, without the prior written permission of the publisher, except in the case of brief quotations embedded in critical articles or reviews.

Every effort has been made in the preparation of this book to ensure the accuracy of the information presented. However, the information contained in this book is sold without warranty, either express or implied. Neither the author nor **Orange Education Pvt Ltd** or its dealers and distributors, will be held liable for any damages caused or alleged to have been caused directly or indirectly by this book.

Orange Education Pvt Ltd has endeavored to provide trademark information about all of the companies and products mentioned in this book by the appropriate use of capital. However **Orange Education Pvt Ltd** cannot guarantee the accuracy of this information. The use of general descriptive names, registered names, trademarks, service marks, etc. in this publication does not imply, even in the absence of a specific statement, that such names are exempt from the relevant protective laws and regulations and therefore free for general use.

Excel®, Microsoft®, Power BI® and other such products/services are trademarks of the Microsoft Corporation, Inc.

First published: December 2023
Published by: Orange Education Pvt Ltd, AVA™
Address: 9, Daryaganj, Delhi, 110002

ISBN: 978-81-96782-61-0

www.orangeava.com

Dedicated To

All Excel and Data Analysis Lovers!

Whether you are a Beginner or an Expert

About the Author

Crispo Mwangi is a globally recognized Microsoft Most Valuable Professional (MVP) in Excel, a distinguished Microsoft Certified Trainer, and an Excel Expert accredited by Microsoft Office. With an illustrious career spanning over a decade, Crispo is not just an expert in Excel but a true trailblazer in the world of technology and data management.

Renowned for his exceptional leadership in the technology community, Crispo is more than just an expert; he is a mentor, guiding individuals worldwide with unparalleled expertise and passion. His commitment to knowledge sharing is unparalleled, evident through his high-quality blogs and comprehensive training programs, which have empowered countless individuals to harness the full potential of Excel.

Beyond his technical prowess, Crispo embodies the spirit of community, always willing to extend a helping hand and provide objective feedback. His ability to unravel complexities and simplify intricate Excel functions has made him a trusted resource for professionals and enthusiasts alike.

About the Technical Reviewers

Vijay A. Verma, an expert in Excel, Power BI, SQL, Python, R, Data Analytics, VBA, and Dashboard, provides support on the Microsoft and Power BI Community for Excel and Power BI. He is widely recognized as Excel BI, running the highly popular and critically acclaimed Excel and Power Query Challenges on LinkedIn. As a moderator on the MS Answers Excel forum and a Super User on the Power BI Forum, he is sought after for his expertise in addressing Excel and Power BI issues by the community. Moreover, he is the author of the popular free-of-cost ebook - Excel Formula Bible. Additionally, he manages a blog - Excel BI Analytics – aimed at benefiting the Excel, Power BI, and Analytics community.

LinkedIn profile: https://www.linkedin.com/in/excelbi/

Shubhi Aggarwal, an accomplished Data Analyst and Microsoft Certified Trainer, excels in the intricate language of data and analytics tools, including Microsoft Excel, PowerPoint, Word, Microsoft Power BI, and Tableau, transforming raw data into meaningful insights. With an intimate understanding of the Extract, Transform, Load (ETL) cycle, she brings a meticulous approach to data analysis, extracting actionable intelligence and decoding complex datasets. Her international experience enriches her analytical toolkit, positioning her as an asset in a data-driven world without boundaries. In her world, every dataset is a canvas for insights. Whether unraveling Excel spreadsheets, crafting compelling stories through PowerPoint presentations, or creating visually stunning dashboards using Power BI and Tableau, she transforms data into powerful narratives.

Shubhi Aggarwal isn't just an analyst; she is a storyteller in the language of data, crafting narratives that empower organizations to make informed decisions.

https://www.linkedin.com/in/shubhi-aggarwal-182a3918/

Acknowledgements

First and foremost, I extend my deepest gratitude to the readers – your curiosity and enthusiasm for Excel and data management inspire me every day. Your continuous support fuels my passion for exploring the limitless possibilities within the realm of Excel.

To my dedicated team of editors, researchers, and illustrators, your meticulous attention to detail and unwavering commitment have transformed ideas into meticulously crafted manuscripts. Your expertise and dedication have been invaluable, and I am fortunate to have had the opportunity to collaborate with each one of you.

I extend my thanks to my mentors and colleagues whose guidance and insights have been instrumental in shaping my understanding of data management. Your wisdom has been a guiding light throughout my journey, and I am deeply appreciative of your generosity in sharing your knowledge.

Special appreciation goes to my family and friends for their unwavering support and encouragement. Your belief in my work has been a driving force, and I cherish the moments of inspiration and camaraderie we have shared.

Lastly, I express my heartfelt thanks to the entire community of data enthusiasts, Excel aficionados, and analytics professionals. Your passion for the subject matter ignites a collective spirit of exploration and learning, and I am honored to be a part of this vibrant community.

This book stands as a testament to the collaborative efforts of many, and I am profoundly grateful to each and every one of you. Together, we continue to push the boundaries of knowledge and redefine the landscape of data management and analytics in Excel.

Preface

In the ever-evolving landscape of data management and analytics, mastering Excel's lookup functions is not just a skill but a cornerstone of efficient data handling. "*Ultimate Excel with Power Query and ChatGPT*" is more than just a book; it's a guide crafted for data enthusiasts, Excel aficionados, and anyone aiming to harness the full potential of Excel's lookup capabilities.

This book embarks on a transformative journey through Excel's lookup functionalities, navigating from the traditional methods to the trailblazing techniques that define the current era of data management. Each chapter unfolds a new dimension, debunking myths, unraveling complexities, introducing nested functions, and providing hands-on solutions to real-world data lookup dilemmas.

By the end of each chapter, you will not only master the focused lookup function but also learn many other nested functions, expanding your knowledge of Excel.

This book is divided into nine chapters. They will cover a range from Excel basics and basic lookup functions to the advanced use of AI in Excel. The details are listed below.

Chapter 1: The chapter will introduce the basics of Excel. You will learn why you need to develop Excel skills and the general steps to follow to master these skills. We will explore the world of Excel formulas and functions, including nesting or combining functions. Additionally, we will cover the basics of Excel cell referencing and using Excel tables.

Chapter 2: The chapter will introduce the most used Lookup function in Excel – VLOOKUP. It will highlight its challenges and provide a workaround to those challenges by showing how nesting other functions can help overcome VLOOKUP default settings.

Chapter 3: The chapter will introduce a combo of functions that Excel users have come to regard as one lookup function – INDEX and MATCH. We will explore how the individual functions work and how their combination is the second most widely used method for looking up data. After that, we will investigate situations where this combo is better than the VLOOKUP function.

Chapter 4: The LOOKUP function is as old as Excel itself. It has been there since 1985. Unlike its successor, VLOOKUP, the LOOKUP function has one unique feature – it can handle arrays. This chapter will investigate its usefulness 35 years later, particularly in areas where it is a better choice.

Chapter 5: Apart from what Excel classifies as lookup functions, there are different ways of looking up data in Excel. This chapter investigates the different ways and functions that one can use to look up data. We will learn some rarely discussed methods, such as the use of Excel intersection, advanced filters, database functions, and the use of pivot tables.

Chapter 6: Released in 2019, XLOOKUP was the most hyped release of any function. It was termed as the most powerful lookup function in Excel. The chapter will investigate scenarios where XLOOKUP could be the preferred lookup function.

Chapter 7: Although it did not receive as much publicity as XLOOKUP, the FILTER function compensates for all the shortcomings in the previous lookup functions. This chapter will explore areas where FILTER is the ultimate lookup function. We will also look at its shortcomings and how to work around them.

Chapter 8: Power Query has been hailed as the ultimate extract, load, and transform add-in for Excel, but it can also be used to look up data. This chapter will explore how Power Query can be used to create solutions for novice users who are afraid of tinkering with the functions.

Chapter 9: This chapter will discuss how to incorporate artificial intelligence (AI) into solving lookup problems in Excel. We will explore topics such as what is ChatGPT and how can we get the best out of it. By the end of this chapter, you will be able to understand the nuances of prompting and leveraging ChatGPT for accurate and tailored responses.

Downloading the code bundles and colored images

Please follow the link to download the
Code Bundles of the book:

https://github.com/ava-orange-education/Ultimate-Excel-with-Power-Query-and-ChatGPT

The code bundles and images of the book are also hosted on
https://rebrand.ly/zlukuby

In case there's an update to the code, it will be updated on the existing GitHub repository.

Errata

We take immense pride in our work at **Orange Education Pvt Ltd,** and follow best practices to ensure the accuracy of our content to provide an indulging reading experience to our subscribers. Our readers are our mirrors, and we use their inputs to reflect and improve upon human errors, if any, that may have occurred during the publishing processes involved. To let us maintain the quality and help us reach out to any readers who might be having difficulties due to any unforeseen errors, please write to us at :

errata@orangeava.com

Your support, suggestions, and feedback are highly appreciated.

DID YOU KNOW

Did you know that Orange Education Pvt Ltd offers eBook versions of every book published, with PDF and ePub files available? You can upgrade to the eBook version at **www.orangeava.com** and as a print book customer, you are entitled to a discount on the eBook copy. Get in touch with us at: **info@orangeava.com** for more details.

At **www.orangeava.com**, you can also read a collection of free technical articles, sign up for a range of free newsletters, and receive exclusive discounts and offers on AVA™ Books and eBooks.

PIRACY

If you come across any illegal copies of our works in any form on the internet, we would be grateful if you would provide us with the location address or website name. Please contact us at **info@orangeava.com** with a link to the material.

ARE YOU INTERESTED IN AUTHORING WITH US?

If there is a topic that you have expertise in, and you are interested in either writing or contributing to a book, please write to us at **business@orangeava.com**. We are on a journey to help developers and tech professionals to gain insights on the present technological advancements and innovations happening across the globe and build a community that believes Knowledge is best acquired by sharing and learning with others. Please reach out to us to learn what our audience demands and how you can be part of this educational reform. We also welcome ideas from tech experts and help them build learning and development content for their domains.

REVIEWS

Please leave a review. Once you have read and used this book, why not leave a review on the site that you purchased it from? Potential readers can then see and use your unbiased opinion to make purchase decisions. We at Orange Education would love to know what you think about our products, and our authors can learn from your feedback. Thank you!

For more information about Orange Education, please visit **www.orangeava.com**.

Table of Contents

1. **Excel Environment** 1
   - Introduction 1
   - Structure 1
   - Reasons for Learning Excel 2
   - How to Master Excel 2
     - STEP 1: Love Mistakes 2
     - STEP 2: Master the Basics 3
     - STEP 3: Progressive Overload 3
     - STEP 4: Learn to Break your Problem into Small Pieces 4
     - STEP 5: Teach 4
     - STEP 6: Participate in Excel Forums 5
     - STEP 7: Daily Intentional Learning 5
   - Introducing Excel formulas and functions 6
   - Nesting functions: When one is not enough 9
     - Resolving Complexity in Nesting Function 10
     - Nesting Function Rules 11
   - Introducing Excel Cell Referencing 11
     - Types of Cell References 12
   - Introducing Excel Tables 14
   - Importance of having lookup skills 18
   - Classification of Lookup Functions 19
   - Conclusion 19
     - Question 20

2. **VLOOKUP Is Dead: Or is it?** 21
   - Introduction 21
   - Structure 21
   - VLOOKUP exact and approximate match 22
     - VLOOKUP approximate match 23
     - Breaking VLOOKUP myths 25

  Myth 1: VLOOKUP cannot do a left lookup 25

  Myth 2: VLOOKUP cannot return multiple columns in a lookup 26

  Myth 3: VLOOKUP cannot use multiple criteria in a lookup 26

  Myth 4: VLOOKUP cannot handle the insertion
  and deletion of olumns in the lookup range 28

  Myth 5: VLOOKUP cannot do a two-way lookup 29

  Myth 6: VLOOKUP cannot do a partial match lookup 30

  Myth 7: VLOOKUP cannot do a case-sensitive partial
  match lookup 32

  Myth 8: VLOOKUP cannot do a case-sensitive lookup 33

  Myth 9: VLOOKUP cannot return multiple results 34

  Myth 10: VLOOKUP cannot lookup from last to first 36

  Myth 11: VLOOKUP cannot lookup the top or bottom N values 37

  Myth 12: VLOOKUP cannot do a reverse lookup 39

  Myth 13: VLOOKUP cannot do a horizontal lookup 41

  Myth 14: VLOOKUP cannot return multiple
  non-contiguous columns 43

  Myth 15: VLOOKUP cannot lookup multiple
  non-contiguous arrays 44

 Conclusion 45

 Points to remember 46

3. INDEX and MATCH **47**

 Introduction 47

 Structure 47

 INDEX, MATCH, and the two-way lookup 48

 Three-way lookup 52

 Reverse-lookup single result 53

 Reverse-lookup multiple results 55

 Multiple criteria lookup 57

 Returning multiple columns 59

 Horizontal lookup 60

 Lookup non-contiguous array 60

 Lookup using wildcards 62

| Lookup based on text length 64
       Lookup items in a list...66
              Lookup unique value...68
       Lookup bottom ***n*** values 69
       Conclusion... 71
       Points to remember 72
4. LOOKUP...**73**
       Introduction.. 73
       Structure... 74
       Lookup the Last Match Using a Criterion 74
       Lookup the Last Blank Cell..77
       Lookup the Last Negative Number or Text 78
       Lookup Approximate Match in an Array..80
       Lookup Most Repeated Item.. 81
       Conclusion...83
       Points to remember 83
       Multiple choice questions 83
       Answers 85
5. Other LOOKUP Methods and Functions...**86**
       Introduction..86
       Structure..86
       Using the advanced filter to lookup items in/not in a list...................... 87
       Using Excel Intersection Operator to do a two-way lookup...................89
       Using Database functions to lookup numeric data................................93
       Using SUMIFS, SUMPRODUCT, AGGREGATE, and
       MAX functions to lookup numeric data..95
       Looking up images...101
       Looking up cell addresses 105
       Using Pivot Table to lookup unique items in a list.............................. 106
       Conclusion... 109
       Points to remember 109

6. XLOOKUP 110

Introduction 110
Structure 110
Exact match default 111
Easily returns multiple adjacent and non-adjacent columns 113
Easily lookup data to the left or right 115
Easily accommodates column insertion/deletion 116
Easily looks up data vertically or horizontally 118
Easily lookup data from the bottom up 118
Easily integrates wildcards in the lookup 120
Returns a cell reference 122
Returns values in case of No Match 124
Easily do a three-way lookup 124
Easily returns non-adjacent columns 126
Returns the last/first non-empty cell 129
Easily lookup non-contiguous array 130
Easily returns duplicate lookup values 131
Conclusion 132
Points to remember 133
Multiple choice questions 133
Answers 134

7. FILTER: The Ultimate Lookup Function 135

Introduction 135
Structure 135
Return multiple columns and rows 136
Return multiple non-adjacent columns and rows 138
Easily use multiple criteria lookups using AND/OR 140
Easily lookup all X and not Y items 142
Easily lookup top or bottom n items 144
Easily lookup X or Y and not both 145
Looking up data using wildcards 146
Looking up weekday or weekend data 147

Looking up data that excludes holidays and weekends 148
Looking up ODD/EVEN numbers 149
Looking up items repeated N times 150
Looking up items based on time 152
Looking up data based on week number, month, and year 153
Lookup common/uncommon items in two lists 155
Return end-of-the-month date items only 156
Conclusion 157
Points to remember 158
Quiz 158
Answers 159

8. Power Query: One-Stop Solution 160

Introduction 160
Structure 161
Installing the Power Query add-in for Excel 2010 and Excel 2013 161
Exact Lookup 162
Return multiple results and multiple columns 168
Approximate Lookup 169
Lookup using table joins 174
Looking up the top or bottom n items 177
Lookup using the List function 179
Looking up Weekday versus Weekend data 182
Looking up date that excludes holidays 184
Looking up items repeated N times 185
Return end-of-month date items only 188
Fuzzy Lookup 190
Conclusion 192
Points to remember 192
Multiple choice questions 193
Answers 194

9. **ChatGPT: Using ChatGPT to solve lookup issues** 195
   Introduction 195
   Structure 196
   Setting up ChatGPT for optimal results 196
   Mastering the perfect ChatGPT prompt 198
   Increasing Accuracy of ChatGPT Prompts 200
   Tips and tricks to advanced ChatGPT usage 202
   Beyond ChatGPT 203
   Conclusion 204
   Points to remember 205
   Multiple choice questions 205
   Answers 206

   Index 207-211

CHAPTER 1
Excel Environment

Introduction

This chapter will introduce us to the basics of Excel. You will learn why you need to develop Excel skills and the general steps to follow to master these skills.

We will explore the world of Excel formulas and functions, including nesting or combining functions. We will also cover the basics of Excel cell referencing and using Excel tables.

Since the book is about the 101 ways to look up anything in Excel, we will dive into the world of Excel lookup skills and why they are a door to mastering Excel. Finally, we will dig into the different classifications of the lookup functions.

Structure

In this chapter, we will discuss the following topics:

- Why you should learn Excel?
- How to Master Excel
- Introducing Excel formulas and functions
- Nesting functions: When one is not enough
- Introducing Excel Cell referencing: full column/row, range reference, named reference, absolute, relative, and mixed references
- Introducing Excel tables
- Importance of having lookup skills
- Classification of lookup functions:
    - Old-Version: Legacy array functions
    - Dynamic Array Functions
    - Power Query

Reasons for Learning Excel

Excel is one of the most powerful spreadsheet tools used by millions of people worldwide to analyze, manage, and visualize data. It is extensively used in different industries, such as finance, engineering, logistics, medicine, mining, and operations.

Surveys conducted by two global research consultants (Spiceworks in 2018 and Censuswide in 2019) reveal that over 69% of professionals use Excel regularly, with 57% using it at least once a day. Additionally, 59% of companies with over 500 employees use Excel for data analysis.

Therefore, you are likely to use Excel if your work involves data manipulation or analysis, irrespective of your industry.

At a personal level, Excel is beneficial for organizing information: it is easy to organize and store data in a structured format, create, retrieve, and simply update information. This makes it helpful in maintaining personal budget keeping, tracking personal items, and even creating daily to-do lists.

Developing your Excel abilities is one of the ways to advance your career in today's data-driven business environment. It enhances your productivity by improving your efficiency and effectiveness at tasks that call for data management, analysis, and reporting. A productive worker is a sure-fire candidate for job promotions.

In conclusion, Excel's ubiquity and versatility make acquiring and advancing Excel-related skills necessary for any professional.

How to Master Excel

Having used and trained others on Excel for over a decade, we have identified six steps to accelerate acquiring and advancing Excel skills.

These are the steps that have been followed and taught to others, resulting in impressive results.

STEP 1: Love Mistakes

Learning from mistakes is one of the most underrated steps in acquiring any skill.

Learning from mistakes contributes far more than one can acquire from reading theories and practicing without making mistakes. Mistakes provide valuable feedback that helps you refine your technique and improve your performance.

Therefore, a love of mistakes frees you from the decapitating fear of failure and helps you build resilience and persistence.

With the ability to love and learn from our mistakes, we can achieve our goal of acquiring and improving any skill in our chosen field. That is why this is the first step towards mastering Excel skills.

STEP 2: Master the Basics

Mastering the basics is one of the most belittled steps in acquiring any skill, as it seems boring and repetitive. Yet, the basics form the foundation for more advanced techniques. With a strong understanding of the fundamentals, it becomes easier to progress and improve in any given area.

Other hindrances to mastering the basics include eagerness to achieve quick results and placing greater value on advanced skills, believing they are more impressive or essential.

For example, a user wants to start using the nested INDEX and MATCH functions without first understanding the basics of nesting functions and using the individual functions.

In this book, we will devote time to building this foundation as it helps build complex functions.

STEP 3: Progressive Overload

Acquiring and advancing a skill is like building muscles. You need to challenge yourself through progressive overload.

Mastering the basics is essential but sticking to the basics is detrimental to mastering Excel and any other skill.

Mastering requires consistent practice, increasing the difficulty gradually, tracking progress, and seeking feedback and guidance from experts and colleagues.

To promote continued growth and improvement, the concepts taught in the book will move from basic to complex.

STEP 4: Learn to Break your Problem into Small Pieces

How do you eat an elephant? The answer is *"One Bite at a Time"*.

In other words, when faced with a big, complex task, it can seem impossible to tackle it all at once. However, if you break it down into smaller, more manageable pieces, you can approach it one step at a time until you eventually achieve your goal.

For example, how easily can you memorize the number "12110081644936251694"?

The hint is to break it down into small pieces and observe the pattern. (See the answer at the end of the chapter).

Complex tasks in Excel require some formulas with over five nested functions. Understanding a nested function is easy if you know how each function contributes to the formula.

Metaphorically speaking, this is the art of seeing single trees in a forest.

STEP 5: Teach

Teaching is one of the scariest things for a novice, yet this is an essential step in advancing any skill. Fear of failure and lack of confidence stop the beginner from reaping the benefits of teaching.

When you teach someone else, you must organize your thoughts and articulate the information clearly and concisely.

Explaining a concept to another person requires you to fully understand the material yourself and anticipate questions and potential misunderstandings that your student may have. By doing this, you can identify gaps in your knowledge and fill in those gaps, thereby improving your understanding.

The statement "*When you teach, you learn twice*" is a common proverb suggesting that teaching others can be a powerful way to reinforce and deepen your understanding of a topic.

To advance your Excel skills, you need to be comfortable teaching others the little you have learned so that it can stick.

STEP 6: Participate in Excel Forums

Online connections have made the world a village. You can access world-class experts, discussions, and training from anywhere.

Joining and participating in Excel forums is vital for two reasons as follows:

1. It gives you access to online students where you can practice your teaching. As discussed in the previous section, teaching is essential to mastering Excel.

2. It provides an excellent opportunity for passive and unintentional learning. In these forums, you will encounter many lessons, tips, and tricks you would never have thought of.

Some recommended forums are Excel Microsoft Answers, Excel Microsoft Tech Community, Excel Stack Overflow, and Reddit Excel.

STEP 7: Daily Intentional Learning

Intentional learning differs from spontaneous learning in that purposeful learning is a conscious effort to acquire knowledge for a specific purpose.

For example, every chapter in this book covers a different method of looking up data in Excel. You will engage in intentional learning if you set a specific period daily to study each chapter.

It involves setting clear goals, actively seeking information, and engaging in deliberate practice to improve one's abilities. This requires the willingness to invest time and effort in the learning process.

Daily intentional learning improves the learner's confidence in teaching others, leading to deeper understanding. The user enter the productivity circle of learning to teach and teaching to learn:

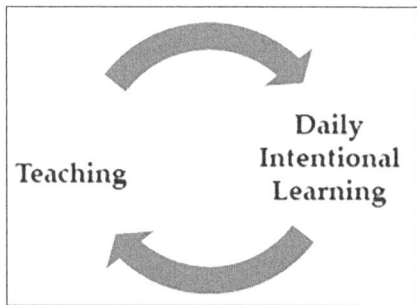

Figure 1.1: *Productivity circle*

This is not an attempt to downplay the benefits of incidental learning (learning something unintentionally while engaged in some other activity) or accidental learning (learning something by chance). Benefits can be gained from these as well, but the intentional learning benefits outweigh all other forms of learning.

Introducing Excel formulas and functions

Excel formulas and functions are the core of Excel. You must learn formulas and functions to fully utilize Excel and improve productivity.

In Excel, a formula combines operations used for calculations, data manipulation, or generating results from data on a worksheet. It may contain cell references, arithmetic operators, numbers, or functions.

For example, in *Figure 1.2*, how do you get the total payments per invoice using a formula?

	A	B	C	D	E	F	G	H
1				Daily Payments				formula
2			Invoice #	2/1/23	2/15/23	3/1/23	3/20/23	3/5/23	Total Payment
3			100	70,000	35,000	55,800	60,900	45,000	266,700
4			101	16,000	77,100	88,900	95,200	18,800	296,000
5			102	54,200	93,500	89,300	67,100	19,300	323,400
6			103	69,600	17,900	54,700	11,000	24,900	178,100
7			104	14,300	29,900	53,000	74,800	82,200	254,200

H3 fx =C3+D3+E3+F3+G3

Figure 1.2: *Using a formula in Excel*

The formula used in the figure contains the arithmetic operators (=, +) and cell references (C3, D3, E3, F3, G3). We will discuss more cell references later in the chapter.

On the other hand, a function is a pre-defined set of instructions or formulas **already built-in** and can be used to perform various operations on data.

For example, in *Figure 1.3*, how do you get the total payments per invoice using a function?

Excel Environment

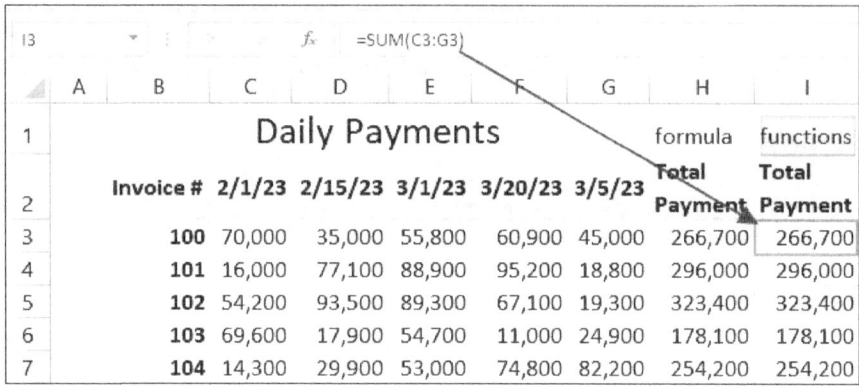

Figure 1.3: *Using a Sum function in Excel*

The function used in *Figure* 1.3 contains the arithmetic operators (=), cell range references (C3:G3), and an inbuilt function name (**SUM**).

NOTE

Both the formula and the function should start with an equal sign (=).

Some users start with a plus sign (+), and others go overboard by starting with both equal and plus sign (= +)

We can also have a complex formula, which will be a combination of operations and functions.

Excel has over 500 functions, but you only need to learn some to be productive. This number keeps growing with the introduction of the LAMBDA function, which gives users the power to create their own functions.

These functions are classified as mathematical, statistical, financial, logical, text, date and time, lookup and reference, engineering, and more. This book focuses on the lookup and reference group and how they relate to the other groups.

The following are the most common features of all functions:

- **Composition**: All Excel functions have a standard structure that determines how they are entered into a cell, that is, always starting with an equal sign, followed by the function name, and then one or more or no arguments in parentheses, separated by commas.

    For example, the IF function has three arguments, which Excel IntelliSense will outline, while the **TODAY** function has zero arguments:

    ```
    =IF(Logical_Test, Value_if_True, Value_if_False)
    =Today()
    ```

- **Arguments:** Arguments are the values or cell references the function uses to perform a specific calculation. Each function has a different number and type of arguments required to work correctly. Any argument inside the square brackets means it is optional and thus can be skipped, and the function still works well.
- **Results:** Every Excel function returns a result based on the input arguments and the functional classification. For example, all functions classified as text functions will always result in text data type results.
- **Compatible:** Excel functions work well together, allowing you to utilize the result of one function as the input for another function. This is called nesting functions, which will be covered later in the chapter. Nesting capability permits you to design intricate calculations and formulas.
- **Built-in:** All Excel functions are built-in, meaning they are part of the Excel software and do not need to be installed separately. However, functions are only available in different versions of Excel. For example, you can only access dynamic array formulas in Office 365.
- **Accessibility:** Excel functions are easily accessible through the Formula bar (*Figure* 1.4) and the Function Wizard:

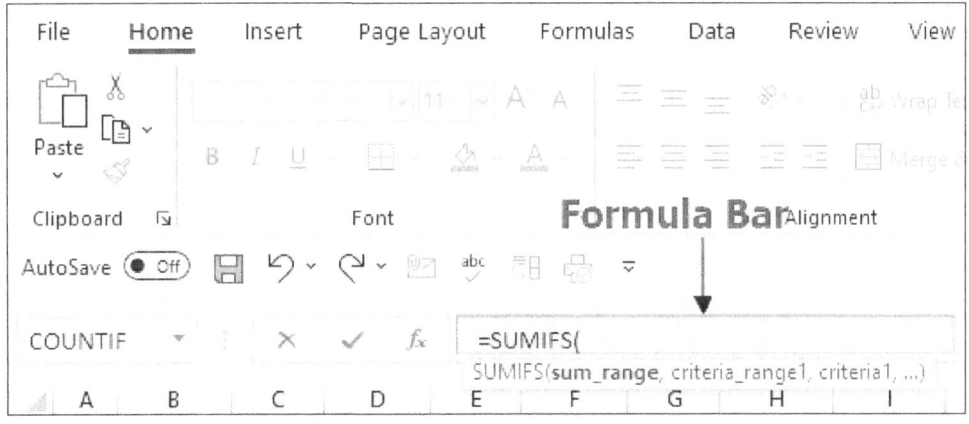

Figure **1.4**: *Accessing function through the formula bar*

Or, by typing the function directly into a cell (*Figure* 1.5):

Excel Environment

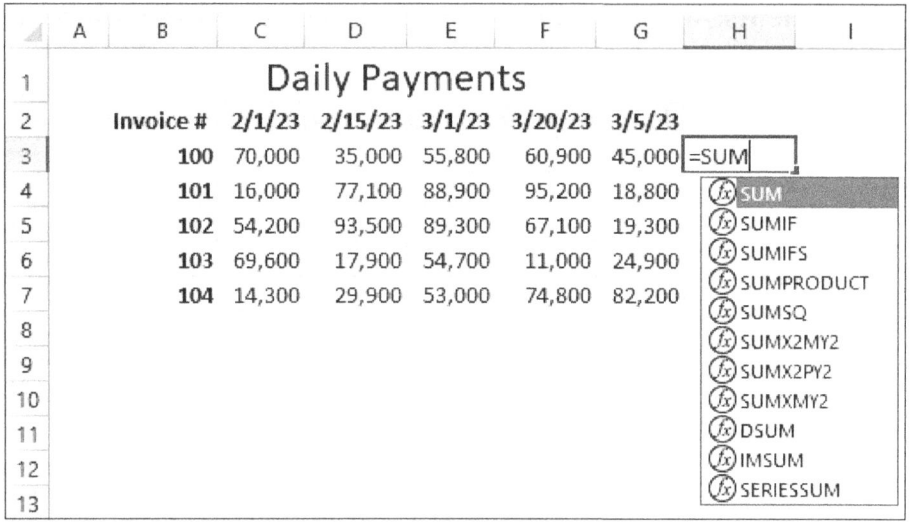

Figure 1.5: Accessing function by typing directly into a cell

Nesting functions: When one is not enough

Nesting functions in Excel are the ultimate skill for performing complex calculations and manipulating data. By using multiple functions in combination, you can perform tasks that would be difficult or impossible to do with just one function alone.

So, what does it mean to nest a function?

To nest a function in Excel is to use the result of one function as an input for another function. You can do this as often as possible to create complex formulas that perform multiple calculations.

For example, in *Figure 1.6*, how do we mark only invoices due in January with an amount greater than or equal to 50,000 as a priority?

What you will realize is that there is no single function in Excel that will help you solve the preceding task. This calls for a nested formula, as shown here:

```
=IF(
AND(MONTH(I3)=1, J3>=50000 ),
"YES","NO")
```

How does this function work?

First, you need to realize that the IF function on its own can only handle a single logical test. Since our task has two analytical tests, you need to nest the **AND** function inside the IF function.

Secondly, you will realize that the first logical test requires a month comparison, yet your data contains dates. Therefore, you must convert the dates to months by nesting the **MONTH** function inside the **AND** function.

In summary, here is how the three functions work together, starting from the innermost function:

- **MONTH** function returns the moth part of a date. These results are used in the first logical test of the **AND** function to check if the month is January (1).
- AND function evaluates the two logical tests (check if the month is January and the amount is greater than or equal to 50,000) and returns a TRUE/FALSE result used by the IF function to determine whether the priority is **YES/NO**.

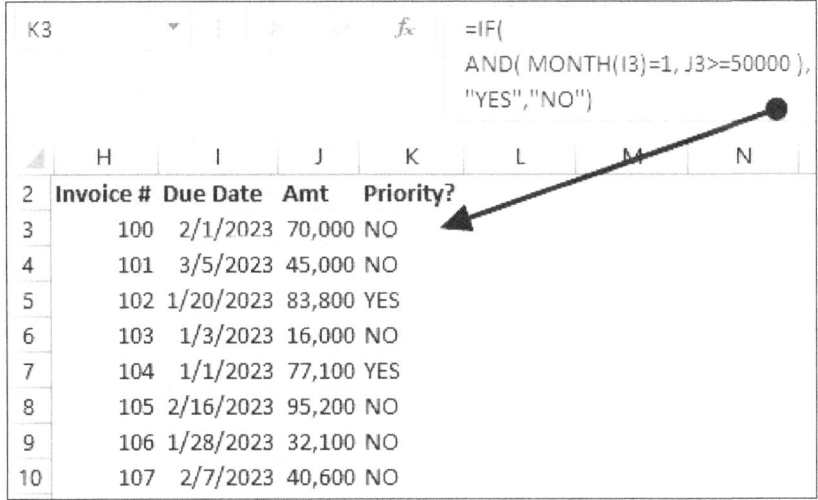

Figure 1.6: *Nesting function*

Resolving Complexity in Nesting Function

Let's learn how to solve complexity in nesting function:

- Use brackets color codes to ensure that all nested function arguments are within brackets. The outermost function's brackets are always black; for the nested functions, the opening and closing brackets are the same color.

- Another option is to ensure that every time you write a function, it is followed by opening and closing brackets before you key in the arguments.
- Utilize Excel's function IntelliSense to show which function and what argument you are working on.
- Use named ranges and tables' structured references to make your functions more readable.
- Always use the F9 shortcut to evaluate the results of each function.

Nesting Function Rules

Here are some rules to follow in nesting functions:

- An equal sign should not precede all nested functions. Only the outermost function should be preceded by an equal sign.
- All nested functions **MUST** return the same data type as the argument it replaces in the function. Using our preceding example, the **AND** function must return a Boolean data type since this is what the logical test argument in the **IF** function requires.
- All nested functions must follow Excel's order of operation: PEDMAS (Parentheses, Exponents, Multiplication, Division, Addition, Subtraction)
- Nested functions get evaluated from the innermost to the outermost function.

Introducing Excel Cell Referencing

Each cell in Excel is identified by a unique combination of a column letter and a row number called "cell address".

For example, the cell located in the first column and the first row is called "A1", and the cell located in the second column and the third row is called "B3".

When you create a formula in Excel, you can either hardcode the data (for example, `SUM(10, 12)`) or refer to data stored in cells by their cell addresses (for example, `SUM(A1, A2)`). This is called a cell reference.

Cell references are an essential concept in Excel, and understanding how to use them effectively can help you manipulate and analyze data with greater efficiency and accuracy.

Types of Cell References

The following types of cell references are observed in Excel:

- **Full Row/Full Column reference**: If you want to select all 1,048,576 rows in column A, then use a full-column reference (**A:A**). Otherwise, if you want to select all the data in 16,384 columns in row one, use the full row reference (**1:1**).

    We highly discourage the use of full-row and full-column references for two reasons:

    o There could be an invalid value far in the column/row beyond your view, affecting your analysis.

    o It can cause slow spreadsheet calculation because Excel has to check all 1,048,576 rows or 16,384 columns.

- **Cells Range reference**: It refers to a block of cells on a worksheet with a starting and ending cell address, unlike a full column/row reference. It can be a block in the same column (for example, A1:A26), a block in the same column (for example, A1:K1), or a combination of rows and columns (for example, A1:F26).

    This allows you to perform calculations, formatting, or other operations on multiple cells at once, instead of having to do them individually.

    For example, in *Figure 1.7*, the sum per invoice (=SUM(C3:G3), a cell range in a row), sum per date (=SUM(C3:C7), a cell range in a column), and overall totals (=**SUM**(C3:G7), cell ranges in both columns and rows).

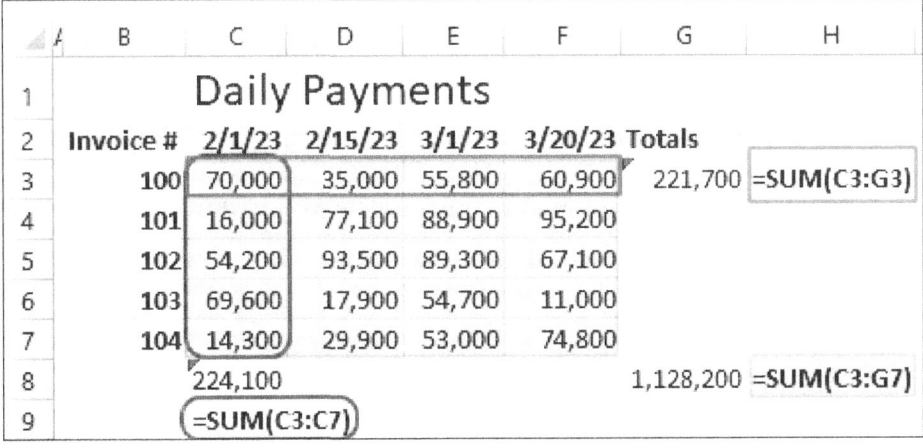

Figure 1.7: *Cell Range Reference*

- **Named Range reference**: This is a way to refer to a range of cells in a spreadsheet by a name instead of using the traditional cell reference discussed here. To create a named range in Excel, perform the following steps:
  - Select the range of cells you want to name, then go to the "Formulas" tab and click on "Define Name". Alternatively, you can use the keyboard shortcut **Alt + M + M + D**.
  - In the new name pop-up window, give your range a name and define its scope (do you want to access it in the whole workbook or just the worksheet it is created).

  Once created, these named ranges can be used in formulas and functions just like you use a cell reference. For example, if you have named a range `Invoice100` created from cell range C3:G3, you could refer to it in a formula like this:

  `=SUM(Invoice100)`

  This formula works like the `=SUM(C3:G3)` discussed earlier. Using named ranges can make your formulas and functions easier to read and understand.

  Here are some rules to consider while creating named ranges:
  - The name should be descriptive, without spaces or special characters, and not start with a number.
  - Avoid relative cell references and use absolute cell references for your named range. The difference between relative and absolute references is discussed in the next section.
  - Finally, keep your names as short, simple as possible, and consistent across your workbook.
- **Relative, Absolute, and Mixed Cell references**: All cell references default to relative reference, that is, they change their location relative to the position of the formula when copied or moved to a new cell.

  For example, if you have a formula in cell C1, references of cell range A1:B1, and copy the formula to cell D1, the reference will change to B1:C1.

  On the other hand, absolute references always point to the same cell or range, regardless of where the formula is copied or moved. To tell if it is an absolute reference, check if there is a dollar sign ($) before the column letter and row number.

For example, if you want to make a cell range A1:B1 absolute, the easiest way is to highlight the range and press F4, which changes to **$A$1: $B$1**. When the formula is copied or moved, the reference will remain **$A$1: $B$1**.

Mixed references have a combination of relative and absolute components, with either the row or column reference being absolute while the other is relative.

For example, if you have a formula that references cell A1:A10 and you want the column to be absolute but the row to be relative, you would use **$A1:$A10**. When the formula is copied or moved, it will always reference column A, but the row reference will change according to the position of the formula.

Otherwise, if you want the columns to be relative and rows absolute, use **A$1: B$1**. When the formula is copied or moved, it will always reference row 1, but the column reference will change according to the position of the formula.

Introducing Excel Tables

Assume you want to carry ten bulky items; what will be easier? Putting them in a container or trying to arrange them on your hands? Of course, putting them in a container is the easiest method.

Excel tables are just containers that help you easily organize, analyze, and present data concisely, saving you time by automating specific tasks. In addition, it allows for quick sorting and filtering of data, which can help you find patterns or trends in your data.

Furthermore, Excel tables also allow you to use structured references in formulas, making your formulas more readable and easier to maintain. For example, instead of referencing cells by their cell addresses, you can use a formula like **=SUM (tblSales[Amount])**, that is, total all data in a column called **Amount** in a table called Sales.

Excel Environment

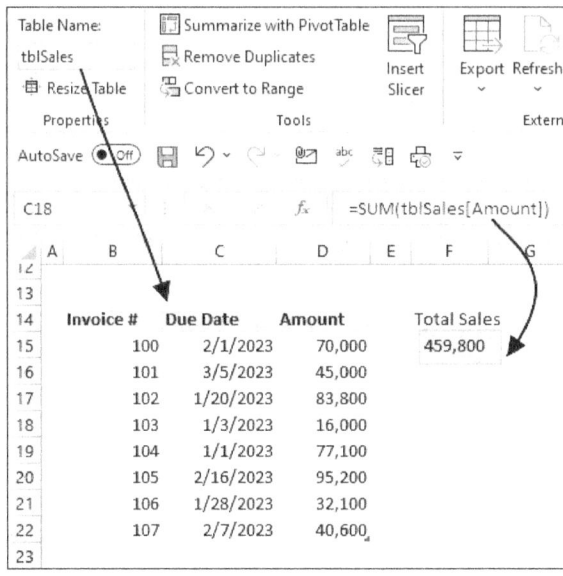

Figure 1.8: Use structured references in formulas

Perform the following steps to Create Tables:

- Ensure there is no blank row or column in between your data.
- Select All using the shortcut **Ctrl + A**.
- Go to the Home tab, select Format as a Table, or use the shortcut **Ctrl + T**. A pop-up window will appear (see *Figure* 1.9) showing the data range formatted as a table. If the first row in your data range contains the heading, tick the My table has headers checkbox. Otherwise, Excel will create an extra row for headers on top of your range.

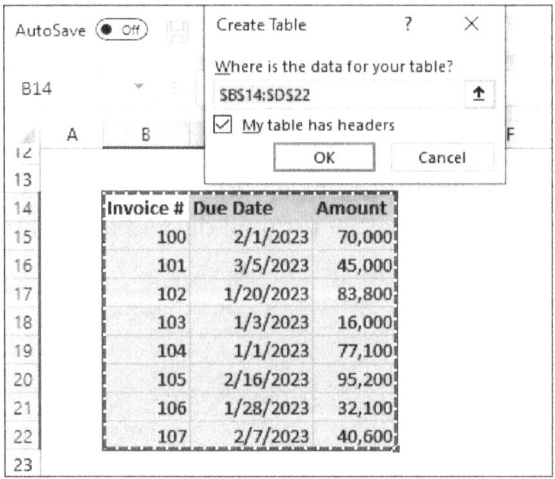

Figure 1.9: Creating a table in Excel

- Click anywhere on the table, go to the **Table Design** tab, and assign a descriptive name to your table. By default, Excel gives a generic table (see *Figure 1.10*):

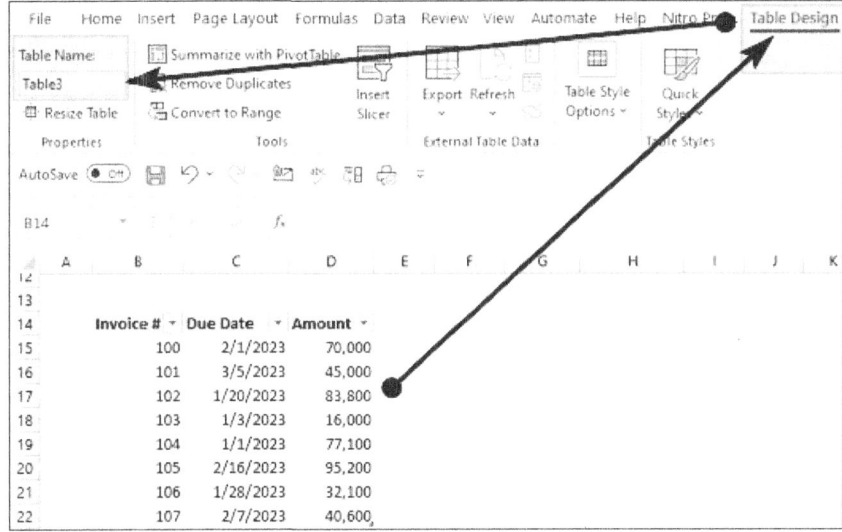

Figure 1.10: *Renaming your table*

- To convert the table back to a range, go to the **Table Design** tab and click convert to the range:

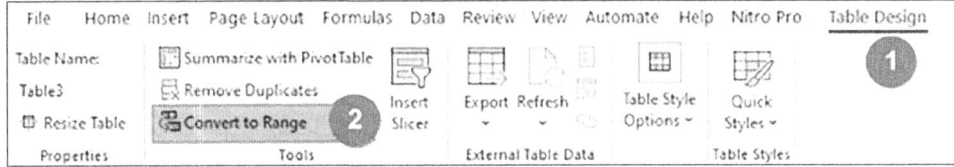

Figure 1.11: *Converting a table to a range*

Now, let's see the reasons for using Tables:

- They are essential source data for pivot tables and charts since they dynamically expand.
- They can be quickly and easily formatted.
- You can easily select the entire table, column, or row with just one click. To select the entire table, hover over the top left corner and click (see *Figure 1.12*).

Excel Environment

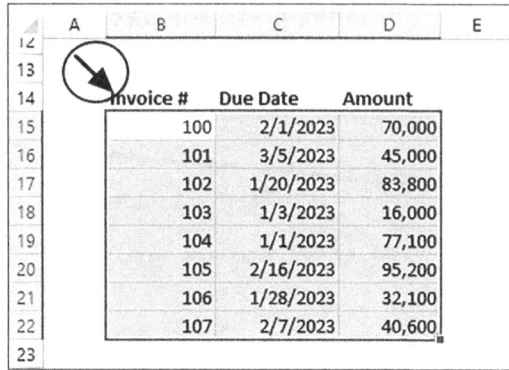

Figure 1.12: *Selecting the entire table*

To select only the column range with data, hover over the column header and click once (see *Figure 1.13*).

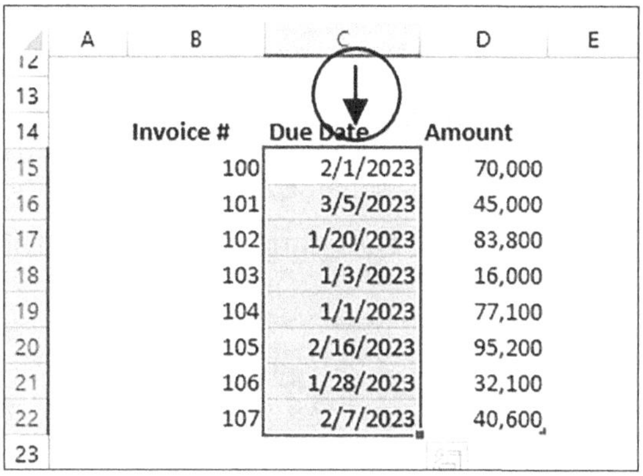

Figure 1.13: *Selecting the entire Column*

Hover over the table's left edges for the row range and click (see *Figure 1.14*).

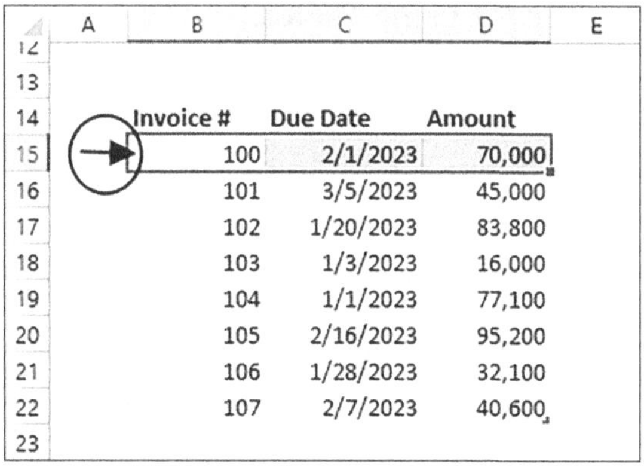

Figure 1.14: *Selecting the entire Row*

- Excel tables use structured referencing, making creating complex formulas easier. Structured referencing uses table column names and functions to simplify formulas, saving time and reducing errors.

Importance of having lookup skills

This book aims to build the user's lookup skills as a way of setting them on the path of mastering Excel.

So, why are lookup functions so important to any Excel user?

Here are the 11 top reasons:

- **Fast, efficient, and effective data retrieval**: Excel lookup functions can speed up finding and retrieving specific data from an extensive dataset, across worksheets or workbooks, thus reducing manual data search and retrieval time.
- **Increases the overall data analysis accuracy**: By using these functions, you can also reduce errors that may arise during manual data searches and ensure that you access the correct data accurately.
- **Enhances better data analysis and reporting**: Lookup functions help you compare and analyze data from different sources and consolidate them into a single report with minimal errors.
- **Improved decision-making**: Accurate and timely information is critical for making informed decisions. Also, having a big picture from consolidated data is critical to better decision-making. Lookup functions are essential in data consolidation, time-saving, and accurate data retrieval.
- **Increased productivity**: With lookup functions, you can work faster and more accurately, leading to increased productivity and better performance.
- **Flexible and easy to learn**: Excel lookup functions are relatively easy to learn, and once you understand them, you can use used in a variety of ways, making them flexible and adaptable to different situations.
- **Error reduction**: Lookup functions help to reduce the risk of errors in your data analysis by providing accurate and reliable results.
- **Enhanced data visualization**: Lookup functions allow you to create dynamic reports and charts that update automatically as new data is added, enhancing the visualization and presentation of data.
- **Better data organization**: By automating data retrieval and organization, lookup functions can help keep data more organized and easier to manage.

- **Allows for more complex calculations**: With lookup functions, users can perform more complex calculations that would otherwise be time-consuming or impossible to do manually.
- **Increases Excel proficiency**: Different lookup methods integrate many functions in Excel functions. Learning these methods can improve your overall Excel proficiency and make you more efficient and effective in using Excel.

Classification of Lookup Functions

Excel functions can be broadly divided into three categories as follows:

- Dynamic array functions (automatically spill their results into adjacent cells)
- Legacy array functions (require the use of keyboard shortcuts **Ctrl + Shift + Enter** to enter them if they are required to spill results to adjacent cells)
- M function (functions used in Power Query to perform data transformations)

In this book, we will learn lookup skills using a variety of methods from all three categories.

We will start by learning legacy array functions, starting with the most popular `VLOOKUP`, followed by a popular combination of `INDEX` and `MATCH`, and then the oldest lookup function, `LOOKUP`. Finally, we will learn unique ways of retrieving data using Database functions, Aggregate functions, Math functions, and some Text functions.

Later, we will jump into time-saving and dynamic array functions, starting with the most popular `XLOOKUP` and then the handy `FILTER` function. In the process, we will learn how to nest other dynamic functions like `VSTACK`, `HSTACK`, and `SEQUENCE` to create efficient lookup formulas.

Finally, we will explore looking up data using Power Query table joins, list functions, grouping, and how to create dynamic criteria in Power Query.

Conclusion

Excel skills are essential to any professional whose line of duty includes any form of data manipulation. Furthermore, these skills can be used to manage personal data, such as budgets, track daily habits, and make to-do lists.

Among all the Excel skills to learn, learning lookup skills can have an instant impact on your productivity and data analysis accuracy.

In the next chapter, we will delve deep into one of the most popular Excel functions: VLOOKUP.

Question

Did you find the trick to memorizing this number "12110081644936251694"?

Solution:

Break it down into these groups →121 | 100 | 81 | 64 | 49 | 36 | 25 | 16 | 9 | 4

Can you see a pattern yet?

These are the square of numbers from 11 to 2. That is how simple an issue becomes if you break it down into small pieces.

CHAPTER 2
VLOOKUP Is Dead: Or is it?

Introduction

This chapter will introduce us to the most popular Excel lookup function – **VLOOKUP**. We will learn its basic structure and inherent weaknesses, as well as how we can nest it with other functions to overcome its weaknesses.

In addition, since the book is about Mastering Excel, we will dig into the different Excel functions.

Structure

In this chapter, we will discuss the following topics:

- **VLOOKUP** exact and approximate match
- Breaking **VLOOKUP** myths
    - Myth 1: **VLOOKUP** cannot do a left lookup
    - Myth 2: **VLOOKUP** cannot return multiple columns in a lookup
    - Myth 3: **VLOOKUP** cannot do a multiple criteria lookup
    - Myth 4: **VLOOKUP** cannot handle inserting and deleting columns in the lookup range
    - Myth 5: **VLOOKUP** cannot do a two-way lookup
    - Myth 6: **VLOOKUP** cannot do a partial match lookup
    - Myth 7: **VLOOKUP** cannot do a case-sensitive partial match lookup
    - Myth 8: **VLOOKUP** cannot do a case-sensitive lookup
    - Myth 9: **VLOOKUP** cannot return multiple results

- Myth 10: **VLOOKUP** cannot lookup from last to first
- Myth 11: **VLOOKUP** cannot lookup the top or bottom N values
- Myth 12: **VLOOKUP** cannot do a reverse lookup
- Myth 13: **VLOOKUP** cannot do a horizontal lookup
- Myth 14: **VLOOKUP** cannot return multiple non-contiguous columns
- Myth 15: **VLOOKUP** cannot lookup multiple non-contiguous arrays

VLOOKUP exact and approximate match

As we learned in the previous chapter, mastering the basics is the initial step to mastering any skill. So, here is what you need to know about **VLOOKUP**.

VLOOKUP allows you to search for a specific value in the leftmost column (that is, *lookup value*) in a table (that is, *table array*) and then return a value from a specified column on the right (that is, *column index number*) in the same row as the lookup value. You can specify whether you want an approximate or exact match (that is, *range lookup*).

By default, **VLOOKUP** will do an approximate match.

Syntax:

```
=VLOOKUP(lookup value, table array, column index number, [range lookup])
```

Point to note:

- The lookup value **must be in the first column** of the table. In *Figure 2.1*, since the invoice number is the lookup value, all invoices are stored in the first column of our table.
- There are only two essential columns in our table – the one storing the lookup value and the one storing the value to return. In *Figure 2.1*, our formula would still have worked even if we did not have the third column.
- Since we want an exact match for our lookup value, we select **FALSE** as the lookup range. You can replace **FALSE** with zero **0**, as follows:

    ```
    =VLOOKUP(F3 , tblSales , 2 , 0)
    ```

Note: Excel stores Boolean values as integers, with a value of **0** representing **FALSE** and any other value representing TRUE. When you enter **TRUE** or **FALSE** in a cell, Excel automatically converts them to their equivalent integer.

G3 =VLOOKUP(F3,tblSales,2,FALSE)

Invoice #	Due Date	Amount
100	2/1/2023	70,000
101	3/5/2023	45,000
102	1/20/2023	83,800
103	1/3/2023	16,000
104	1/1/2023	77,100
105	2/16/2023	95,200
106	1/28/2023	32,100
107	2/7/2023	40,600
108	1/1/2023	18,100
109	2/16/2023	32,683
110	1/28/2023	28,600
111	2/7/2023	24,517
112	1/1/2023	20,433
113	2/16/2023	16,350
114	1/28/2023	12,267

Invoice	Due Date
107	2/7/2023

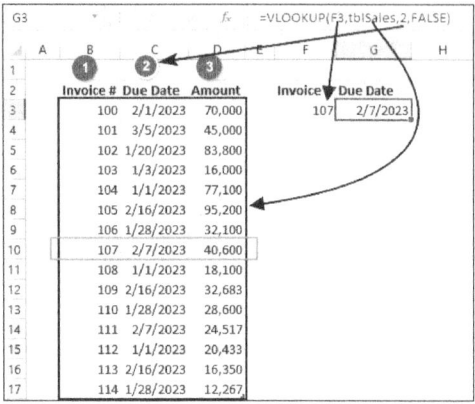

***Figure 2.1**: Basic VLOOKUP exact match*

VLOOKUP approximate match

By default, the **VLOOKUP** function is set to return an approximate match. On the brighter side, when working with a large numerical and sorted dataset, and you can tolerate some errors, **VLOOKUP** is very fast.

However, most searches require an exact match. In addition, an approximate search will return the wrong results if the following requirements are not met:

- Data table must be sorted in ascending order by the lookup value.
- Data table should only have unique values in the lookup values columns.
- Data table lookup range should be in the same data type as the lookup value.

Nonetheless, an approximate match is beneficial when grouping data (for example, when assigning grades to students; *Figure* 2.2).

K3 =VLOOKUP(J3,tblGrades,2)

Student	Marks	Grade
Emily	71	B
Theodore	45	E
Luna	83	A
Penelope	16	E
Austin	77	B
Joshua	95	A
Ruby	52	D
Luke	40	E
Gupta	87	A

Marks	Grade
0	E
50	D
60	C
70	B
80	A

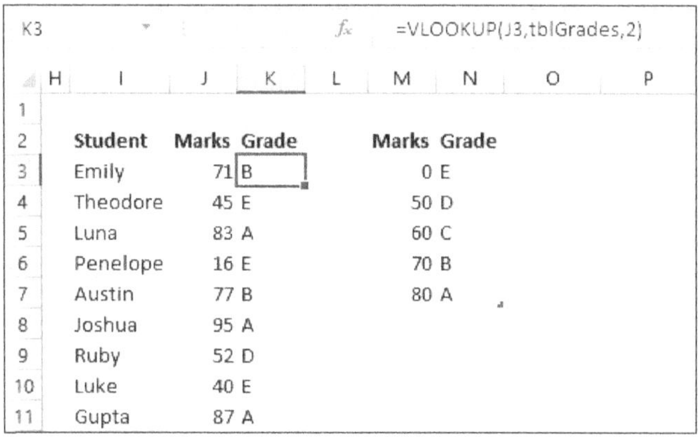

***Figure 2.2**: VLOOKUP approximate match data grouping*

Approximate Match is also applicable when searching for a value within a range (for example, when giving a discount based on sales range; *Figure* 2.3):

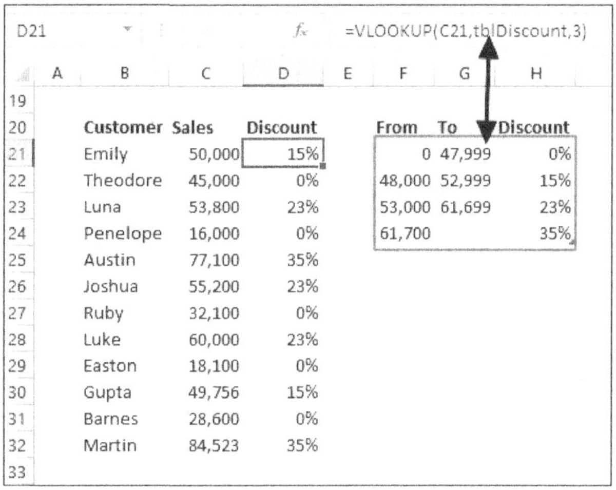
D21 =VLOOKUP(C21,tblDiscount,3)

Customer	Sales	Discount
Emily	50,000	15%
Theodore	45,000	0%
Luna	53,800	23%
Penelope	16,000	0%
Austin	77,100	35%
Joshua	55,200	23%
Ruby	32,100	0%
Luke	60,000	23%
Easton	18,100	0%
Gupta	49,756	15%
Barnes	28,600	0%
Martin	84,523	35%

From	To	Discount
0	47,999	0%
48,000	52,999	15%
53,000	61,699	23%
61,700		35%

***Figure 2.3**: VLOOKUP approximate match value from a range*

Note: When using VLOOKUP for an approximate range, you can skip the last range lookup argument, and the formula will still be ok.

Any argument between square brackets means it is optional.

```
=VLOOKUP(lookup value, table array, column index number, [range lookup])
```

Tip: VLOOKUP approximate match is a good alternative to the nested IF function since it calculates faster.

For example, to get the same results, as shown in *Figure* 2.2, you can either use the following nested IF function or VLOOKUP:

```
=IF(J3>=M7, N7, IF(J3>=M6,N6,IF(J3>=M5,N5,IF(J3>=M4,N4,$N3))))
=VLOOKUP(J3, tblGrades,2)
```

Because of the aforementioned limitation, there are many myths about what `VLOOKUP` can or cannot do.

In the next section, we explore the full potential of the `VLOOKUP` function when nested with other functions.

Breaking VLOOKUP myths

Myths are stories that people from a particular culture have been telling for a long time. These stories usually majorly involve teaching why things are the way they are based on history. These are sometimes half-truths or pure lies.

A lot of teachings regarding how **VLOOKUP** functions are shrouded by half-truths and sometimes pure lies, giving the **VLOOKUP** function a bad name.

In this section, we will learn the full truth about **VLOOKUP** by busting the existing myths one by one.

Myth 1: VLOOKUP cannot do a left lookup

In *Figure* 2.4, the lookup value (sales date) is not in the first column of the table; instead, we have the return value (customer) there.

In such a situation, the default **VLOOKUP** function will not work. You must nest the IF function, as shown in the following figure:

		fx	=VLOOKUP(T3, IF({1,0},tblTrans[Sales Date],tblTrans[Customer]), 2,0)		
P	Q	R	S	T	U	V
Customer	Sales Date	Amount		Sales Date	Customer
Emily	1/12/2010	50,000		1/24/2010	Gupta
Theodore	1/5/2010	45,000			
Luna	1/11/2010	53,800			
Penelope	1/8/2010	16,000			
Austin	1/17/2010	77,100			
Joshua	1/20/2010	55,200			
Ruby	1/18/2010	32,100			
Luke	1/10/2010	60,000			
Easton	1/14/2010	18,100			
Gupta	1/24/2010	49,756			
Barnes	1/21/2010	28,600			
Martin	1/15/2010	84,523			

Figure 2.4: VLOOKUP left lookup

The trick is creating a custom table array using the **IF** function.

The **IF** function returns a two-column table with the Sales Date being the first column and the Customers as the second Column.

This column rearrangement tricks **VLOOKUP** into looking to the Left while assuming it is looking to the right.

Myth 2: VLOOKUP cannot return multiple columns in a lookup

In *Figure* 2.5, you must return the Sales Date and Amount given for a specific customer.

By default, you can only return one value at a time, as the `column_index` argument in VLOOKUP only accepts a single value.

However, you can wrap more than one `column_index` value in curly braces and return multiple columns.

If you do not have Office 365 subscription, perform the following steps:
- Highlight the cells to return the multiple values.
- Go to the formula bar and key in the following formula.
- Click **Ctrl + Shift + Enter** to return the following values:

Customer	Sales Date	Amount		Customer	Sales Date	Amount
Emily	1/12/2010	50,000		Penelope	1/8/2010	16,000.00
Theodore	1/5/2010	45,000				
Luna	1/11/2010	53,800				
Penelope	1/8/2010	16,000				
Austin	1/17/2010	77,100				
Joshua	1/20/2010	55,200				
Ruby	1/18/2010	32,100				
Luke	1/10/2010	60,000				
Easton	1/14/2010	18,100				
Gupta	1/24/2010	49,756				
Barnes	1/21/2010	28,600				
Martin	1/15/2010	84,523				

Formula: `=VLOOKUP(T3,tblTrans,{2,3},0)`

Figure 2.5: *VLOOKUP returns multiple columns*

Myth 3: VLOOKUP cannot use multiple criteria in a lookup

If your data has duplicates, as shown in *Figure* 2.6, the **VLOOKUP** function will return the first value that meets a criterion.

For example, if you looked up the sales amount for customer "Carl Jackson", the VLOOKUP function will return 45,000 since this is the first occurrence.

VLOOKUP Is Dead: Or is it?

What if you want to look up the sales amount for customer "Carl Jackson" for "1/14/2010"?

By default, VLOOKUP cannot look up multiple values. You can modify it as follows:

- Combine the multiple values using an ampersand. Using our preceding example, our lookup value now will be Carl Jackson1/14/2010.
- Create a custom two-column table array using the IF function. The first column should contain a combination of two columns that contain the lookup values, that is, tblSales[Customer]&tblSales[Sales Date] in that order, similar to the lookup value combo. The second column should contain the lookup value.
- With the combo lookup value and custom table array, write your VLOOKUP as shown in *Figure 2.6*. Remember that this is an array function; therefore, click **Ctrl + Shift +Enter** if you do not have an Office 365.

```
=VLOOKUP( T19&U19,
    IF({1,0}, tblSalesT[Customer]&tblSalesT[Sales Date],
tblSalesT[Amount]), 2, 0 )
```

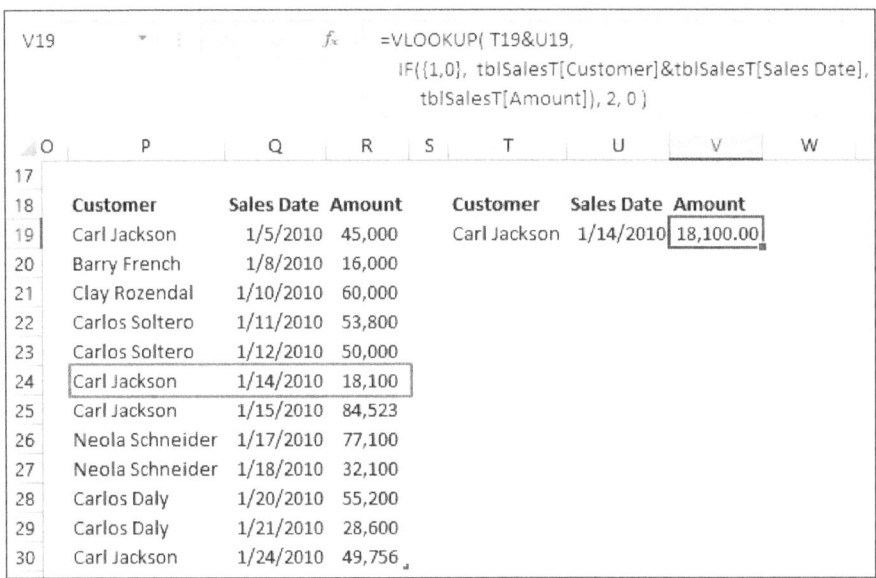

Figure 2.6: VLOOKUP *multiple criteria*

Myth 4: VLOOKUP cannot handle the insertion and deletion of columns in the look-up range

So far, we have been hard coding the column index number in the function, that is, the number of the column that contains the return value.

This poses a problem when you insert or delete a column before this column, as it breaks the VLOOKUP function.

Therefore, for VLOOKUP to handle insertion and deletion, we need to make the column index number dynamic using the MATCH Function, as shown in *Figure* 2.7:

```
=VLOOKUP(E3,tblSale,
    MATCH(F2,tblSale[#Headers],0),
        FALSE)
```

Note: The **MATCH** function looks up a value in a range and returns its relative position.

```
=MATCH(F2,tblSale[#Headers],0)=2
```

In our case, the **MATCH** function looks for the text **Amount** stored in cell F2 among the sales table headers and will always return its position, making it dynamic.

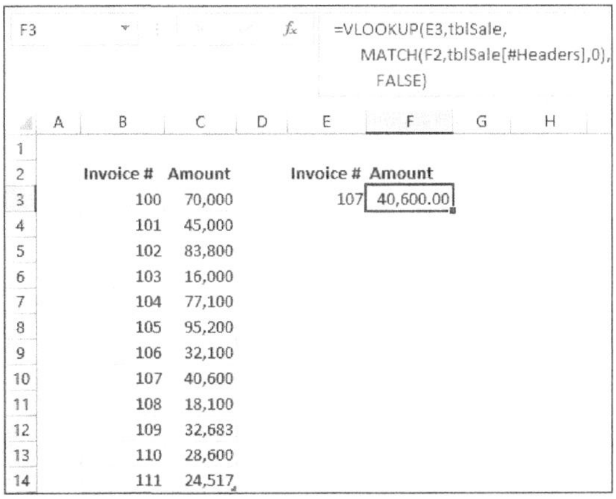

	A	B	C	D	E	F	G	H
1								
2		Invoice #	Amount		Invoice #	Amount		
3		100	70,000		107	40,600.00		
4		101	45,000					
5		102	83,800					
6		103	16,000					
7		104	77,100					
8		105	95,200					
9		106	32,100					
10		107	40,600					
11		108	18,100					
12		109	32,683					
13		110	28,600					
14		111	24,517					

F3 — fx =VLOOKUP(E3,tblSale, MATCH(F2,tblSale[#Headers],0), FALSE)

Figure 2.7: *VLOOKUP handle insertion and deletion*

Myth 5: VLOOKUP cannot do a two-way lookup

Hard coding the column index number in the **VLOOKUP** function makes it almost impossible to do a two-way lookup.

However, if we nest the **MATCH** function, as we have learned from the previous section, the **VLOOKUP** function can easily do a two-way lookup (see *Figure 2.8*).

Our Task is to look up sales for a specific customer (Joshua) from the Customers List and for a specific region (Western).

Since the customers' list is stored in the first column of our SalesRegion table, the lookup value will be the specific customer in cell G38. As for the regions, we shall use the MATCH function to return the relative column index for the specific region.

```
=VLOOKUP(G38,SalesRegion,
MATCH(G40, SalesRegion[#Headers],0),0)
```

Note: The MATCH function always returns the first TRUE match.

And since we cannot have duplicates in table headers, the MATCH function will always return the correct column number.

	A	B	C	D	E	F	G	H	I
36									
37		Customer	Eastern	Western	Southern		Customer	Amount	
38		Emily	70,000	50,000	45,000		Joshua		
39		Theodore	45,000	45,000	16,000		**Region**	55,200.00	
40		Luna	83,800	53,800	60,000		Western		
41		Penelope	16,000	16,000	53,800				
42		Austin	77,100	77,100	50,000				
43		Joshua	95,200	55,200	18,100				
44		Ruby	32,100	32,100	84,523				
45		Luke	40,600	60,000	77,100				
46		Easton	18,100	18,100	32,100				
47		Gupta	32,683	49,756	55,200				
48		Barnes	28,600	28,600	28,600				
49		Martin	24,517	84,523	49,756				

Figure 2.8: VLOOKUP two-way Lookup

Myth 6: VLOOKUP cannot do a partial match lookup

VLOOKUP has only an Approximate and Exact Match but can also do a partial match.

A partial match is possible if you combine the lookup value with a wildcard, as shown in *Figure 2.9*.

Note: Wildcards are special characters representing one or multiple characters in a text string. The most common wildcards are the asterisk (*) and a question mark (?).

- Asterisk (*): This wildcard represents one or more characters in a text string. For example, "`P*`" will find any word that *starts with* the letter P, `*P` will find any word that *ends with* the letter P, and `*P*` will find any word that *contains* the letter P.

- Question mark (?): The question mark wildcard represents a single character in a text string. For example, the search term `H??t` will find any four-letter word that starts with "H", ends with "t", and has two characters in between, such as "Heat" or "Host".

- You can combine the asterisk and the question marks to define your search. For example, `???T*` will search for any string where T is the fourth character but ends with any number of characters, such as Mas**ts**, Coa**t**ing, Soo**t**hing, and so on. Another example is `*T???` This will search for any string where T is the fourth last character but starts with any number of characters, such as Bea**t**ing, Charac**t**ers, Assis**t**ing.

    ```
    =VLOOKUP(  "*" & E54 & "*",  tblinvoices, 2, 0 )
    ```

In the following example (*Figure 2.9*), we look up the amount for an invoice containing the letter P. We know this because we have put an asterisk before and after our criterion stored in cell E54.

Therefore, *P* means there could be many characters before and after the letter "P".

Please note that the formula returns the first TRUE value. Later in the chapter, we will learn how to return multiple values in case of duplicates.

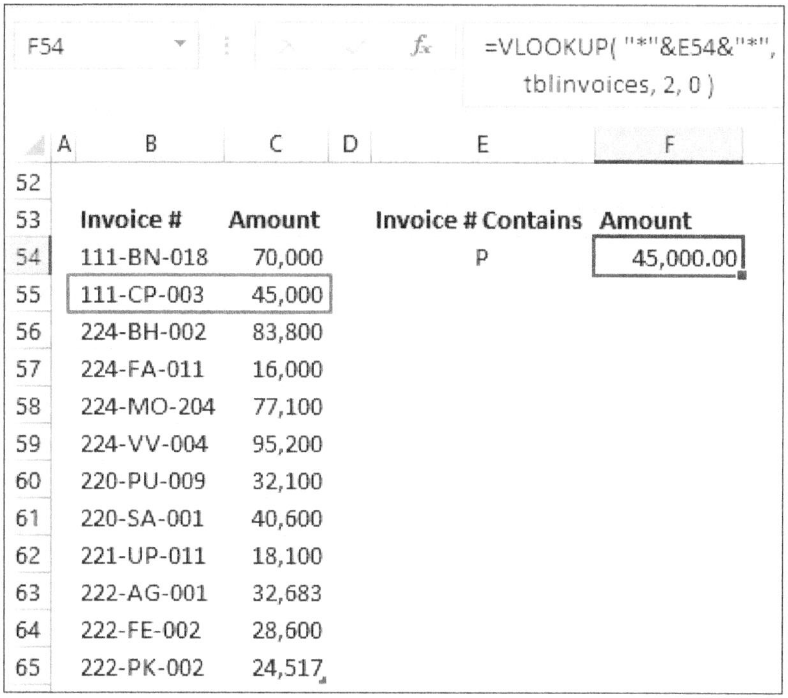

VLOOKUP Is Dead: Or is it?

	A	B	C	D	E	F
52						
53		Invoice #	Amount		Invoice # Contains	Amount
54		111-BN-018	70,000		P	45,000.00
55		111-CP-003	45,000			
56		224-BH-002	83,800			
57		224-FA-011	16,000			
58		224-MO-204	77,100			
59		224-VV-004	95,200			
60		220-PU-009	32,100			
61		220-SA-001	40,600			
62		221-UP-011	18,100			
63		222-AG-001	32,683			
64		222-FE-002	28,600			
65		222-PK-002	24,517			

Cell F54: =VLOOKUP("*"&E54&"*", tblinvoices, 2, 0)

Figure 2.9: VLOOKUP Partial Match

Suppose you want to look up values for an invoice whose fifth character is the letter "P"?

In such a scenario, we shall use the question mark (?) as the wildcard character to represent any single character.

=VLOOKUP("????"&E57&"*", tblinvoices, 2, 0)

As shown in *Figure 2.10*, Invoice number "220-PU-009" is the first invoice, where the letter "P" is the fifth character. We know this is the correct invoice because we put four question marks before our criterion (P) stored in cell E57.

Remember, since the invoice does not end with the letter "P", we must insert an asterisk after the criterion to represent any number of characters after it.

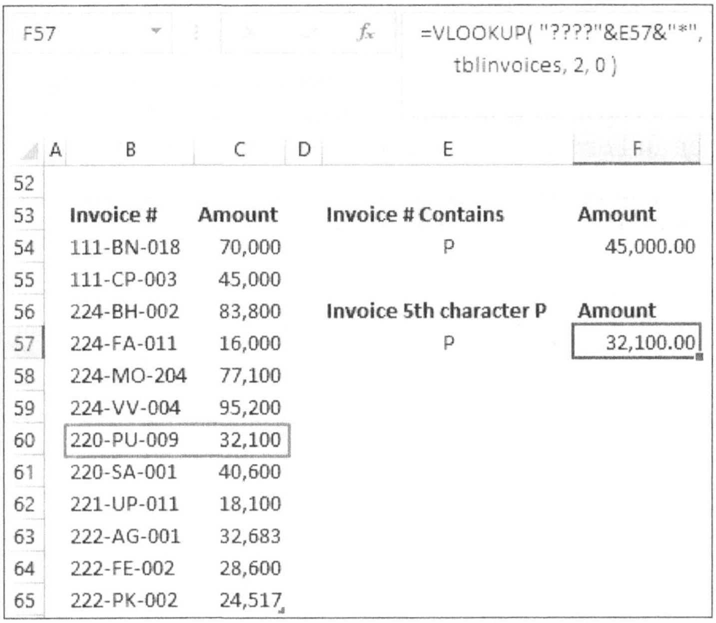

Figure 2.10: VLOOKUP Partial Match single characters

Note: Since the **VLOOKUP** function is not case-sensitive, the preceding examples will search for the letter "P" irrespective of whether it is uppercase or lowercase.

Myth 7: VLOOKUP cannot do a case-sensitive partial match lookup

Excel has two popular case-sensitive functions: **FIND** and **EXACT**.

Since **VLOOKUP** is not case-sensitive, we must nest one of the preceding functions when doing a case-sensitive partial match lookup.

As *Figure 2.11* exemplifies, we need to look up an invoice that contains the lowercase letter "p".

```
=VLOOKUP(TRUE, IF( {1,0},
ISNUMBER(FIND(K54,tblpay[Invoice'#])),
tblpay[Amount]),2,0)
```

Here is how the preceding function works:

- `FIND(K54, tblpay[Invoice'#])` returns an array of numbers and errors. Numbers representing the position of lowercase "p" in the invoice number and errors for any invoice missing a lowercase "p."
- `ISNUMBER(FIND(K54,tblpay[Invoice'#]))` converts this array of numbers and errors into a `TRUE/FALSE` array. TRUE for any number and FALSE for the errors.
- Create a custom two-column table array using the IF function. The first column contains this array of `TRUE/FALSE` (lookup values column), and the second contains the Invoices amount (return values column).
- Since our lookup values are `TRUE/FALSE` values, the `VLOOKUP` function should look up a `TRUE` value and return the first TRUE value.
- Since this is an array function, click **Ctrl + Shift + Enter** if you do not have an Office 365 subscription.

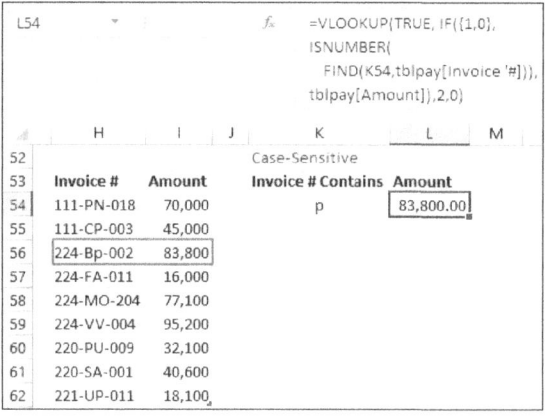

Figure 2.11: VLOOKUP Partial Case-Sensitive Match

Myth 8: VLOOKUP cannot do a case-sensitive lookup

As we have learned from the previous section, the `FIND` function will help the `VLOOKUP` function to do a partial case-sensitive lookup.

We must use the `EXACT` function to do an entire case-sensitive lookup (see *Figure 2.12*):

```
=VLOOKUP(TRUE,
IF({1,0},
```

```
EXACT(Q54,Payment[Product]),
Payment[Amount]),2,0)
```

Here is how the preceding function operates:

- **EXACT(Q54, Payment[Product])** returns an array of **TRUE** and **FALSE**. **TRUE** represents the product, which is precisely equal to the proper case Furniture else **FALSE**.
- Create a custom two-column table array using the IF function. The first column contains this array of **TRUE/FALSE** (lookup values column), and the second contains the Invoices amount (return values column).
- Since our lookup values are **TRUE/FALSE** values, the **VLOOKUP** function should look up a **TRUE** value and return the first **TRUE** value.
- Since this is an array function, click **Ctrl + Shift + Enter** if you do not have an Office 365 subscription.

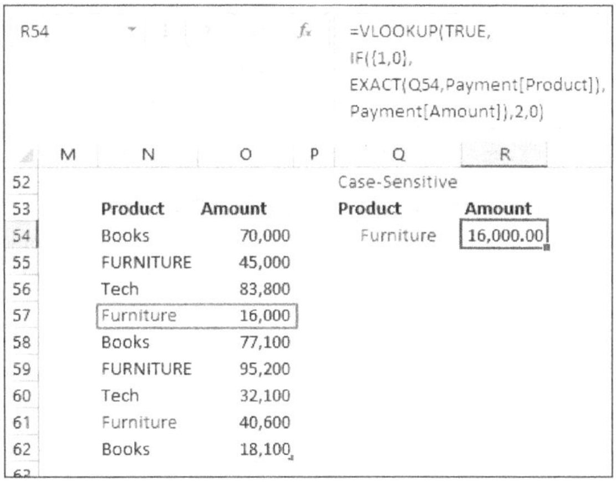

Figure 2.12: VLOOKUP Full Case-Sensitive Match

Note: Since **VLOOKUP** is not case-sensitive, without the use of the **EXACT** function as shown earlier, it would have returned the amount for the first instance where the product is furniture, that is, 45,000.

Myth 9: VLOOKUP cannot return multiple results

By default, **VLOOKUP** returns the first **TRUE** value. So, if you have duplicate items and want to return all **TRUE** values, you must nest the **SMALL** and **IF** functions as shown in *Figure 2.13*:

```
=VLOOKUP(
SMALL(IF($F$70=tbl[Customer],
ROW(tbl[Customer])), ROW(A1)),
IF({1,0},ROW(tbl[Customer]),tbl[Amount]),
2,0)
```

Here is how the preceding function works:

- **IF($F$70=tbl[Customer], ROW(tbl[Customer]))** checks for our criterion customer "Carl Jackson" among the customers' list, and IF true, it returns the row number where the customer is found. Since we have duplicate customers, this function will return multiple row numbers.
- We need to iterate over this row numbers list and return one at a time as the lookup value for VLOOKUP. We use the SMALL function for this task, which returns the row numbers from the smallest to the largest. Note that ROW(A1) evaluates to 1, and as you drag the function down, it increases until the complete list is iterated:

SMALL(IF($F$70=tbl[Customer],ROW(tbl[Customer])), ROW(A1))

- Create a custom two-column table array using the IF function. The first column contains Customers' row numbers (lookup values column), and the second contains the Invoices amount (return values column).
- VLOOKUP function uses each row number returned by the SMALL function and returns the corresponding amount.
- Please note that after all amounts have been returned, the VLOOKUP function returns the #NUM error.
- Since this is an array function, click **Ctrl + Shift + Enter** if you do not have an Office 365 subscription.

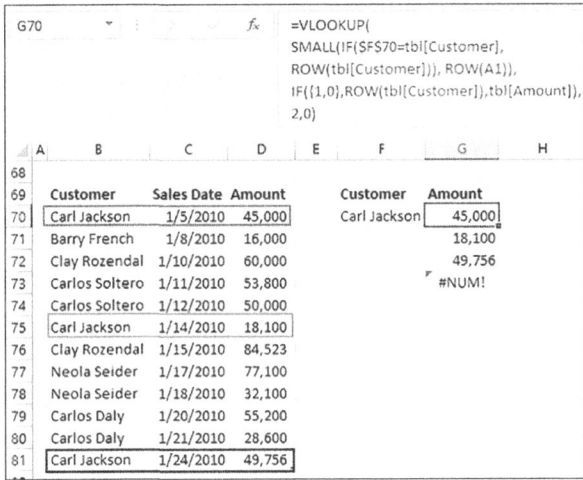

Figure 2.13: VLOOKUP Multiple Results

Myth 10: VLOOKUP cannot lookup from last to first

By default, VLOOKUP looks up values from top to bottom and returns the first TRUE value.

To search from the last to the first, we nest the LARGE function in VLOOKUP.

Using the example from the previous chapter, all we need to do to search from last to first is to replace the SMALL function with the LARGE function, as shown in Figure 2.14:

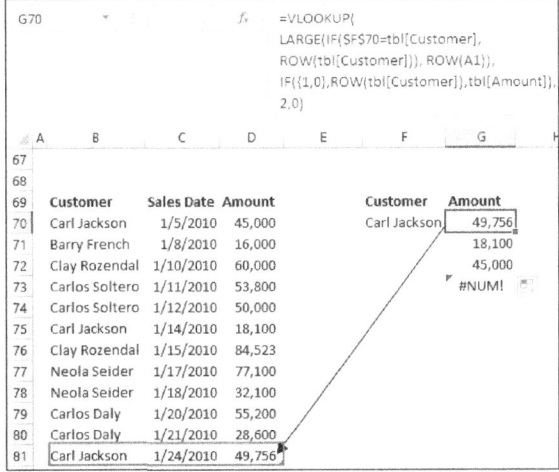

Figure 2.14: VLOOKUP Multiple Results

Here is how the preceding function works:

- **IF($F$70=tbl[Customer], ROW(tbl[Customer]))** checks for our criterion customer "Carl Jackson" among the customers' list, and IF true, it returns the row number where the customer is found. Since we have duplicate customers, this function will return multiple row numbers
- We need to iterate over this row numbers list and return one at a time as the lookup value for VLOOKUP. We use the LARGE function for this task, which returns the row numbers from the largest to the smallest. Note that ROW(A1) evaluates to 1, and as you drag the function down, it increases until the complete list is iterated.
- Create a custom two-column table array using the IF function. The first column contains Customers' row numbers (lookup values column), and the second contains the Invoices amount (return values column).
- VLOOKUP function uses each row number returned by the LARGE function and returns the corresponding amount.
- Please note that after all amounts have been returned, the VLOOKUP function returns the #NUM error.
- Since this is an array function, click **Ctrl + Shift + Enter** if you do not have an Office 365 subscription.

Myth 11: VLOOKUP cannot lookup the top or bottom N values

By nesting the SMALL or LARGE function, VLOOKUP can quickly return the top or bottom N amounts in an unsorted list (see *Figure* 2.15):

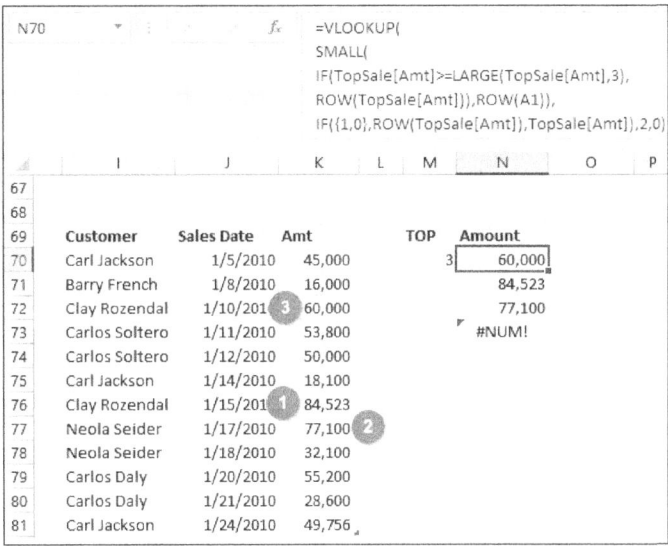

Figure 2.15: VLOOKUP top three sales amount

```
=VLOOKUP(
SMALL(IF(TopSale[Amt]>=LARGE(TopSale[Amt],3),ROW(TopSale[Amt])),ROW(A1)),
IF({1,0},ROW(TopSale[Amt]),TopSale[Amt]),2,0)
```

Here is how the preceding function performs:

- **TopSale[Amt]>=LARGE(TopSale[Amt],3)** checks if the sales amount is greater or equal to the third largest sales amount and returns an array of TRUE/FALSE.
- The IF function returns a list of row numbers for all sales amounts that are larger or equal to the third-largest sales amount.
- We need to iterate over this row numbers list and return one at a time as the lookup value for VLOOKUP. For this task, we use the SMALL function, which returns the row numbers from the smallest to the largest. Note that ROW(A1) evaluates to 1, and as you drag the function down, it increases until the complete list is iterated.

SMALL(IF(TopSale[Amt]>=LARGE(TopSale[Amt],3),ROW(TopSale[Amt])),ROW(A1))
- Create a custom two-column table array using the IF function. The first column contains Amounts' row numbers (lookup values column), and the second contains the Invoices amount (return values column).

- VLOOKUP function uses each row number returned by the SMALL function and returns the corresponding amount.
- Please note that after all amounts have been returned, the VLOOKUP function returns the #NUM error.
- Since this is an array function, click Ctrl + Shift + Enter if you do not have an Office 365 subscription.

Myth 12: VLOOKUP cannot do a reverse lookup

In Excel, a reverse lookup is a way to look up a value in a table based on a known result. This is the reverse of the two-way lookup discussed in the previous section (see Myth 5).

For example, as shown in *Figure 2.16*, you are looking for a Doctor and a Corresponding session given to the patient.

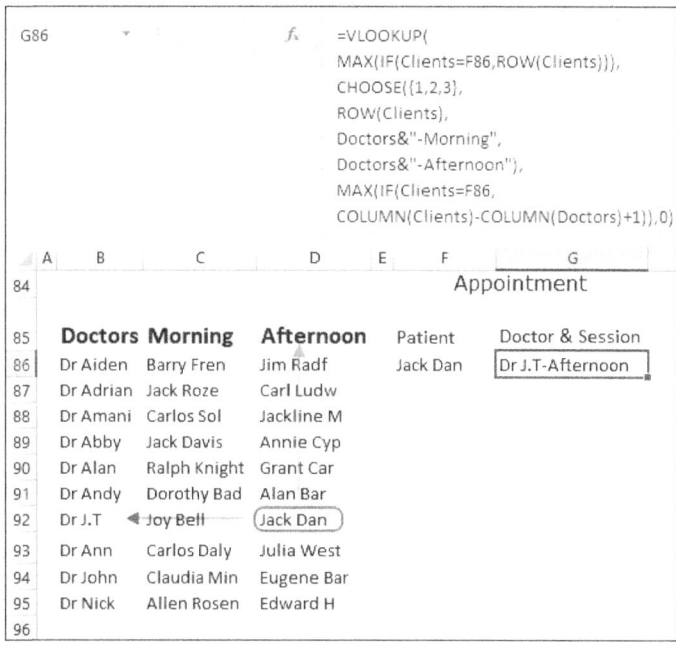

Figure 2.16: VLOOKUP reverse lookup

```
=VLOOKUP(
MAX(IF(Clients=F86,ROW(Clients))),
CHOOSE({1,2,3},
ROW(Clients),
```

Doctors&"-Morning",

Doctors&"-Afternoon"),

MAX(IF(Clients=F86, COLUMN(Clients)-COLUMN(Doctors)+1)),0)

Before we start learning how the formula works, let us learn about the named ranges that we have used:

- Clients = C86:D95
- Doctors = B86:B95

Now, the preceding function performs in the following way:

- **IF(Clients=F86, ROW(Clients))** checks if the client in cell F86 is in the array of clients in the named range. Assuming no duplicates, the IF function returns the row number of the client; otherwise, it returns FALSE values (see *Figure 2.17*):

G86			fx	=IF(Clients=F86,ROW(Clients))		
A	B	C	D	E	F	G	H
84						Appointment	
85	**Doctors**	**Morning**	**Afternoon**	Patient		Doctor & Session	
86	Dr Aiden	Barry Fren	Jim Radf		Jack Dan	FALSE	FALSE
87	Dr Adrian	Jack Roze	Carl Ludw			FALSE	FALSE
88	Dr Amani	Carlos Sol	Jackline M			FALSE	FALSE
89	Dr Abby	Jack Davis	Annie Cyp			FALSE	FALSE
90	Dr Alan	Ralph Knight	Grant Car			FALSE	FALSE
91	Dr Andy	Dorothy Bad	Alan Bar			FALSE	FALSE
92	Dr J.T	Joy Bell	Jack Dan			FALSE	92
93	Dr Ann	Carlos Daly	Julia West			FALSE	FALSE
94	Dr John	Claudia Min	Eugene Bar			FALSE	FALSE
95	Dr Nick	Allen Rosen	Edward H			FALSE	FALSE
96							

Figure 2.17: Return Client Row

- **MAX(IF(Clients=F86, ROW(Clients))):** the MAX function ignores the FALSE values and returns the row number. This becomes the lookup value for the VLOOKUP function.
- **CHOOSE({1,2,3}, ROW(Clients), Doctors&"-Morning", Doctors&"-Afternoon"):** the CHOOSE creates a table array for VLOOKUP function with clients row numbers as lookup values column and the two-column array combining the doctors with the sessions as return values columns.

VLOOKUP Is Dead: Or is it?

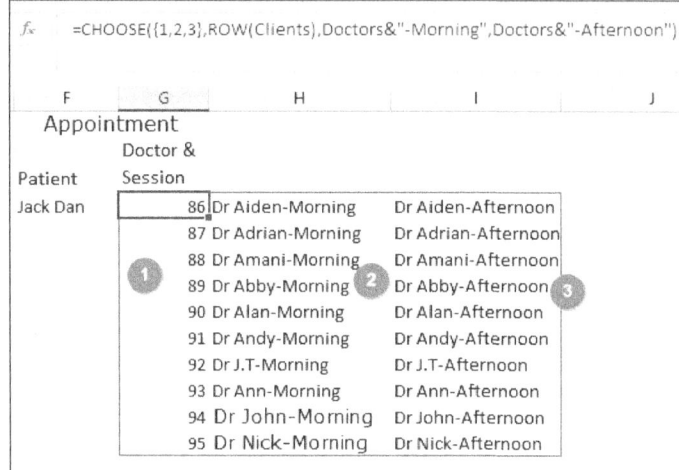

Figure 2.18: VLOOKUP Custom Table Array

- `MAX(IF(Clients=F86, COLUMN(Clients)-COLUMN(Doctors)+1))` checks if the client in cell F86 is in the array of clients in the named range and returns the column number of the client; otherwise, it returns FALSE values. Please note that we must adjust the column counts by deducting the doctor's column and adding 1.
- Using the preceding inputs, the `VLOOKUP` function can do reverse lookup.

Myth 13: VLOOKUP cannot do a horizontal lookup

In Excel, many horizontal lookups are left for the `HLOOKUP` function, but this should not be the case anymore, as the `VLOOKUP` function can also do a horizontal lookup, as shown in *Figure 2.19*.

In the following example, you are supposed to look up the representative who quoted the least per item.

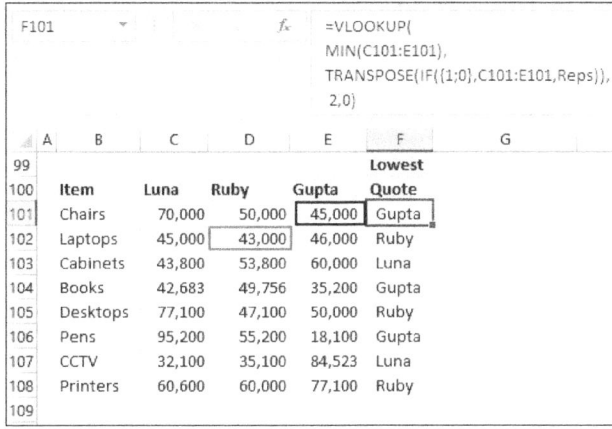

Figure 2.19: VLOOKUP horizontal lookup

```
=VLOOKUP(
MIN(C101:E101),
TRANSPOSE(IF({1;0},C101:E101,Reps)),
 2,0)
```

This function works as follows:

- **MIN(C101:E101)** returns the minimum amount per item. This becomes the lookup value for the VLOOKUP function.
- **IF({1;0}, C101:E101, Reps)** returns a two-row table array, where the first row contains the quoted prices and the second row contains the representatives (see *Figure 2.20*):

Figure 2.20: Two-row table array

- Since VLOOKUP only looks up data vertically, we need to transpose the two-row table to a two-column table using the TRANSPOSE function (see *Figure* 2.21):

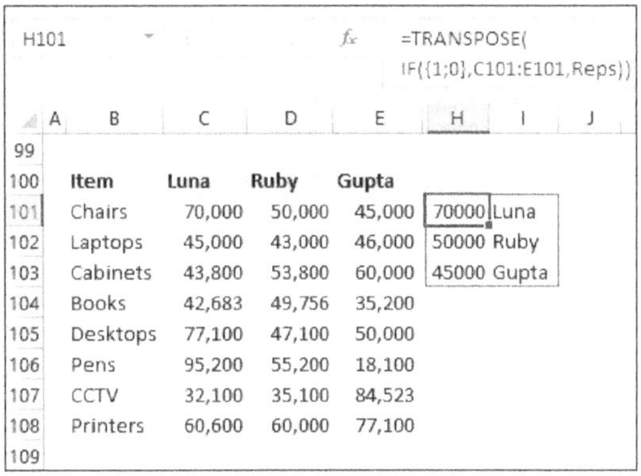

H101 =TRANSPOSE(IF({1;0},C101:E101,Reps))

	A	B	C	D	E	H	I	J
99								
100		Item	Luna	Ruby	Gupta			
101		Chairs	70,000	50,000	45,000	70000	Luna	
102		Laptops	45,000	43,000	46,000	50000	Ruby	
103		Cabinets	43,800	53,800	60,000	45000	Gupta	
104		Books	42,683	49,756	35,200			
105		Desktops	77,100	47,100	50,000			
106		Pens	95,200	55,200	18,100			
107		CCTV	32,100	35,100	84,523			
108		Printers	60,600	60,000	77,100			
109								

Figure 2.21: *Two-column table array*

- Using the Minimum quoted price as the Lookup value and the transposed table as the Table array, the VLOOKUP function quickly returns the representative with the least quotation.

Myth 14: VLOOKUP cannot return multiple non-contiguous columns

In the previous section, Myth 2, we discussed returning multiple contiguous columns. Now, let us discuss further how to return multiple non-contiguous columns.

In our example (*Figure* 2.22), we must return the Amount and the Region column data:

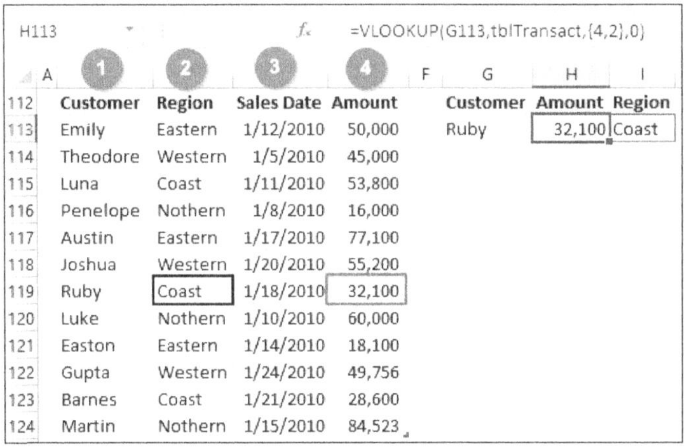

H113 =VLOOKUP(G113,tblTransact,{4,2},0)

	A	1	2	3	4	F	G	H	I
112		Customer	Region	Sales Date	Amount		Customer	Amount	Region
113		Emily	Eastern	1/12/2010	50,000		Ruby	32,100	Coast
114		Theodore	Western	1/5/2010	45,000				
115		Luna	Coast	1/11/2010	53,800				
116		Penelope	Nothern	1/8/2010	16,000				
117		Austin	Eastern	1/17/2010	77,100				
118		Joshua	Western	1/20/2010	55,200				
119		Ruby	Coast	1/18/2010	32,100				
120		Luke	Nothern	1/10/2010	60,000				
121		Easton	Eastern	1/14/2010	18,100				
122		Gupta	Western	1/24/2010	49,756				
123		Barnes	Coast	1/21/2010	28,600				
124		Martin	Nothern	1/15/2010	84,523				

Figure 2.22: VLOOKUP *non-contiguous columns*

```
=VLOOKUP(G113, tblTransact,{4,2},0)
```

The only trick we must remember is to put the required column numbers in curly braces. Also, if you do not have an Office 365 subscription, first highlight the column, go to the formula bar, write the above formula, and finally, **click Ctrl + Shift +Enter**.

If you want the returned values row-wise, the only trick to remember is to have a semi-colon (;) instead of a comma (,) as a separator between your column numbers (see *Figure 2.23*):

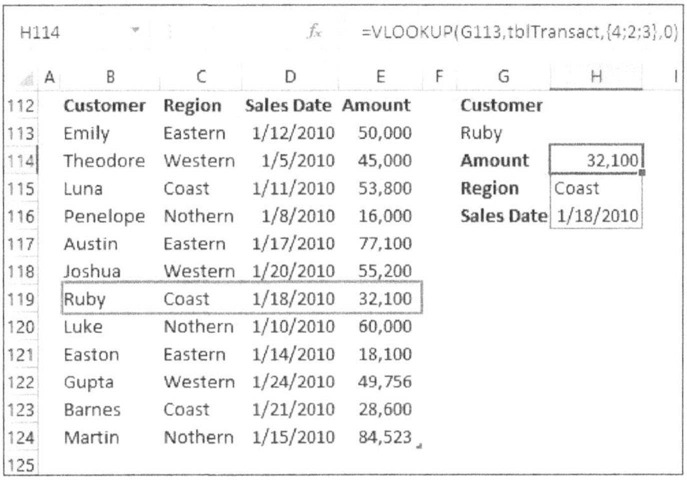

Figure 2.23: VLOOKUP non-contiguous columns row-wise

Myth 15: VLOOKUP cannot lookup multiple non-contiguous arrays

Dynamically looking up non-contiguous tables requires more functions nesting, as shown in *Figure 2.24*:

```
=VLOOKUP([@Amount],
   CHOOSE(MATCH([@Product],{"Chairs","Laptops"},0),
       Chairs_Discount, Laptops_Discount), 2, TRUE)
```

This function works as follows:

- **MATCH([@Product],{"Chairs", "Laptops"},0)** dynamically returns the position of the product in the lookup array, that is, Chairs = 1, Laptops =2.

- **CHOOSE(MATCH([@Product],{"Chairs", "Laptops"},0), Chairs_Discount, Laptops_Discount))**: the CHOOSE function uses the position returned by the MATCH function to determine the lookup table array, that is, 1= Chairs Discount, 2= Laptops Discount.
- **VLOOKUP** function then checks the sales amount in the selected discount table amount, and it returns the approximate discount.

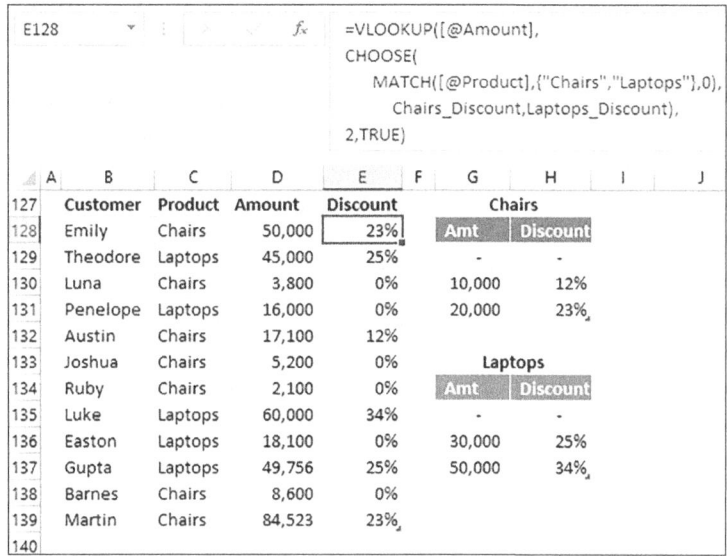

Figure 2.24: VLOOKUP non-contiguous lookup tables

Conclusion

In this chapter, we have learned to look beyond the common knowledge about VLOOKUP and seek to unleash its full potential.

We discovered that by creating a custom table array using the IF function, there is no need to rearrange our columns to make VLOOKUP lookup to the left. Furthermore, we can return more than one column by having the required return columns in curly braces.

Also, you do not need to struggle with the HLOOKUP function to do a horizontal lookup; instead, you can simply Transpose your data.

When combined with the MATCH function, VLOOKUP performs all tasks equal to the combination of INDEX + MATCH.

In the next chapter, we will investigate why many Excel users prefer the combination of the INDEX and MATCH functions over VLOOKUP and MATCH.

Points to remember

- Every Excel function has its limits, but most of them can be adjusted by nesting another function. This is why we pointed out the need for every Excel user to hone their function nesting skills in the first chapter.
- Using the IF function to create a custom table array for the VLOOKUP function makes it more flexible and able to look to the left. However, the IF function is limited to returning only a two-column table. If we need more columns, we use the CHOOSE function.
- VLOOKUP function defaults to an approximate search. This is one of its biggest weaknesses, and it's important for any user to be aware of it.
- Finally, never accept a function's weakness without challenging it first.

CHAPTER 3
INDEX and MATCH

Introduction

This chapter will introduce what is regarded as the **VLOOKUP** function replacement – **INDEX** and **MATCH**. These nested functions are so popular in such a way that some users think of them as individual functions. We shall first analyze these two functions individually and later see why they are such a powerful combination.

In addition, since the book is about Mastering Excel, we will learn how to combine them with other functions to solve complex lookup issues.

Structure

In this chapter, we will discuss the following topics:
- INDEX, MATCH, and the two-way lookup
- Three-way lookup
- Reverse-lookup single result
- Reverse-lookup multiple results
- Multiple criteria lookup
- Returning multiple columns
- Horizontal lookup
- Lookup non-contiguous array
- Lookup using wildcards
- Lookup based on text length
- Lookup items in a list
- Lookup unique values

INDEX, MATCH, and the two-way lookup

A two-way lookup is used to find a specific value by matching two criteria. It's commonly used when you have a data table and need to retrieve a value at the intersection of a row and column.

The INDEX function returns the data at the intersection of a given row and column. Therefore, the function requires an array of data, an optional row number (if it is a **single-row array**), *and an optional column number (if it is a single-column array)*.

We will start by looking up a multiple-row and multiple-column array, as shown in *Figure 3.1*. We are trying to answer the question, *"What amount did customer Gupta buy from the Western region?"*:

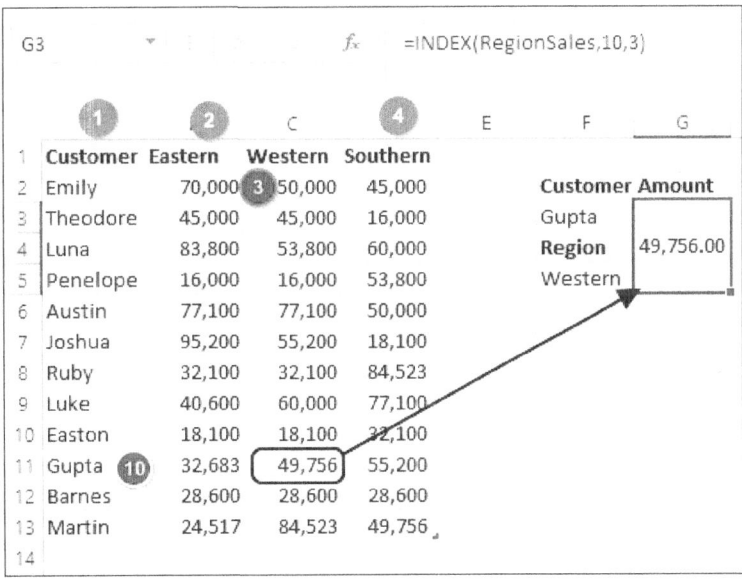

Figure 3.1: INDEX *multiple rows and columns lookup*

```
=INDEX(RegionSales,10,3)
```

Note: If your data is in a table (this is the date in range A2:D13), the row count starts after the header.

This is why in *Figure 3.1*, Gupta is in row 10, not 11.

Instead of selecting the whole table, we can select the column or row you want.

INDEX and MATCH

For example, in *Figure 3.2*, since we know we want Western region sales, we can select the entire column and provide only the row number containing our customer:

```
=INDEX(RegionSales[Western],10)
```

Note: If your data is in a single column, you only need to provide the row number.

You can input 1 as the column number, but it is unnecessary since you have selected only one column – Western Region data.

For example, you can re-write the preceding function as follows:

```
=INDEX(RegionSales[Western],10,1)
```

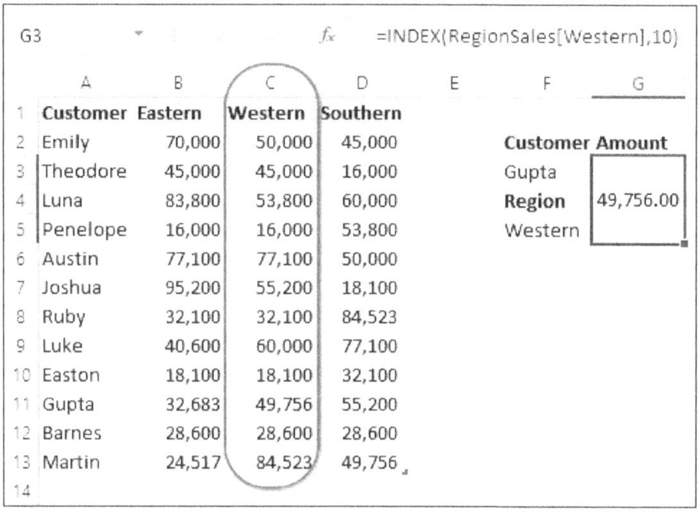

	A	B	C	D	E	F	G
1	Customer	Eastern	Western	Southern			
2	Emily	70,000	50,000	45,000		Customer	Amount
3	Theodore	45,000	45,000	16,000		Gupta	
4	Luna	83,800	53,800	60,000		Region	49,756.00
5	Penelope	16,000	16,000	53,800		Western	
6	Austin	77,100	77,100	50,000			
7	Joshua	95,200	55,200	18,100			
8	Ruby	32,100	32,100	84,523			
9	Luke	40,600	60,000	77,100			
10	Easton	18,100	18,100	32,100			
11	Gupta	32,683	49,756	55,200			
12	Barnes	28,600	28,600	28,600			
13	Martin	24,517	84,523	49,756			
14							

Figure 3.2: INDEX single-column lookup

Alternatively, you can select the entire row that contains customer **"Gupta"** and only provide the column number, as shown in *Figure 3.3*:

```
=INDEX( A11:D11 , , 3 )
```

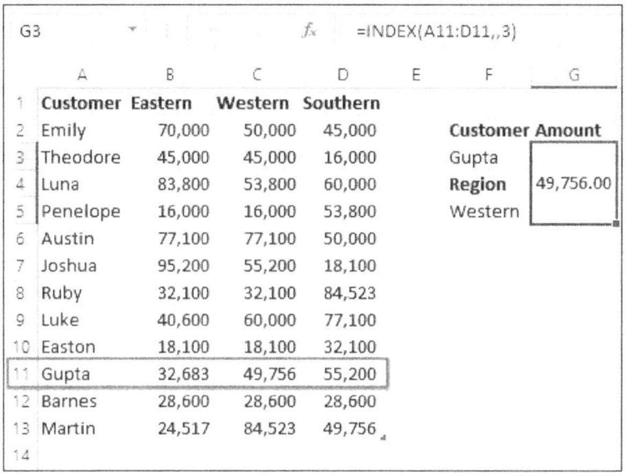

Figure 3.3: INDEX single-row lookup

Note: If your data is in a single row, you need only provide the column number.

You can input 1 as the row number, but it is unnecessary.

For example, you can re-write the preceding function as follows:

=INDEX(A11:D11,1,3)

Now that we have learned how the INDEX function works, let us revise the MATCH function.

As we learned in *Chapter 2*, "VLOOKUP IS DEAD: *Or is it*", the MATCH function returns the relative position of an item in an array. For example, in *Figure 3.2*, we can dynamically get the row number instead of hardcoding it. We achieve this using the MATCH function, as shown in *Figure* 3.4:

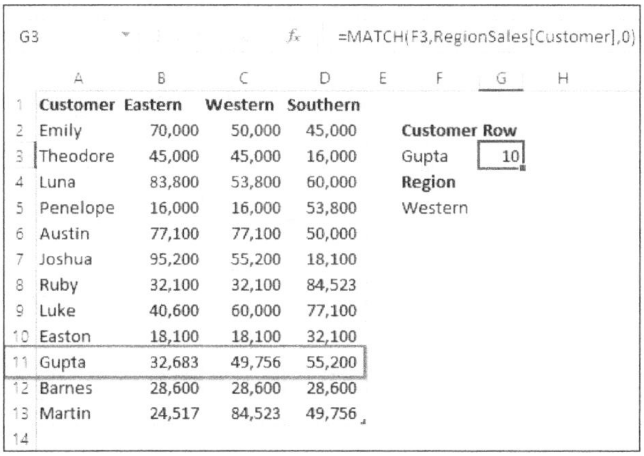

Figure 3.4: MATCH function gets the row number

Note: The **`MATCH`** function returns row 10, yet from the figure, we can see that the customer is in row 11.

As we noted earlier, this is because the MATCH function returns the relative position of the value within the lookup array. Since the header data is not within the lookup array, the `MATCH` function has ignored it.

Knowing the **`MATCH`** function can automate the hardcoding of the row number in the **`INDEX`** function, let us substitute the row number with it (see *Figure* 3.5):

```
=INDEX(RegionSales[Western],
MATCH(F3,RegionSales[Customer],0))
```

This is the optimal way of writing a simple INDEX and MATCH combo:

- Select only the column/row you require.
- Use the **`MATCH`** function to get the criterion row/column instead of hardcoding it.

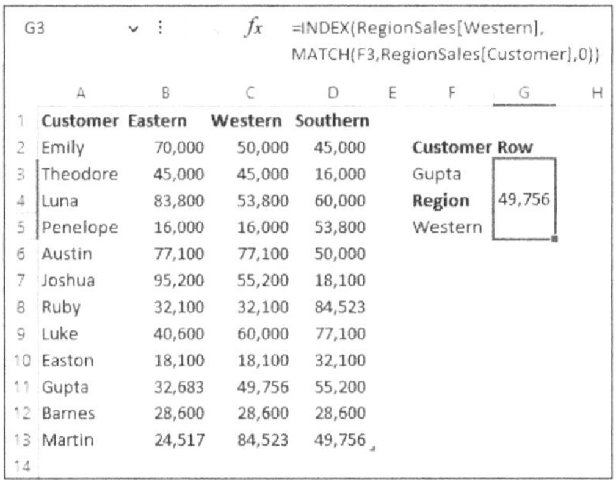

	A	B	C	D
1	Customer	Eastern	Western	Southern
2	Emily	70,000	50,000	45,000
3	Theodore	45,000	45,000	16,000
4	Luna	83,800	53,800	60,000
5	Penelope	16,000	16,000	53,800
6	Austin	77,100	77,100	50,000
7	Joshua	95,200	55,200	18,100
8	Ruby	32,100	32,100	84,523
9	Luke	40,600	60,000	77,100
10	Easton	18,100	18,100	32,100
11	Gupta	32,683	49,756	55,200
12	Barnes	28,600	28,600	28,600
13	Martin	24,517	84,523	49,756

Figure 3.5: *INDEX and MATCH function*

We are not limited to selecting single-column or single-row arrays. We can select a complete table and nest two MATCH functions to make our solution dynamic (see *Figure* 3.6):

```
=INDEX(RegionSales,
MATCH(F3,RegionSales[Customer],0),
MATCH(G3,RegionSales[#Headers],0))
```

H3 fx =INDEX(RegionSales,
MATCH(F3,RegionSales[Customer],0),
MATCH(G3,RegionSales[#Headers],0))

	A	B	C	D	E	F	G	H
1	**Customer**	**Eastern**	**Western**	**Southern**				
2	Emily	70,000	50,000	45,000		**Customer**	**Region**	**Amount**
3	Theodore	45,000	45,000	16,000		Gupta	Western	49756
4	Luna	83,800	53,800	60,000				
5	Penelope	16,000	16,000	53,800				
6	Austin	77,100	77,100	50,000				
7	Joshua	95,200	55,200	18,100				
8	Ruby	32,100	32,100	84,523				
9	Luke	40,600	60,000	77,100				
10	Easton	18,100	18,100	32,100				
11	Gupta	32,683	49,756	55,200				
12	Barnes	28,600	28,600	28,600				
13	Martin	24,517	84,523	49,756				
14								

Figure 3.6: *Dynamic two-way lookup*

Three-way lookup

A three-way lookup formula allows you to get data from a table using three criteria (see *Figure 3.7*):

```
=INDEX(RegionSales,
MATCH(G18&H18,RegionSales[Product]&RegionSales[Customer],0),
MATCH(G20,RegionSales[#Headers],0))
```

I18 fx =INDEX(RegionSales,
MATCH(G18&H18,RegionSales[Product]&RegionSales[Customer],0),
MATCH(G20,RegionSales[#Headers],0))

	A	B	C	D	E	F	G	H	I	J	K
16											
17	**Product**	**Customer**	**Jan**	**Feb**	**Mar**		**Product**	**Customer**	**Amount**		
18	Chairs	Emily	70,000	50,000	45,000		Chairs	Ruby	84,523.00		
19	Chairs	Luna	83,800	53,800	60,000		**Month**				
20	Chairs	Austin	77,100	77,100	50,000		Mar				
21	Chairs	Ruby	32,100	32,100	84,523						
22	Chairs	Easton	18,100	18,100	32,100						
23	Chairs	Barnes	28,600	28,600	28,600						
24	Laptops	Theodore	45,000	45,000	16,000						
25	Laptops	Penelope	16,000	16,000	53,800						
26	Laptops	Joshua	95,200	55,200	18,100						
27	Laptops	Luke	40,600	60,000	77,100						
28	Laptops	Gupta	32,683	49,756	55,200						
29	Laptops	Martin	24,517	84,523	49,756						
30											

Figure 3.7: *Dynamic three-way lookup*

The preceding function performs as follows:

- `G18&H18` returns a single combined criterion, that is, "ChairsRuby."
- `RegionSales[Product]&RegionSales[Customer]` joins the two columns and return a one-way array of products and customers that we can use to look up the combo criterion (see **Figure 3.8**):

Tip: When creating a one-way array, follow the **same order** as when creating the combo criteria.

In our example, the combo criterion is a join between `Product and Customer` (`ChairsRuby`); this is the reason we have followed the same order when creating the single array.

- `MATCH(G18&H18,    RegionSales[Product]&RegionSales[Customer],0)` returns the row number in the custom one-way array that contains the combo criterion.
- `MATCH(G20, RegionSales[#Headers],0))` returns the column number in the table headers that contain the month criterion.
- Remember that this is an array function since we are doing the criteria and columns joining. Therefore, if you do not have an Office 365 subscription, remember to click **Ctrl + Shift + Enter** when you complete writing it.

Product	Customer	Jan	Feb	Mar	One way Array
Chairs	Emily	70,000	50,000	45,000	ChairsEmily
Chairs	Luna	83,800	53,800	60,000	ChairsLuna
Chairs	Austin	77,100	77,100	50,000	ChairsAustin
Chairs	Ruby	32,100	32,100	84,523	ChairsRuby
Chairs	Easton	18,100	18,100	32,100	ChairsEaston
Chairs	Barnes	28,600	28,600	28,600	ChairsBarnes
Laptops	Theodore	45,000	45,000	16,000	LaptopsTheodore
Laptops	Penelope	16,000	16,000	53,800	LaptopsPenelope
Laptops	Joshua	95,200	55,200	18,100	LaptopsJoshua
Laptops	Luke	40,600	60,000	77,100	LaptopsLuke
Laptops	Gupta	32,683	49,756	55,200	LaptopsGupta
Laptops	Martin	24,517	84,523	49,756	LaptopsMartin

Figure 3.8: One-way array

Reverse-lookup single result

A reverse lookup is the opposite of the two-way lookup function discussed earlier. You start with data in an intersection and return the row and column headers.

For example, in *Figure 3.10*, we know the exam, but we must look up the tutor and the hall:

=INDEX(Tutors&"-"&Halls,
SUM((Exams=E33)*ROW(Exams))-ROW(Halls),
SUM((Exams=E33)*COLUMN(Exams))-COLUMN(Tutors))

Here is how the preceding function works:

- **Tutors&"-"&Halls** returns a custom table containing the combination of every tutor and the hall.
- **(Exams=E33)*ROW(Exams)** checks if our criteria exam is in the list of exams and returns an array of **TRUE / FALSE**, which, when multiplied by the exam rows, returns 0 where FALSE and the row number where TRUE (see **Figure 3.9**).
- We **SUM** the array to get a single row number from the preceding step. Since **INDEX** starts counting row numbers from the header, we then deduct the row of the header: SUM((Exams=E33) * ROW(Exams)) - ROW(Halls)
- Similar steps to the ones mentioned earlier are repeated to get the column number: SUM((Exams=E33) * COLUMN(Exams))- COLUMN(Tutors))
- Remember that this is an array function since we create the custom tutors and sessions table. Therefore, if you do not have an Office 365 subscription, remember to click **Ctrl + Shift + Enter** when you complete writing it.

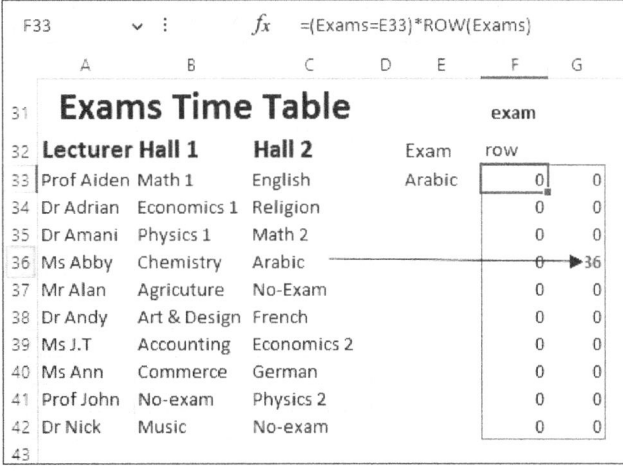

Figure 3.9: *Exam row number*

Tip: Always deduct Row or Column headers in your count if you have yet to include them in the table array.

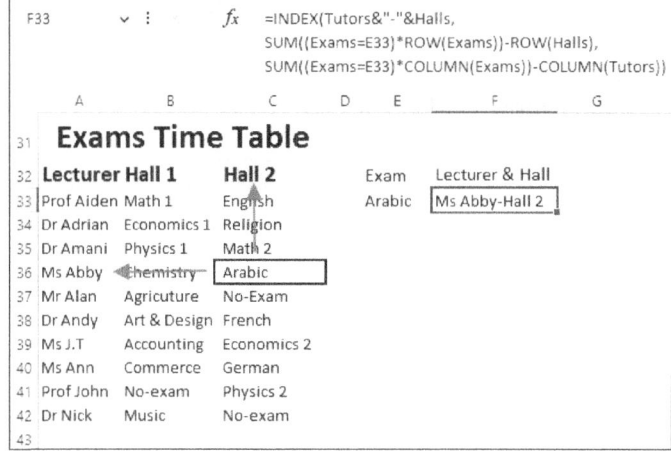

Figure 3.10: *Reverse lookup*

Reverse-lookup multiple results

Now, let us learn how to return multiple items if you have duplicates in your data.

Using the example in the previous section, assume patient `Jack Dan` had two appointments. *Figure* 3.12 shows how to return the two appointments:

=INDEX(Doctor&" "&session,
MATCH(TRUE,
    INDEX(Patients,, LARGE(IF(Patients=$G$47,COLUMN(Patients)-COLUMN(Doctor)),ROW(A1)))=$G$47,0),
LARGE((Patients=$G$47)*COLUMN(Patients)-COLUMN(Doctor),ROW(A1)))

This function works as follows:
- `Doctor&" "&session` returns a custom table containing the combination of every doctor and the session.
- `IF(Patients=$G$47, COLUMN(Patients)-COLUMN(Doctor))` checks if our criteria patient is in the list of patients and returns the column numbers where this is **TRUE**, else **FALSE** (see *Figure* **3.11**):

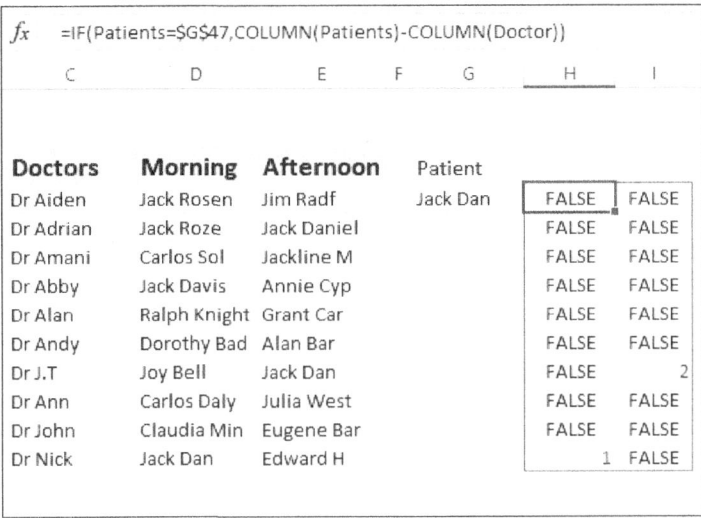

Figure 3.11: Check columns

- `LARGE(IF(Patients=$G$47,COLUMN(Patients)-COLUMN(Doctor)),ROW(A1))` returns the largest column number, that is, 2. We use `ROW(A1)`, which returns 1, and the number increments as we scroll our formula down.
- `INDEX(Patients,,LARGE(IF(Patients=$G$47,COLUMN(Patients)-COLUMN(Doctor)),ROW(A1)))` use the `INDEX` function to filter the data per column (see *Figure 3.12*):

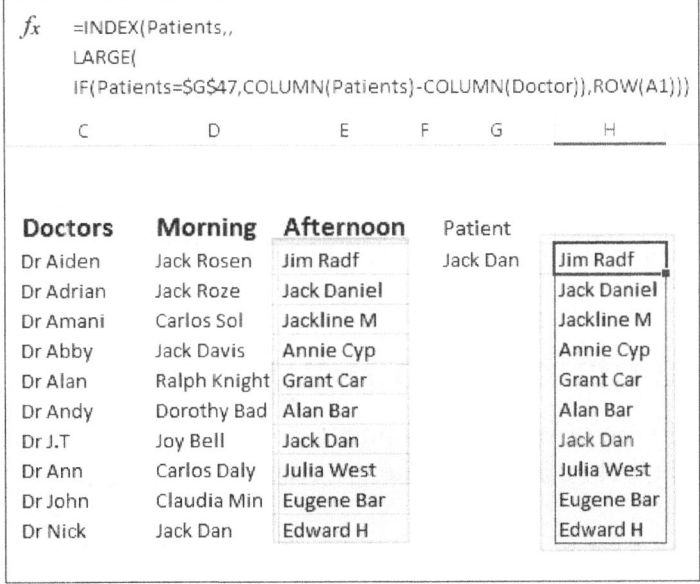

Figure 3.12: Filter one column at a time

INDEX and MATCH

- `MATCH(TRUE, INDEX(Patients,, LARGE(IF(Patients=$G$47, COLUMN(Patients)-COLUMN(Doctor)), ROW(A1)))=$G$47,0)`, checks if the patient is in the filtered column and returns an array of `TRUE/FALSE`. The `MATCH` function returns the relative position of the only `TRUE` value, which forms our row number for the `INDEX` function.
- Now that we have the row number, the last part is to get the column number using the `LARGE`: `LARGE(IF(Patients=$G$47,COLUMN(Patients)-COLUMN(Doctor)), ROW(A1))`
- Fill the formula downward to return all the appointments.
- Remember that this is an array function since we create the custom doctors and sessions table. Therefore, if you do not have an Office 365 subscription, remember to click **Ctrl + Shift + Enter** when you complete writing it.

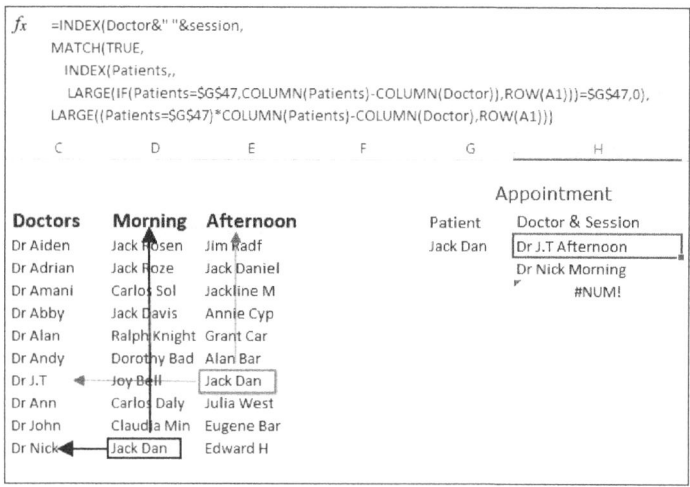

Figure 3.13: Reverse-lookup multiple items

Note: When all appointments have been returned, the INDEX function starts to return the `#NUM` error.

Multiple criteria lookup

As we learned in the previous section on three-way lookup, the trick to doing a multiple criteria lookup is joining the criteria into one using the ampersand (&) (see *Figure 3.14*):

```
=INDEX(tblSalesT20[Amount],
MATCH(E60&F60,tblSalesT20[Customer]&tblSalesT20[Sales Date],0))
```

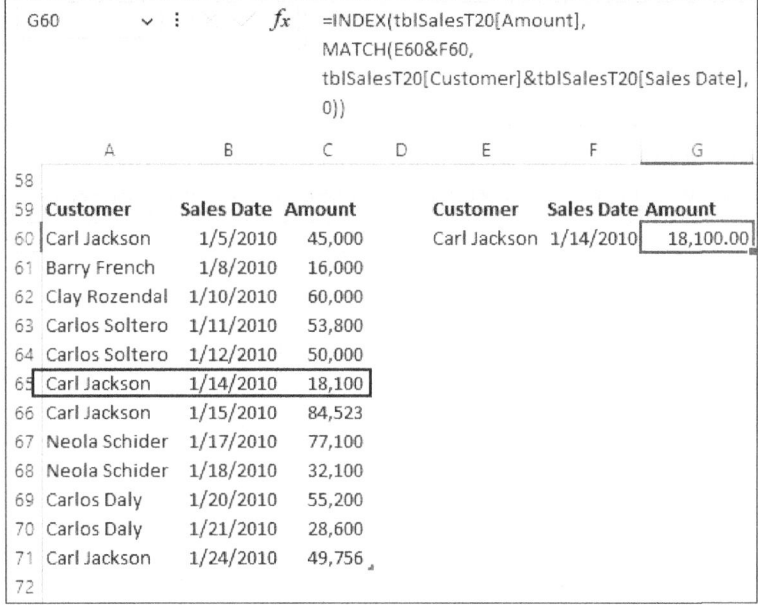

Figure 3.14: Multiple criteria lookup

The preceding function performs as follows:

- **E60&F60** returns a single combo criterion for the customer and dates **"Carl Jackson40192."**
- **tblSalesT20[Customer]&tblSalesT20[Sales Date]** returns a single combo array for the customer and dates (see *Figure* 3.15):

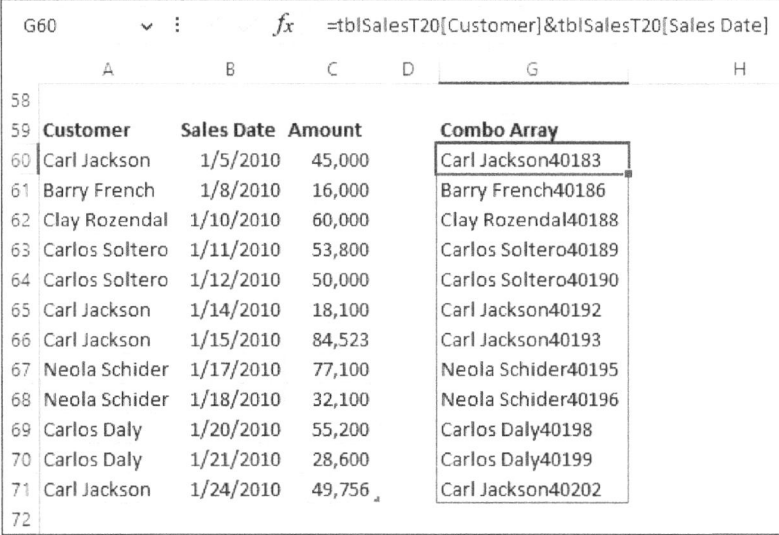

Figure 3.15: Combo array

- `MATCH(E60&F60,tblSalesT20[Customer]&tblSalesT20[Sales Date],0))`
  The **MATCH** function returns the row number of the combo criterion in the combo array.
- Remember that this is an array function since we create the custom combo array. Therefore, if you do not have an Office 365 subscription, remember to click **Ctrl + Shift + Enter** when you complete writing it.

Returning multiple columns

By default, the **INDEX** and **MATCH** combo returns a single column. If we want multiple columns, we must modify the **MATCH** function, as shown in *Figure 3.16*:

```
=INDEX(RegionSale21,
MATCH(F75,RegionSale21[Customer],0),
MATCH(G74:H74,RegionSale21[#Headers],0))
```

	A	B	C	D	E	F	G	H
73								
74	Customer	Jan	Feb	Mar		Customer	Jan	Feb
75	Emily	70,000	50,000	45,000		Ruby	32,100	49,100
76	Luna	83,800	53,800	60,000				
77	Austin	77,100	77,100	50,000				
78	Ruby	32,100	49,100	84,523				
79	Easton	18,100	18,100	32,100				
80	Barnes	28,600	28,600	28,600				
81	Theodore	45,000	45,000	16,000				
82	Penelope	16,000	16,000	53,800				
83	Joshua	95,200	55,200	18,100				
84	Luke	40,600	60,000	77,100				
85	Gupta	32,683	49,756	55,200				
86	Martin	24,517	84,523	49,756				

Figure 3.16: *Multiple columns*

The only trick is finding the relative positions of the multiple columns using the MATCH function, `MATCH(G74:H74,RegionSale21[#Headers],0))`, by highlighting the two criteria (G74:H74), the **MATCH** function returns an array of columns ({2,3}), which forces the **INDEX** function to return both columns.

This is also an array function; therefore, if you do not have an Office 365 subscription, remember to click **Ctrl + Shift + Enter** when you complete writing it.

Horizontal lookup

Unlike the VLOOKUP function, the **INDEX** function is not limited to a vertical lookup. The return array can be stored in any direction if you provide the correct column or row number (see *Figure* 3.17):

```
=INDEX(Suppliers,,
MATCH( MIN(B91:D91),B91:D91,0))
```

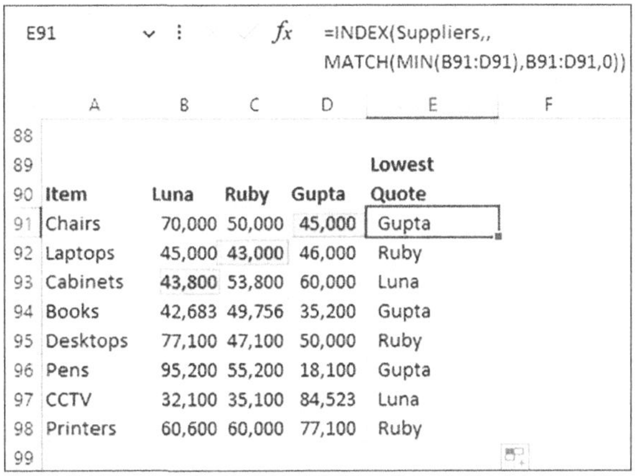

E91 =INDEX(Suppliers,, MATCH(MIN(B91:D91),B91:D91,0))

Item	Luna	Ruby	Gupta	Lowest Quote
Chairs	70,000	50,000	45,000	Gupta
Laptops	45,000	43,000	46,000	Ruby
Cabinets	43,800	53,800	60,000	Luna
Books	42,683	49,756	35,200	Gupta
Desktops	77,100	47,100	50,000	Ruby
Pens	95,200	55,200	18,100	Gupta
CCTV	32,100	35,100	84,523	Luna
Printers	60,600	60,000	77,100	Ruby

Figure 3.17: *Horizontal lookup*

The only trick here is using the MIN function to return the lowest quoted price per item. This price becomes our lookup value for the **MATCH** function. The **MATCH** function then returns the relative position of this minimum price.

Note: Since the suppliers are in a single-row array, we can skip the row number, as shown in the preceding formula.

Lookup non-contiguous array

As shown in *Figure* 3.18, the INDEX function has two syntax options:

- Array Option, which expects single or multiple contiguous arrays of data.
- Reference Option, which expects references to cells or a range of non-contiguous cells. Here are some important points to note on non-contiguous ranges:
    - Ranges must be enclosed in parentheses and separated by commas.
    - Ranges must be on the same worksheet; otherwise, the function will result in a **#VALUE** error.

INDEX and MATCH

- Ranges can be of different lengths but must contain the referenced row or column number. An out-of-range reference will result in a **#REF** error.
- Ranges are selected in the `[area_num]` argument of the **INDEX** function.

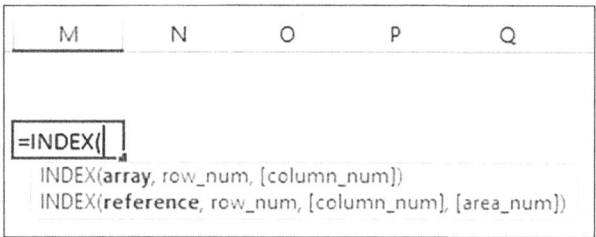

Figure 3.18: INDEX reference option

The example given in *Figure* 3.19 shows different discounts for chairs and laptops. We can use the following function to look up the different tables:

=INDEX((Chairs_Disc[Disc],Laptops_Disc[Disc]),

MATCH([@Amount],

CHOOSE(IF([@Product]="Chairs",1,2),Chairs_Disc[Amt],Laptops_Disc[Amt]),1),,

IF([@Product]="Chairs",1,2))

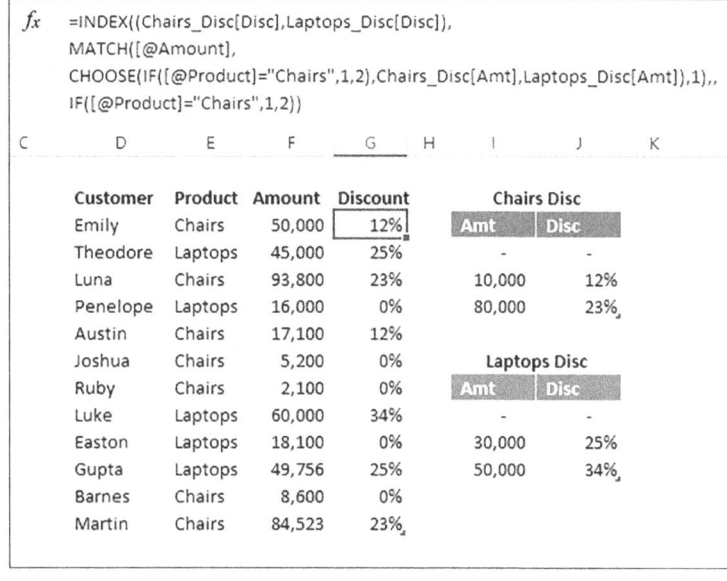

Figure 3.19: INDEX non-contiguous array

The preceding function works as follows:

- (`Chairs_Disc[Disc]`, `Laptops_Disc[Disc]`) returns the two non-contiguous discount columns for Chairs and Laptops.
- **IF([@Product]="Chairs",1,2),** returns a 1 if the product on the table is chairs; otherwise, it returns 2. This is the index that the **CHOOSE** function will determine to select the amount column in either the Chairs or Laptops table.
- `MATCH([@Amount],CHOOSE(IF([@Product]="Chairs",1,2),Chairs_Disc[Amt],Laptops_Disc[Amt]),1)` MATCH function returns the approximate relative position of the amount in the discount table amount column.
- Since we are selecting single-column arrays, we can ignore the column index argument and jump to the area number argument.
- **IF([@Product]="Chairs",1,2),** return a 1 if the product on the table is chairs; otherwise, it returns 2. This determines which of the two non-contiguous discount columns for Chairs and Laptops will be selected.

Lookup using wildcards

As learned in the last chapter, specifically in the **VLOOKUP** partial lookup section, the **INDEX-MATCH** combo can also use the two popular wildcard characters (? *).

For example, in *Figure* 3.20, we want to look up the amount for an invoice containing the letter "P":

Invoice #	Amount	Invoice # Contains	Amount
111-BN-018	70,000	P	45,000
111-KP-003	45,000		
224-BP-002	83,800		
224-FA-011	16,000		
224-PO-204	77,100		
224-VV-004	95,200		
220-PU-009	32,100		
220-SA-001	40,600		
221-UP-011	18,100		
222-AG-001	32,683		
222-FE-002	28,600		
222-PK-002	24,517		

formula: =INDEX(tblinvoicez[Amount], MATCH("*"&G117&"*",tblinvoicez[Invoice '#],0))

***Figure* 3.20**: INDEX *using an asterisk wildcard character*

```
=INDEX(tblinvoicez[Amount],
MATCH("*"&G117&"*",tblinvoicez[Invoice '#],0))
```

Here are some points to remember while using Wildcard characters:

- **Asterisk (*)**: The asterisk wildcard represents zero or more characters in a text string.
- **Question mark (?)**: The question mark wildcard represents a single character in a text string.
- You can combine the asterisk and the question marks to define your search further.

Here is how the preceding function works:

- **"*"&G117&"*"** returns *P*, which means there could be many characters before and after the letter **P**.
- **MATCH** function returns the first invoice's relative row position whose invoice number contains the letter **P**.
- **INDEX** function returns the invoice amount in the same row number.

Suppose you want to look up values for an invoice number whose fifth character is the letter "P"?

In such a scenario, we shall use the question mark (?) as the wildcard character to represent any single character (see **Figure 3.21**):

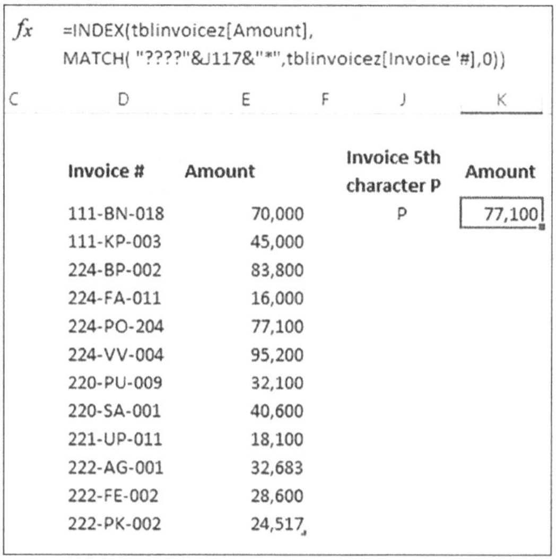

Invoice #	Amount	Invoice 5th character P	Amount
111-BN-018	70,000	P	77,100
111-KP-003	45,000		
224-BP-002	83,800		
224-FA-011	16,000		
224-PO-204	77,100		
224-VV-004	95,200		
220-PU-009	32,100		
220-SA-001	40,600		
221-UP-011	18,100		
222-AG-001	32,683		
222-FE-002	28,600		
222-PK-002	24,517		

Formula: `=INDEX(tblinvoicez[Amount], MATCH( "????"&J117&"*",tblinvoicez[Invoice '#],0))`

Figure 3.21: INDEX using mixed wildcard characters

```
=INDEX(tblinvoicez[Amount],
MATCH("????"&J117&"*",tblinvoicez[Invoice '#],0))
```

Here is how the preceding function works:

- **"????"&J117&"*"** returns ????P*, which means any four characters could be before the letter "P". Therefore, "P" is the fifth character, but there are multiple characters after it.
- MATCH function returns the first invoice's relative row position where an invoice number's fifth character is the letter "P".
- INDEX function returns the invoice amount in the same row number.

Lookup based on text length

In *Figure 3.22*, we assume all invoice back-orders can be identified by the length of the invoice number (that is, 8 characters):

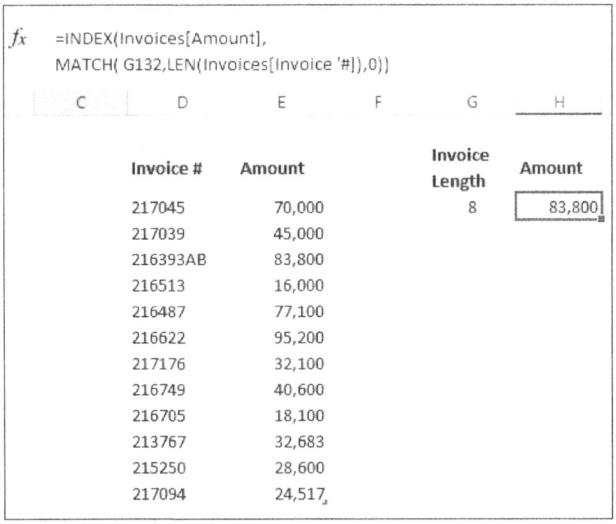

Invoice #	Amount	Invoice Length	Amount
217045	70,000	8	83,800
217039	45,000		
216393AB	83,800		
216513	16,000		
216487	77,100		
216622	95,200		
217176	32,100		
216749	40,600		
216705	18,100		
213767	32,683		
215250	28,600		
217094	24,517		

fx =INDEX(Invoices[Amount],
MATCH(G132,LEN(Invoices[Invoice '#]),0))

Figure 3.22: *Lookup text based on Length*

To look up these back-ordered invoices, we use the following formula:

```
=INDEX(Invoices[Amount],
MATCH( G132,LEN(Invoices[Invoice '#]),0))
```

Here is how the preceding function works:

- **LEN(Invoices[Invoice '#]), the** LEN function returns an array of

INDEX and MATCH

invoice number lengths. This becomes the lookup array argument for the MATCH function.

- **MATCH** function returns the first invoice's relative row position, whose length is 8 characters.
- **INDEX** function returns the invoice amount in the same row number.

Assuming you had multiple back-ordered invoices, as shown in *Figure 3.23*. Let us learn how to return the last match with the help of the **MAX** function:

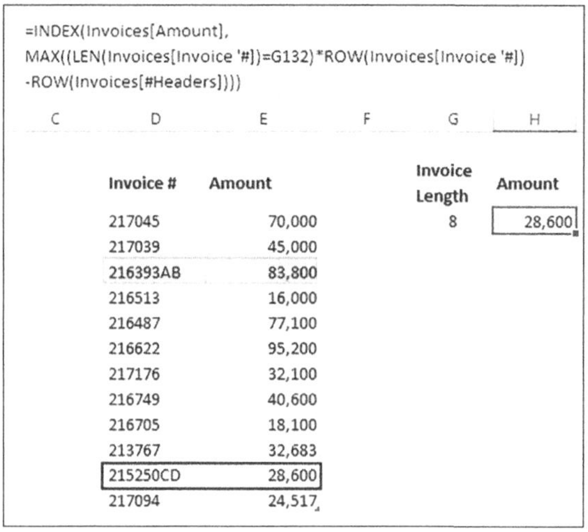

```
=INDEX(Invoices[Amount],
MAX(
(LEN(Invoices[Invoice '#])=G132)*ROW(Invoices[Invoice '#])
-ROW(Invoices[#Headers])
))
```

Figure 3.23: Lookup the last match

Here is how the preceding function works:

- **LEN(Invoices[Invoice '#])** LEN function returns an array of invoice number lengths.
- **LEN(Invoices[Invoice '#])=G132** checks which invoice length is equal to 8 and returns an array of **TRUE/FALSE**
- Get the row numbers by multiplying the TRUE/FALSE array with row numbers: **(LEN(Invoices[Invoice '#])=G132)*ROW(Invoices[Invoice '#])**

- Adjust the row numbers count by deducting the header row.
- To get the last low, use the **MAX** function.
- **INDEX** function returns the invoice amount in the last matching row number returned by the **MAX** function.

Lookup items in a list

Looking up items in a list is relatively easy when you understand the **COUNTIF** function.

In *Figure 3.24*, we want to look up the first customer who bought from us using any of the currencies in the list in cell G:

fx	=INDEX(Sales_Currency[Customer], MATCH(1,COUNTIF(List,Sales_Currency[Currency]),0))					
	C	D	E	F	G	H
	Customer	Currency	Amount		List	Customer
	Emily	RUPEE	45,000		ZAR	Barnes
	Luna	KES	16,000		USD	
	Austin	SSD	60,000		CHF	
	Ruby	MGA	53,800			
	Easton	KES	50,000			
	Barnes	CHF	18,100			
	Theodore	KES	84,523			
	Penelope	ZAR	77,100			
	Joshua	TSH	32,100			
	Luke	KES	55,200			
	Gupta	MGA	28,600			
	Martin	USD	49,756			

Figure 3.24: *Lookup item in a list*

```
=INDEX(Sales_Currency[Customer],
MATCH(1,COUNTIF(List, Sales_Currency[Currency]),0))
```

Here is how the preceding function works:

- **COUNTIF(List, Sales_Currency[Currency]) COUNTIF** function returns an array of 1/0, where 1 is the count of the currency if it is found in the list, else 0. This becomes the lookup array argument for the **MATCH** function.

- **MATCH** function returns the first invoice's relative row position whose count is 1.
- **INDEX** function returns the customer in the same row number.

If we want to return all the items and not just the first match, we must modify our formula, as shown in *Figure 3.25*:

=INDEX(
Sales_Currency[Customer],
LARGE(
COUNTIF(List, Sales_Currency[Currency])
*ROW(Sales_Currency[Currency])-ROW(Sales_Currency[#Headers]), ROW(A1))
)

Here is how the preceding function works:

- COUNTIF(List, Sales_Currency[Currency])

  *ROW(Sales_Currency[Currency]) **COUNTIF** function returns an array of 1/0, where 1 is the count of the currency if it is found in the list, else 0. Multiply this array with row numbers to return a list of row numbers that contain the items in the list. Remember to adjust the row numbers to start the count after the headers by deducting the header row number.

- We need to iterate over this row numbers list and return one at a time as the row argument for the **INDEX** function. We use the LARGE function for this task, which returns the row numbers from the largest to the smallest. Note ROW(A1) evaluates to 1, and as you drag the function down, it increases until the full list is iterated.

- **INDEX** function uses each row number returned by the LARGE function and returns the corresponding customer.

- Please note that the **INDEX** function returns the **#VALUE** error after all customers have been returned.

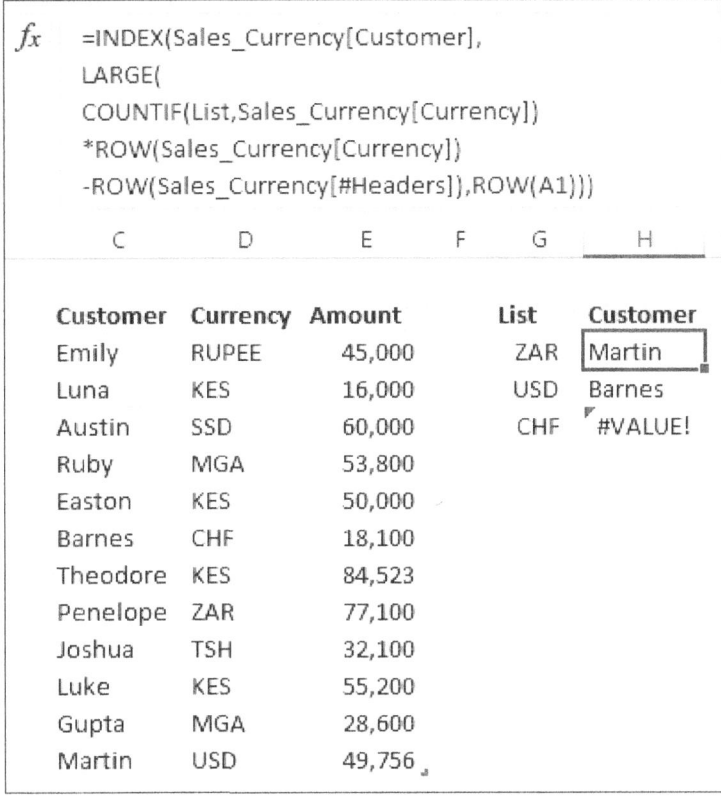

Figure 3.25: Lookup multiple items in a list

If we do not want the formula to return the error, we could nest it in the **IFERRROR** function, as shown in the following syntax. The **IFERROR** function now returns blanks instead of errors:

=IFERROR(
INDEX(Sales_Currency[Customer],
LARGE(
COUNTIF(List,Sales_Currency[Currency])
*ROW(Sales_Currency[Currency])
-ROW(Sales_Currency[#Headers]),ROW(A1))),
"")

Lookup unique value

Mastering the **COUNTIF** function is a big step in enhancing our lookup skills. For example, if you want to look up a unique value in Excel, you must utilize the **COUNTIF** function, as shown in *Figure 3.26*:

=INDEX(Sales[Customer],
MATCH(TRUE, COUNTIF(Sales[Currency],Sales[Currency])=1,0))

Here is how this function works:

- **COUNTIF(Sales[Currency],Sales[Currency]) COUNTIF** function returns an array of counts for each currency in the column. Since we are looking for the unique values, we check which count is equal to 1 ▶ **COUNTIF(Sales[Currency],Sales[Currency])=1**. This comparison returns an array of TRUE/FALSE, where TRUE=UNIQUE and FALSE=DUPLICATES.
- **MATCH** functions return the relative row position of the *first* **TRUE** value in the preceding array.
- **INDEX** function returns the customer in the same row number.

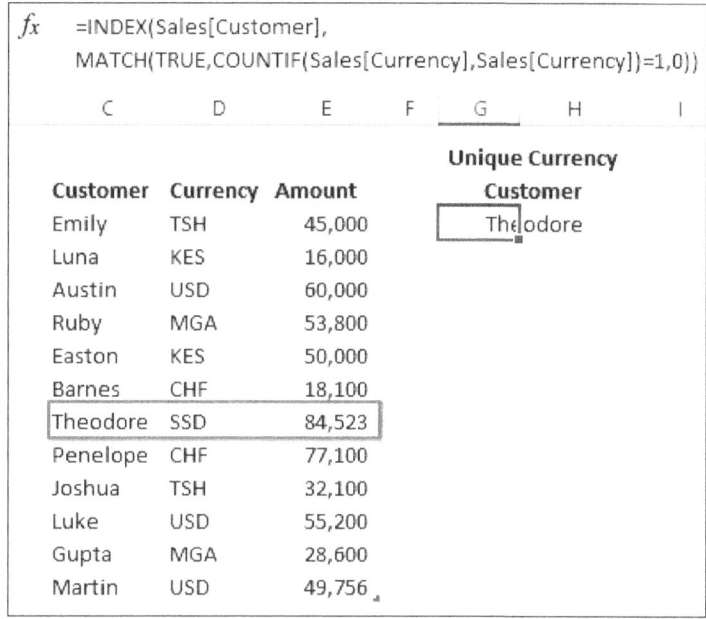

Figure 3.26: Lookup unique items

Lookup bottom *n* values

Looking up the bottom values is relatively easy if we first understand the **IF** and **SMALL** functions. For example, in *Figure 3.27*, we look up the three customers with the least sales:

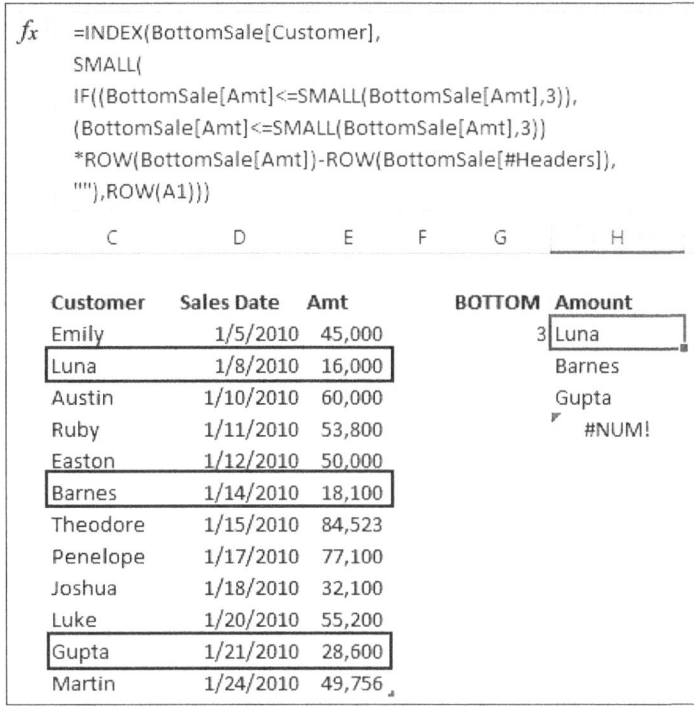

Figure 3.27: Lookup bottom items

```
=INDEX(BottomSale[Customer],
SMALL(
IF((BottomSale[Amt]<=SMALL(BottomSale[Amt],3)),
(BottomSale[Amt]<=SMALL(BottomSale[Amt],3))*ROW(BottomSale[Amt])-ROW(BottomSale[#Headers]),
""),ROW(A1)))
```

Here is how the preceding function works:

- **SMALL(BottomSale[Amt],3)** the SMALL function returns the third smallest amount – 28,600. The next step is to check which amount is less or equal to this third smallest amount ▶ **(BottomSale[Amt]<=SMALL(BottomSale[Amt],3))**. This comparison returns an array of TRUE/FALSE.

- **BottomSale[Amt]<=SMALL(BottomSale[Amt],3))*ROW(BottomSale[Amt]))-ROW(BottomSale[#Headers])** To get an array of row numbers, we multiply the TRUE/FALSE array with the amounts' row numbers. Remember to adjust the row numbers to start the count after the headers by deducting the header row number.

- The next step is to replace the negative values in the preceding array with blanks using the IF function: `IF((BottomSale[Amt]<=SMALL(BottomSale[Amt],3)), (BottomSale[Amt]<=SMALL(BottomSale[Amt],3))*ROW(BottomSale[Amt])-ROW(BottomSale[#Headers]), "")`
- We need to iterate over this row numbers list and return one at a time as the row argument for the INDEX function. For this task, we use the SMALL function, which returns the row numbers from the smallest to the largest. Note ROW(A1) evaluates to 1, and as you drag the function down, it increases until the full list is iterated.
- **INDEX** function uses each row number returned by the **SMALL** function and returns the corresponding customer.
- Please note that the **INDEX** function returns the "#NUM" error after all customers have been returned.

As we learned in the previous section, if you do not want the INDEX function to return an error, nest it in the IFERROR function, as follows:

```
=IFERROR(
INDEX(BottomSale[Customer],
SMALL(
IF((BottomSale[Amt]<=SMALL(BottomSale[Amt],3)),
(BottomSale[Amt]<=SMALL(BottomSale[Amt],3))
*ROW(BottomSale[Amt])-ROW(BottomSale[#Headers]),
""),ROW(A1))),
"")
```

Conclusion

This chapter offers a better lookup method for VLOOKUP – INDEX/MATCH combination.

There are three primary reasons why this combination is the better option: (i) It allows us to select not only a two-column table but also a single column/row array; (ii) The ability to select a single column/row array makes it flexible to look up not only to the left or right but also vertically or horizontally; (iii) Since it does not default to an approximate match, this combination is less prone to errors.

For those without an Office365 subscription, this combination of INDEX/MATCH is the most efficient lookup method.

In the next chapter, we will investigate why some Excel users still use one of the oldest legacy lookup functions – `LOOKUP` and `HLOOKUP`.

Points to remember

- Similar to the `VLOOKUP` function, the `INDEX/MATCH` combination returns the first match single value by default. If we want multiple values to nest, we can use the SMALL/LARGE functions.

- Unlike the `VLOOKUP` function, the `INDEX/MATCH` function row count is based on the array selected, not the default row number returned by the ROW function. Therefore, you must adjust the row count if your data does not start from the topmost row.

CHAPTER 4
LOOKUP

Introduction

In this chapter, we will discuss the LOOKUP function, which has been in Excel since its earliest version. The **LOOKUP** function's longevity and continued presence in Excel prove its value and widespread adoption as a fundamental tool for data retrieval and spreadsheet analysis.

You can use the **LOOKUP** function in both the Vector form and Array form.

In the Vector form, you search for an item in one column/row and return an item from the same position in another column/row.

The syntax is as follows:

=LOOKUP (lookup_value, lookup_vector, [result_vector])

Where:

- **lookup_value**: The value you want to find.
- **lookup_vector**: The single column/row containing the values to be searched (Note: It should be sorted in ascending order).
- **result_vector**: The single column/row containing the values to be returned.

Note

- Vector form is most appropriate If you want to specify a column/row containing the values you want to search.
- If the lookup value is not found, the **LOOKUP** function matches the next biggest value smaller than the lookup value.
- If the lookup value is not found and is smaller than the smallest value in the lookup range, the **LOOKUP** function will return the #N/A error value.
- **Lookup_vector** and **result_vector** range must be of the same size.

In the Array form, we search for an item in the first column/row of a table array (rows and columns) and return values in the same position as the last column/row of a table array.

The syntax is as follows:

=LOOKUP (lookup_value, array)

Where:

- **lookup_value:** The value you want to find.
- **Array:** Columns/rows containing the values to be searched.

Note:

- Values in the first Row/Column must be sorted in ascending order.
- The determination of whether the search will be horizontal or vertical depends on the number of rows vs. columns. If the array has more rows than columns, then **LOOKUP** searches the first column; otherwise, it searches the first row.
- If the lookup value is not found and is smaller than the smallest value in the lookup range, the **LOOKUP** function will return the **#N/A** error value.
- If the lookup value is not found, the **LOOKUP** function matches the next biggest value smaller than the lookup value.

Structure

In this chapter, we will discuss the five cases where we should use the **LOOKUP** function:

- Lookup the last match using a criterion
- Lookup the last empty cell
- Lookup the last negative number or text
- Lookup approximate match in an array
- Lookup the most repeated item

Lookup the Last Match Using a Criterion

One everyday use of the LOOKUP function is retrieving the last matching value. In this example, we shall use the Vector form.

We are trying to find the last subject offered by Ms Abby in *Figure 4.1*:

LOOKUP

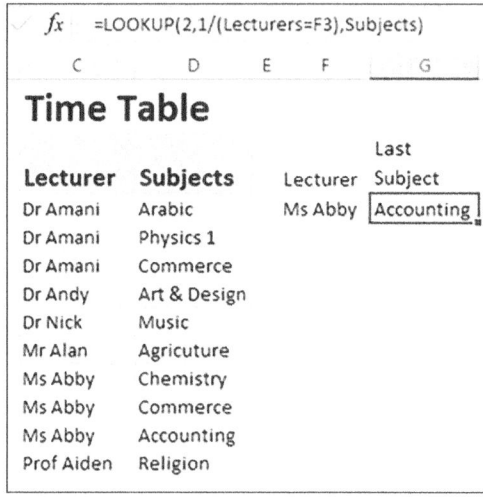

Figure 4.1: Lookup the last match in the column

```
=LOOKUP(2,1/(Lecturers=F3), Subjects)
```

Here is how the preceding function works:

- 2 represents a big value that we are sure will not be found in the lookup vector.
- `Lecturers=F3` returns an array of TRUE/FALSE, where TRUE represents the criteria being met, that is, lecturer = Ms Abby; otherwise, it returns FALSE (see *Figure 4.2*):

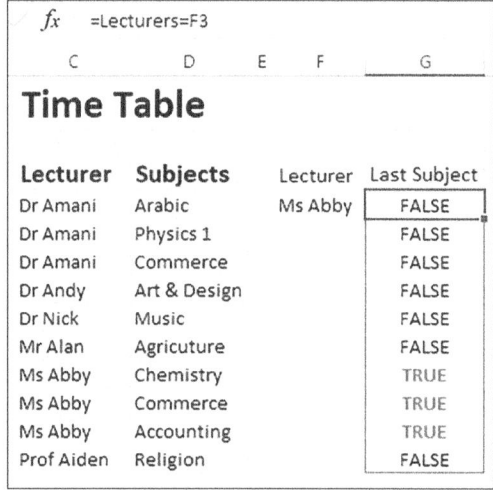

Figure 4.2: Check if the criterion is met

- **1/(Lecturers=F3)** convert the TRUE/FALSE into numeric equivalent by dividing 1 by each value (see *Figure 4.3*):

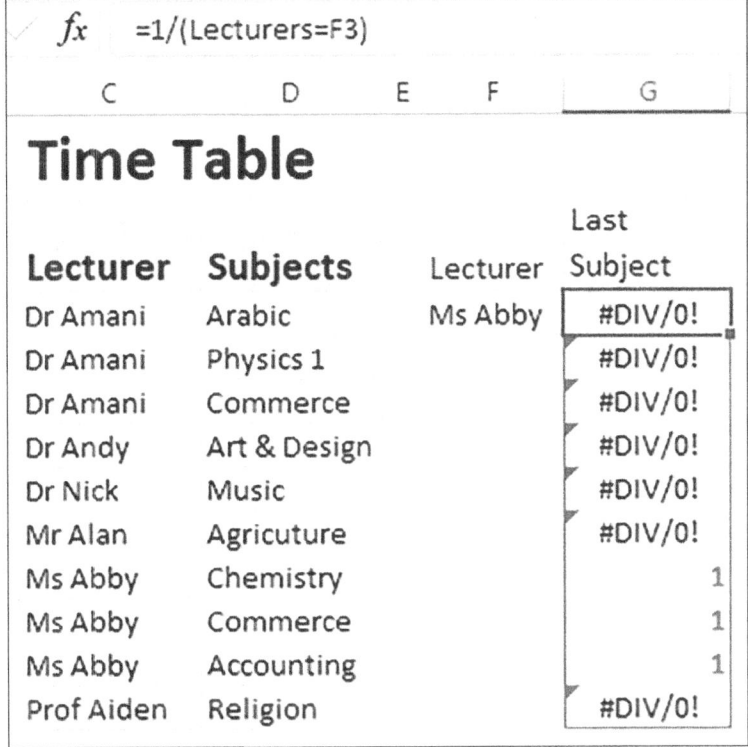

Figure 4.3: *Convert the TRUE/FALSE into numeric equivalent*

Note: There are four ways to convert boolean values to the numeric equivalent:
- By adding Zero: **(Lecturers=F3)+0**
- By multiplying with One: **(Lecturers=F3)*1**
- Using the double Unary method: --**(Lecturers=F3)**
- By dividing with One: 1/**(Lecturers=F3)**
- We should opt for the last method because it is the only method that does not include a zero in the results; including a zero in the lookup vector may disrupt the ascending order and cause the function to return unexpected results or an error.
- Since 2 is not found, and the largest value in lookup_vector is 1, the LOOKUP function matches the last 1 in the array and returns values in the same position in the result vector.

We are not limited to using a single criterion. For example, in *Figure 4.4*, we want to know the last date on which the customer Luke bought the chairs:

LOOKUP

```
fx  =LOOKUP(2,
        1/((tbl_Sales[Customer]=H16)*(tbl_Sales[Product]=H18)),
        tbl_Sales[Date])
```

Customer	Date	Product	Amount		Customer	Last Date
Austin	6/2/2021	Chairs	17,100		Luke	9/6/2021
Barnes	1/5/2021	Chairs	8,600		Product	
Easton	6/8/2021	Laptops	18,100		Chairs	
Gupta	12/8/2021	Laptops	49,756			
Luke	1/5/2021	Laptops	60,000			
Luke	5/5/2021	Chairs	5,200			
Luke	9/6/2021	Chairs	50,000			
Luna	5/3/2021	Chairs	93,800			
Martin	6/8/2021	Chairs	84,523			
Penelope	10/4/2021	Laptops	16,000			
Ruby	5/7/2021	Chairs	2,100			
Theodore	11/1/2021	Laptops	45,000			

Figure 4.4: *Lookup the last match using multiple criteria*

```
=LOOKUP(2,
1/((tbl_Sales[Customer]=H16)*(tbl_Sales[Product]=H18)),
tbl_Sales[Date])
```

Here is how the preceding function works:

- **2** represents a big value that we are sure will not be found in the lookup vector.
- **(tbl_Sales[Customer]=H16)*(tbl_Sales[Product]=H18)** returns an array of 1/0, where 1 represents the row's position where the customer is Luke and the product is chairs.
- **1/((tbl_Sales[Customer]=H16)*(tbl_Sales[Product]=H18))** We divide the preceding array with 1 to exclude all zeros. Including a zero in the lookup vector may disrupt the ascending order and cause the function to return unexpected results or an error.
- Since 2 is not found, and the largest value in lookup_vector is 1, the **LOOKUP** function matches the last 1 in the array and returns values in the same position in the result vector.

Lookup the Last Blank Cell

Lookup, the last blank in an array, is similar to the preceding example, with the only difference being the logical tests. Similar to the preceding example, we will use the vector form of the LOOKUP function to do a horizontal lookup.

In *Figure 4.5*, we look up the last month a customer made the payment, that is, the last non-blank month:

	C	D	E	F	G	H	I	J
	Customer	Jan	Feb	Mar	Apr	May		Last Payment
	Emily	4,500	1,600	6,000	5,380	5,000		May
	Luna		5,380	5,000	1,810			Apr
	Austin	8,452	7,710					Feb
	Ruby		8,452		3,210			Apr
	Easton	6,700		5,520	2,860			Apr
	Barnes			1,810	8,452			Mar
	Luke				3,210	5,520		May

fx =LOOKUP(2,1/(D33:H33<>""),$D$32:$H$32)

Figure 4.5: *Lookup the last non-blank*

```
=LOOKUP(2, 1/(D33:H33<>""),  $D$32:$H$32 )
```

Here is how this function works:

- **2** represents a big value that we are sure will not be found in the lookup vector.
- **D33:H33<>""** returns an array of TRUE/FALSE, where TRUE represents non-blank cells in the row.
- **1/(D33:H33<>"")** We divide the preceding array with 1 to convert the Boolean array to its numeric equivalent as well as to exclude all zeros. Including a zero in the lookup vector may disrupt the ascending order and cause the function to return unexpected results or an error.
- Since 2 is not found, and the largest value in lookup_vector is 1, the LOOKUP function matches the last 1 in the array and returns values in the same position in the result vector, that is, **$D$32:$H$32**.

Lookup the Last Negative Number or Text

The vector form of the LOOKUP function is the most robust function to look up any last value in an array. The only trick we need to learn is creating complex logical tests for the lookup vector.

LOOKUP

For example, in *Figure 4.6*, we want to look up the last date we had a negative temperature:

C	D	E	F	G	H
Temp°	Date	Crop	Production		Last Negative Temp°
13.00	1/5/2021	Traka	8,600		10/4/2021
32.00	1/5/2021	Cucumber	60,000		
(4.00)	5/3/2021	Zucchini	93,800		
(1.00)	5/5/2021	Eggplant	5,200		
10.00	5/7/2021	Traka	2,100		
7.00	6/2/2021	Zucchini	17,100		
31.00	6/8/2021	Traka	18,100		
(14.00)	6/8/2021	Zucchini	84,523		
36.00	9/6/2021	Traka	50,000		
(11.00)	10/4/2021	Zucchini	16,000		
14.00	11/1/2021	Traka	45,000		
14.00	12/8/2021	Zucchini	49,756		

Formula: `=LOOKUP(2,1/(tblHarvest[Temp0]<0),tblHarvest[Date])`

Figure 4.6: Lookup the last negative number

```
=LOOKUP(2,1/(tblHarvest[Temp0]<0),tblHarvest[Date])
```

This formula works in the same way as the others in the preceding examples, except for the logical test. In this example, **tblHarvest[Temp0]<0** returns an array of **TRUE/FALSE**, where TRUE represents all values that are less than zero.

To look up the last text, as shown in *Figure 4.7*, use the ISTEXT function to return an array of TRUE/FALSE values, where TRUE represents the text functions.

Every other aspect of the function is the same as the ones explained earlier.

```
=LOOKUP(2,1/ISTEXT(D59:D74),D59:D74)
```

Figure 4.7: Lookup the last text

Lookup Approximate Match in an Array

In all our previous examples, we have used the vector form of the LOOKUP function. Now, let us learn how to use an array form to look up an approximate match in an array.

For example, in *Figure 4.8*, we are looking up the discount percentage from the Discounts table using an approximate Match.

Customer	Sales	Discount		From	Discount
Emily	50,000	15%		0	0%
Theodore	45,000	0%		48,000	15%
Luna	53,800	23%		53,000	23%
Penelope	16,000	0%		61,700	35%
Austin	77,100	35%			
Joshua	55,200	23%			
Ruby	32,100	0%			
Luke	60,000	23%			
Easton	18,100	0%			
Gupta	49,756	15%			
Barnes	28,600	0%			
Martin	84,523	35%			

Formula: =LOOKUP(D78,Discounts)

Figure 4.8: Lookup approximate match in an array

```
=LOOKUP(D78, Discounts)
```

Here is how this function works:

- Sales Values stored in column D are used as the lookup value.
- The LOOKUP function uses the first column of the discount table as the lookup array and returns the approximate values in the same position of the last column.
- Remember that the values in the first column of the table array must be sorted in ascending order.

Lookup Most Repeated Item

This is another example of using the LOOKUP function's array form. In *Figure 4.9*, we are looking for the most frequent customer:

Name	Sales Date	Amt		Most Frequent Customer
Penelope	1/5/2010	45,000		Penelope
Luna	1/8/2010	16,000		
Austin	1/10/2010	60,000		
Penelope	1/11/2010	53,800		
Easton	1/12/2010	50,000		
Luna	1/14/2010	18,100		
Theodore	1/15/2010	84,523		
Penelope	1/17/2010	77,100		
Joshua	1/18/2010	32,100		
Penelope	1/20/2010	55,200		
Austin	1/21/2010	28,600		
Luna	1/24/2010	49,756		

Formula: `=LOOKUP(MODE(MATCH(Customer[Name],Customer[Name],0)), CHOOSE({1,2},MATCH(Customer[Name],Customer[Name],0),Customer[Name]))`

Figure 4.9: *Lookup most repeated item*

```
=LOOKUP(MODE(MATCH(Customer[Name],Customer[Name],0)),
CHOOSE({1,2},MATCH(Customer[Name],Customer[Name],0),Customer[Name]))
```

Here is how the preceding function works:

- **MATCH(Customer[Name], Customer[Name],0)** The MATCH function returns an array equal to the customers' number, where every item in this array represents the first position at which a customer name appears in the data (see *Figure 4.10*).

Name	Sales Date	Amt	Most Frequent Customer
			=MATCH(Customer[Name],Customer[Name],0)
Penelope	1/5/2010	45,000	1
Luna	1/8/2010	16,000	2
Austin	1/10/2010	60,000	3
Penelope	1/11/2010	53,800	1
Easton	1/12/2010	50,000	5
Luna	1/14/2010	18,100	2
Theodore	1/15/2010	84,523	7
Penelope	1/17/2010	77,100	1
Joshua	1/18/2010	32,100	9
Penelope	1/20/2010	55,200	1
Austin	1/21/2010	28,600	3
Luna	1/24/2010	49,756	2

Figure 4.10: *Customers' position*

- `MODE(MATCH(Customer[Name], Customer[Name],0)` the MODE function returns the most repeated item in the array.
- We then create a two-column table array using the CHOOSE function, whereColumn 1 is the customers' position, while Column 2 is the customers' name (see *Figure 4.11*).

=CHOOSE({1,2},MATCH(Customer[Name],Customer[Name],0),Customer[Name])

Name	Sales Date	Amt	2 column table array	
Penelope	1/5/2010	45,000	1	Penelope
Luna	1/8/2010	16,000	2	Luna
Austin	1/10/2010	60,000	3	Austin
Penelope	1/11/2010	53,800	1	Penelope
Easton	1/12/2010	50,000	5	Easton
Luna	1/14/2010	18,100	2	Luna
Theodore	1/15/2010	84,523	7	Theodore
Penelope	1/17/2010	77,100	1	Penelope
Joshua	1/18/2010	32,100	9	Joshua
Penelope	1/20/2010	55,200	1	Penelope
Austin	1/21/2010	28,600	3	Austin
Luna	1/24/2010	49,756	2	Luna

Figure 4.11: *Two-column table array*

- The **LOOKUP** function uses the first column of the two-column table as the lookup array and returns the customer name in the second column in the same position as the last match value.

Conclusion

In this chapter, we learned that the **LOOKUP** function is the best when looking up the last match. Whether we are using the Vector or Array form, the **LOOKUP** function can be used to look up data vertically or horizontally, provided that the lookup array data is sorted in ascending order.

Due to its limitations, it is only recommended for approximate matches and looking up the last match.

In the next chapter, we will investigate other functions that can be used to look up data, although they are not classified as lookup functions.

Points to remember

- Excel **LOOKUP** functionality is limited and thus not recommended for day-to-day use. As an alternative, consider using the **VLOOKUP** or **INDEX/MATCH** function.
- The **LOOKUP** function has no option for an exact match; all of its uses default to an approximate match.

Multiple choice questions

1. What is the result of the following formula:

    =LOOKUP(0, {1,2,3,4,5}, {"A","B","C","D","E"})?

    a. A
    b. B
    c. C
    d. D
    e. E
    f. #N/A

2. What is the result of the following formula:

   =LOOKUP("Z", {"A","B","C","D","E"}, {1,2,3,4,5})?

   a. 1
   b. 2
   c. 3
   d. 4
   e. 5
   f. #N/A

3. What is the result of the following formula:

   =LOOKUP(5, {1,2,3,4,6}, {"A","B","C","D","E"})?

   a. A
   b. B
   c. C
   d. D
   e. E
   f. #N/A

4. What is the difference between the Vector form and the Array form of the LOOKUP function?

   a. The Vector form searches for an item in one column/row and returns an item from the same position in another column/row, while the Array form searches for an item in the first column/row of a table array and returns values in the same position as the last column/row of a table array.

   b. The Vector form searches for an item in the first column/row of a table array and returns values in the same position as the last column/row of a table array, while the Array form searches for an item in one column/row and returns an item from the same position in another column/row.

c. The Vector form searches for an exact match, while the Array form searches for an approximate match.

d. The Vector form searches for an approximate match, while the Array form searches for an exact match.

Answers

1	f
2	e
3	d
4	a

CHAPTER 5
Other LOOKUP Methods and Functions

Introduction

In this chapter, we will discuss alternative methods and functions that can be used to look up data.

Many Excel users do not look beyond the lookup functions when faced with a lookup problem. This limits their alternatives and chances to learn how other functions work.

Depending on the size of our data or the complexity of the task, certain alternative methods may be more efficient or faster than the known lookup function.

Let us now explore the different approaches that can help us identify the most efficient solution for our situation.

Structure

In this chapter, we will discuss the six unique alternatives and functions to look up data:

- Using the advanced filter to look up items in/not in a list
- Using Excel Intersection operator to do a two-way lookup
- Using Database functions to lookup numeric data

- Using **SUMIFS**, **SUMPRODUCT**, **AGGREGATE**, and **MAX/MAXIFS** to lookup numeric data
- Looking up images
- Looking up cell addresses of an item
- Using a Pivot Table to lookup unique items in a list

Using the advanced filter to lookup items in/not in a list

Many Excel users must work on the advanced filter options in their everyday lookup tasks. Unlike the standard filter, where you only see the filter criteria when you hover a mouse over it, advanced filter options are visible to all.

Figure 5.1 shows the use of the advanced filter to lookup all chair purchases:

	B	C	D	E	F	G	H	I	J
					Criteria		Filtered Data		
	Date	Product	Amount		Product		Date	Product	Amount
	6/2/2021	Chairs	17,100		Chairs		6/2/2021	Chairs	17,100
	1/5/2021	Chairs	8,600				1/5/2021	Chairs	8,600
	6/8/2021	Laptops	18,100				5/5/2021	Chairs	5,200
	12/8/2021	Laptops	49,756				9/6/2021	Chairs	50,000
	1/5/2021	Laptops	60,000				5/3/2021	Chairs	93,800
	5/5/2021	Chairs	5,200				6/8/2021	Chairs	84,523
	9/6/2021	Chairs	50,000				5/7/2021	Chairs	2,100
	5/3/2021	Chairs	93,800						
	6/8/2021	Chairs	84,523						
	10/4/2021	Laptops	16,000						
	5/7/2021	Chairs	2,100						
	11/1/2021	Laptops	45,000						

Figure 5.1: *Lookup items in a table using an advanced filter*

Here are the steps to follow:

1. Click anywhere on the table containing all the data.
2. Go to the data tab and click the Advanced Filter options.
3. On the **Advanced Filter Pop-up Screen** (see *Figure* 5.2):
   a. Click the **Copy to another location**.
   b. The list range will pick automatically if you are using a table and have followed the preceding steps.

c. Select a criteria range – both the header and the cell containing the criteria should be selected. Since the advanced filter reads from the **Criteria range:** to the **List range:**, the headers should be identical.

d. In the **Copy to** field, select a single cell from which to copy the filtered table.

e. Finally, click **OK**.

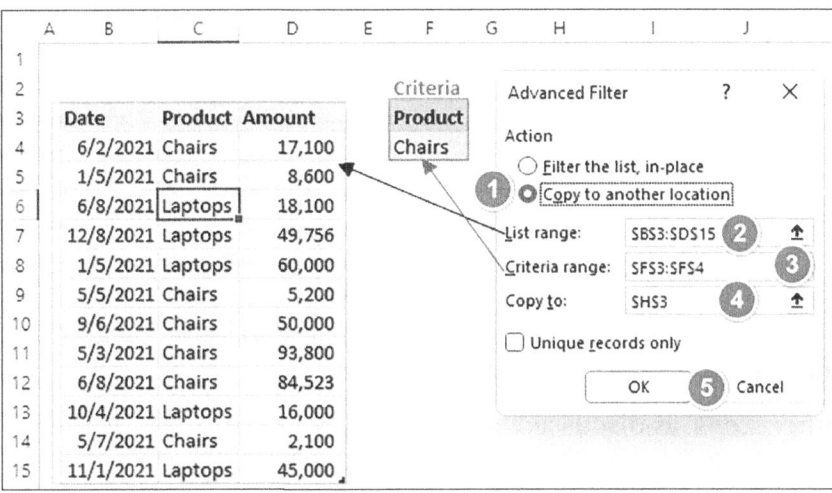

Figure 5.2: Advanced filter options for selecting items in a list

To look up items not in the table, change the criteria to include the "not equal to" operator (<>) and follow the preceding steps.

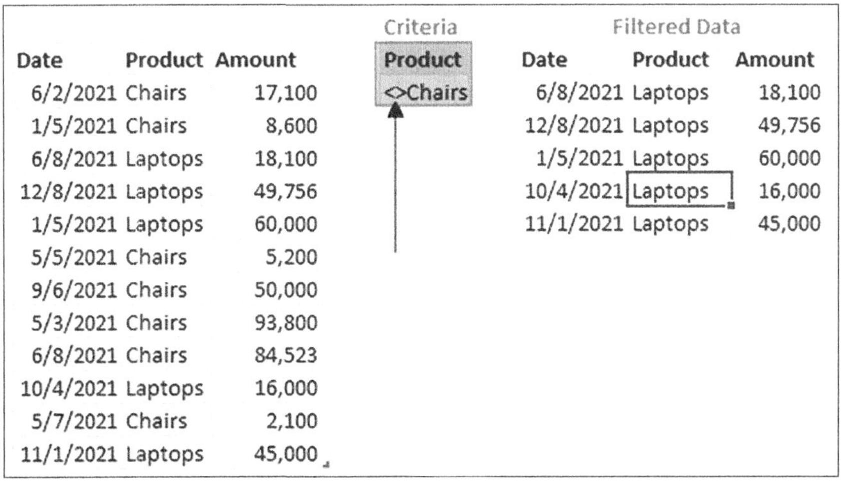

Figure 5.3: Lookup items NOT in a list using an advanced Filter

If we want to look up unique values, Advanced Filter has this option as well. As shown in *Figure* 5.4, suppose we want to know the unique crops that we plant:

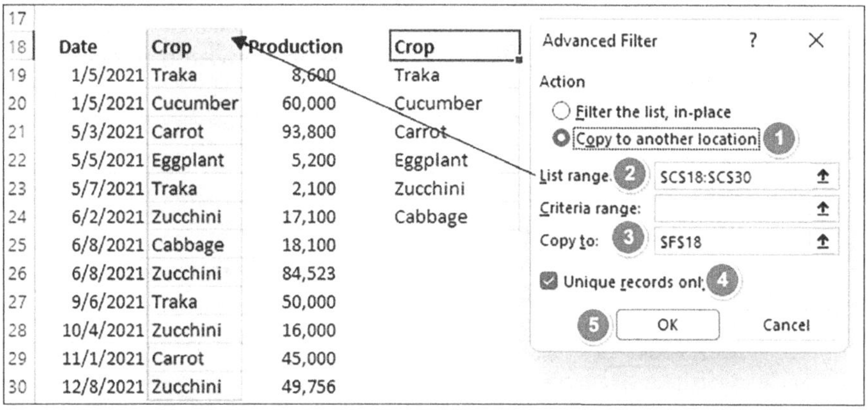

Figure 5.4: Lookup items UNIQUE items in a list using an advanced Filter

Note: With Unique records filtering, we skip the criteria range and click the `Unique record-only` option instead.

All the other steps, as discussed above, apply.

Using Excel Intersection Operator to do a two-way lookup

The Excel intersection operator is one of the least known but ideal ways of solving a two-way lookup problem, that is, finding the intersecting value(s) of two named ranges.

We only need to remember that using **a space character between two named ranges** becomes the Intersect operator.

In *Figure* 5.5, the Intersect operator is used to return the sales in the western region made by customer Joshua:

```
              fx   =Joshua Western

   B          C        D        E     F     G         H
Customer   Eastern  Western  Southern     Customer  Amount
Emily       70,000   50,000   45,000      Joshua    55200
Theodore    45,000   45,000   16,000      Region
Luna        83,800   53,800   60,000      Western
Penelope    16,000   16,000   53,800
Austin      77,100   77,100   50,000
Joshua  ←   95,200   55,200   18,100
Ruby        32,100   32,100   84,523
Luke        40,600   60,000   77,100
Easton      18,100   18,100   32,100
Gupta       32,683   49,756   55,200
Barnes      28,600   28,600   28,600
Martin      24,517   84,523   49,756
```

Figure 5.5: Two-way lookup using Excel Intersection Operation

Here are the steps to follow:

1. Click anywhere on the table containing all the data.

2. Go to the **Formula** tab, and under the **Define Names**, click **Create from Selection**.

3. The **Create Names from Selection** pop-up will appear, as shown in *Figure 5.6*. Select Create names from values in the top row and left columns.

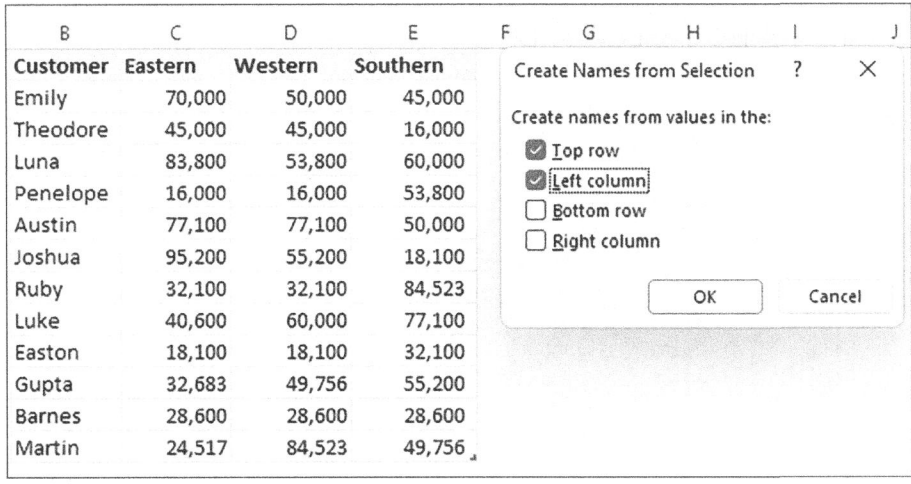

Figure 5.6: Creating names to be used in the Intersection

Other LOOKUP Methods and Functions

4. Once the names have been created, you can use the Intersect operator. Type the Row header (Joshua) and the Column header (Western) separated by the intersection operator, which is a space, as shown in *Figure 5.7*:

	Customer	Eastern	Western	Southern		Customer	Amount
fx	=Joshua Western						
	Emily	70,000	50,000	45,000		Joshua	Western
	Theodore	45,000	45,000	16,000		Region	
	Luna	83,800	53,800	60,000		Western	
	Penelope	16,000	16,000	53,800			
	Austin	77,100	77,100	50,000			
	Joshua	95,200	55,200	18,100			
	Ruby	32,100	32,100	84,523			
	Luke	40,600	60,000	77,100			
	Easton	18,100	18,100	32,100			
	Gupta	32,683	49,756	55,200			
	Barnes	28,600	28,600	28,600			
	Martin	24,517	84,523	49,756			

Figure 5.7: Using the Intersection operation

Intersection operations are not limited to a single criterion operation; we can use it for multiple criteria, as shown in *Figure 5.8*. We want to know the total amount bought by Joshua in the western and southern regions:

=SUM(Joshua Western:Southern)

Customer	Eastern	Western	Southern		Customer		Amount
	fx	=SUM(Joshua Western:Southern)					
Emily	70,000	50,000	45,000		Joshua		73300
Theodore	45,000	45,000	16,000		Region		
Luna	83,800	53,800	60,000		Western & Southern		
Penelope	16,000	16,000	53,800				
Austin	77,100	77,100	50,000				
Joshua	95,200	55,200	18,100				
Ruby	32,100	32,100	84,523				
Luke	40,600	60,000	77,100				
Easton	18,100	18,100	32,100				
Gupta	32,683	49,756	55,200				
Barnes	28,600	28,600	28,600				
Martin	24,517	84,523	49,756				

Figure 5.8: Intersection operation two-way lookup using multiple criteria

How the formula works:

We will follow the same preceding steps to create the named ranges. However, for this solution, we will select two regions separated by a full colon.

This returns the amounts for the two regions, as shown in *Figure 5.9*.

Finally, sum up the amounts to get the totals.

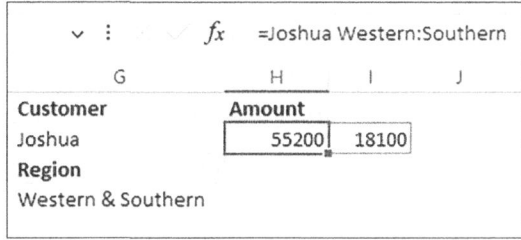

Figure 5.9: Multiple criteria results

We can also look up the total values for non-adjacent columns, as shown in *Figure 5.10*.

In this example, we want to know the total values for Joshua in the Eastern or Southern region.

The only trick to remember here is to use the plus sign (+) as an alternative to the OR logic.

=Joshua Eastern + Joshua Southern

	B	C	D	E	F	G	H
	Customer	Eastern	Western	Southern		Customer	Amount
	Emily	70,000	50,000	45,000		Joshua	113300
	Theodore	45,000	45,000	16,000		**Region**	
	Luna	83,800	53,800	60,000		Eatern & Southern	
	Penelope	16,000	16,000	53,800			
	Austin	77,100	77,100	50,000			
	Joshua	95,200	55,200	18,100			
	Ruby	32,100	32,100	84,523			
	Luke	40,600	60,000	77,100			
	Easton	18,100	18,100	32,100			
	Gupta	32,683	49,756	55,200			
	Barnes	28,600	28,600	28,600			
	Martin	24,517	84,523	49,756			

Figure 5.10: Multiple OR criteria results

Other LOOKUP Methods and Functions 93

Note: Intersection operators work with both cell range references and named ranges.

All you need to remember is to include a space between these ranges.

Using Database functions to lookup numeric data

Database functions have existed since Excel 2007, yet many users do not know their power and potential to look up numeric data.

Database functions perform specific calculations on a specified field (a Column) whose records meet specified criteria.

The syntax is as follows:

= DSUM(Database, Field, Criteria)

Where:

1. Database must be a range of data where every row is considered a record, and every column a field with the top row containing identifiers for the fields.

2. Field is the column that contains the data to look up.

3. Criteria is a range or set of conditions that determine records to look up. It must include a column header, and the criterion must correspond to a field name in the database.

For example, in *Figure 5.11*, we want to look up the amount of pens sold in March:

	A	B	C	D	E	F	G	H
65		Product	Jan	Feb	Mar		Month	Amount
66		Appliances	77,100	77,100	50,000		Mar	53,800
67		Binders	95,200	55,200	18,100		Product	
68		Telephones	32,100	32,100	84,523		Pens	
69		Paper	40,600	60,000	77,100			
70		Envelopes	18,100	18,100	32,100			
71		Bookcases	32,683	49,756	55,200			
72		Tables	28,600	28,600	28,600			
73		Labels	24,517	84,523	49,756			
74		Pens	16,000	16,000	53,800			
75		Copiers	77,100	77,100	50,000			
76		Chairs	95,200	55,200	18,100			
77		Trimmers	32,100	32,100	84,523			
78		Stamp Machines	18,100	18,100	32,100			

H66: fx =DSUM(B65:E78,G66,G67:G68)

Figure 5.11: Multiple OR criteria results

```
=DSUM (B65:E78, G66, G67:G68)
```

Where:

1. **Database**: All the data range, including the headers ▶ B65:E78.
2. **Field**: Header for the column that contains the lookup data ▶ Mar stored in cell G66.
3. **Criteria**: A range that contains a column header and a field value that acts as the criterion. See *Figure 5.12* for more information.

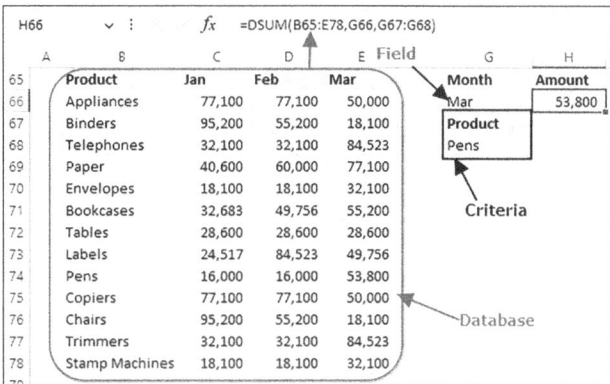

Figure 5.12: Arguments in database function

Database functions are not limited to simple criteria, as shown in the preceding example; you can create complex ones, as shown in *Figure 5.13*:

Figure 5.13: Complex criteria in database function

=DSUM(tbl_Orders[#All],"Qty",F81:I82)

The formula returns orders with a date greater than 1st June and less than 30th June for product Chair, and with a quantity greater than 20.

Here is how the formula works:

1. **Database**: All the data in the table called `tbl_Orders`.
2. **Field**: The column whose header is `Qty`.
3. **Criteria**: All the information contained in cell range F81:I82.

Note: The Criteria area **MUST NOT** include any Blank rows or Columns.

Using SUMIFS, SUMPRODUCT, AGGREGATE, and MAX functions to lookup numeric data

One of the least known facts is that match and trigonometry functions can be better than the lookup function when looking up single numeric values.

For example, in *Figure 5.14*, we want to return the payment amount for invoice "224-VV-004":

=SUMIFS(Payments[Amt],Payments[Invoice],G100)			
D	E	G	H
Invoice	**Amt**	**Invoice #**	**Amount**
111-BN-018	70,000	224-VV-004	95,200
111-CP-003	45,000		
224-BP-002	83,800		
224-FA-011	16,000		
224-MO-204	77,100		
224-VV-004	95,200		
220-PU-009	32,100		
220-SA-001	40,600		
221-UP-011	18,100		
222-AG-001	32,683		
222-FE-002	28,600		
222-PK-002	24,517		

Figure 5.14: *Using SUMIFS function to lookup numeric data*

```
=SUMIFS(Payments[Amt],Payments[Invoice],G100)
```

The **SUMIFS** function calculates the sum of values that meet multiple criteria. It allows you to specify multiple conditions and sum up only the values that satisfy them.

Syntax:

```
=SUMIFS (sum_range, criteria_range1, criteria1, [criteria_range2, criteria2], ...)
```

Where:

1. sum range ▶ the values to be aggregated.
2. criteria range ▶ the values to apply conditions.
3. criteria ▶ the condition to be met.
4. In our preceding example, we check which invoice number stored in the pay is equal to:
5. **Payments[Amt]** is the sum range. It represents the column **Amt** in the **Payments** table. We want to return values from this range based on the given conditions.
6. **Payments[Invoice]** is the first criteria range. It represents the column **Invoice** in the **Payments** table. We want to check this range of cells against a specific condition.
7. **G100** is the criteria. It is a specific value or reference against which the cells in the **Invoice** column will be evaluated.

The function returns the corresponding payment amount since only one invoice number meets the criteria.

Note: If multiple Invoice numbers had met the condition, the function would have returned the total payment amount.

An alternative to the **SUMIFS** function is the **SUMPRODUCT** function (see *Figure 5.15*):

Other LOOKUP Methods and Functions

```
=SUMPRODUCT(Payments[Amt],(Payments[Invoice]=G100)*1)
```

Invoice	Amt	Invoice #	Amount
111-BN-018	70,000	224-VV-004	95,200
111-CP-003	45,000		
224-BP-002	83,800		
224-FA-011	16,000		
224-MO-204	77,100		
224-VV-004	95,200		
220-PU-009	32,100		
220-SA-001	40,600		
221-UP-011	18,100		
222-AG-001	32,683		
222-FE-002	28,600		
222-PK-002	24,517		

Figure 5.15: Using the SUMPRODUCT function to lookup numeric data

```
=SUMPRODUCT(Payments[Amt],(Payments[Invoice]=G100)*1)
```

The **SUMPRODUCT** function is versatile and allows you to multiply corresponding elements in multiple arrays and sum up the products.

It is advantageous when you need to perform calculations on arrays or when you want to apply criteria to multiple ranges simultaneously.

Syntax:

```
=SUMPRODUCT(array1, array2, ...)
```

In the preceding example:

1. **Payments[Amt]** is the first array. It represents the column **Amt** in the **Payments** table. We want to multiply and sum up this array of values.

2. For the second array, we first compare each cell in the **Invoice** column of the **Payments** table to the value in cell G100 and return an array of True and False values **(Payments[Invoice]=G100)**. Multiplying this array by 1 converts True values to 1 and False values to 0 **((Payments[Invoice]=G100)*1)**.

3. Finally, the SUMPRODUCT function multiplies the corresponding values in the **Amt** column and the array of 1s and 0s, then sums up the products. The sum calculation will include only the values in the **Amt** column for the rows where the **Invoice** column matches G100 (see *Figure 5.16*).

Note: Performing a mathematical operation on a Boolean value converts them to their numeric equivalent of 1/0.

Therefore, we could convert the preceding True/False values by adding a zero. `(Payments [Invoice]=G100)+0`.

Payments[Amt]	(Payments[Invoice]=G100)*1	SUMPRODUCT
70,000	0	0
45,000	0	0
83,800	0	0
16,000	0	0
77,100	0	0
95,200	1	95200
32,100	0	0
40,600	0	0
18,100	0	0
32,683	0	0
28,600	0	0
24,517	0	0
		95200

Figure 5.16: SUMPRODUCT arrays multiplication

Finally, let us look at the **AGGREGATE** function and how we can use it to look up numeric values, as shown in *Figure* 5.17:

`=AGGREGATE(14,3,Payments[Amt]*(Payments[Invoice]=G100)*1,1)`

Invoice	Amt	Invoice #	Amount
111-BN-018	70,000	224-VV-004	95,200
111-CP-003	45,000		
224-BP-002	83,800		
224-FA-011	16,000		
224-MO-204	77,100		
224-VV-004	95,200		
220-PU-009	32,100		
220-SA-001	40,600		
221-UP-011	18,100		
222-AG-001	32,683		
222-FE-002	28,600		
222-PK-002	24,517		

Figure 5.17: Using the AGGREGATE function to lookup numeric data

Other LOOKUP Methods and Functions

Unlike the other **SUMPRODUCT** and **SUMIFS** functions, the **AGGREGATE** function performs a wide range of calculations on a dataset.

It allows you to apply 19 functions (see *Table 5.1*) with seven options to ignore errors, hidden values, and subtotals, and apply specific conditions to include or exclude data.

1. AVERAGE	5. MIN	9. SUM	13. MODE.SNGL	17. QUARTILE.INC
2. COUNT	6. PRODUCT	10. VAR.S	14. LARGE	18. PERCENTILE.EXC
3. COUNTA	7. STDEV.S	11. VAR.P	15. SMALL	19. QUARTILE.EXC
4. MAX	8. STDEV.P	12. MEDIAN	16. PERCENTILE.INC	

Table 5.1: Functions to apply in AGGREGATE

Syntax:

=AGGREGATE(function_num, options, array, [k])

Refer to the formula used in *Figure 5.16*.

=AGGREGATE(14,3,Payments[Amt]*(Payments[Invoice]=G100)*1,1)

Here is how the preceding function works:

1. 14 ▶ This argument specifies the **LARGE** function that returns the kth largest value in our data range.

2. 3 ▶ This argument specifies that the function will ignore error values in the data range.

3. For the array, we first compare each cell in the **Invoice** column of the **Payments** table to the value in cell G100 and return an array of True and False values (Payments[Invoice]=G100). Multiplying this array by 1 converts True values to 1 and False values to 0 ((Payments[Invoice]=G100)*1). Then, multiply the corresponding values in the **Amt** column and the array of 1s and 0s.

4. Finally, the function returns the largest value in the preceding final array.

Note: Like the **SUMPRODUCT** function, **AGGREGATE** can natively manage many array operations without using **Ctrl + Shift + Enter**.

Closely related to the preceding functions are the **MAX** and **MAXIFS** functions.

In *Figure 5.17*, we use the **MAX** function to lookup the numeric function.

```
=MAX( Payments[Amt]* (Payments[Invoice]=G100) )
```

Here is how the preceding function works:

1. We first compare each cell in the **Invoice** column of the **Payments** table to the value in cell G100 and return an array of True and False values (Payments[Invoice]=G100).

2. Then, we multiply the corresponding values in the **Amt** column and the array of **TRUE**s and **FALSE**s. This will return an amount value for all **TRUE**s and zeros for all **FALSE**s.

3. The **MAX** function returns the largest value in the preceding array.

=MAX(Payments[Amt]* (Payments[Invoice]=G100))				
D	E	F	G	H
Invoice	Amt		Invoice #	Amount
111-BN-018	70,000		224-VV-004	95,200
111-CP-003	45,000			
224-BP-002	83,800			
224-FA-011	16,000			
224-MO-204	77,100			
224-VV-004	95,200			
220-PU-009	32,100			
220-SA-001	40,600			
221-UP-011	18,100			
222-AG-001	32,683			
222-FE-002	28,600			
222-PK-002	24,517			

Figure 5.18: Using the MAX function to lookup numeric data

The **MAX** function may be hard to understand and explain. The alternative is the **MAXIFS** function, as shown in *Figure 5.19*:0

```
=MAXIFS(Payments[Amt], Payments[Invoice],G100 )
```

Other LOOKUP Methods and Functions

```
=MAXIFS( Payments[Amt], Payments[Invoice],G100 )
```

D	E	F	G	H
Invoice	Amt		Invoice #	Amount
111-BN-018	70,000		224-VV-004	95,200
111-CP-003	45,000			
224-BP-002	83,800			
224-FA-011	16,000			
224-MO-204	77,100			
224-VV-004	95,200			
220-PU-009	32,100			
220-SA-001	40,600			
221-UP-011	18,100			
222-AG-001	32,683			
222-FE-002	28,600			
222-PK-002	24,517			

Figure 5.19: Using the MAXIFS function to lookup numeric data

Syntax:

```
=MAXIFS(max_range, criteria_range1, criteria1, criteria_range2, criteria2,…)
```

In the preceding example, **Amount** values are our max range while the criteria range is the invoice numbers, and our criteria is the value stored in cell G100.

Note: For complex criteria lookup, consider using **MAXIFS** over the **MAX** function.

Looking up images

Lookup capability in Excel is more comprehensive than just text and numbers. We will learn how to look up images, as shown in *Figure 5.20*:

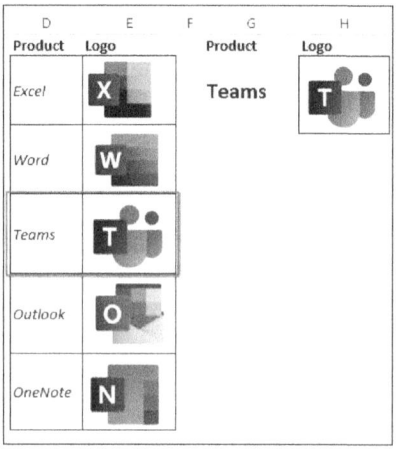

Figure 5.20: Looking up images

Perform the following steps:

1. Create a list of products and an adjacent blank column for logo images.

2. Copy a logo image for each product and paste it on the blank cell adjacent to each product name. Resize it to fit.

3. To lock the image to the cell, right-click and select **Format Picture**. Go to the Format Picture pane, select **Size & Properties**, and select **Move and size with cells** in the **Properties** section (see *Figure* 5.21):

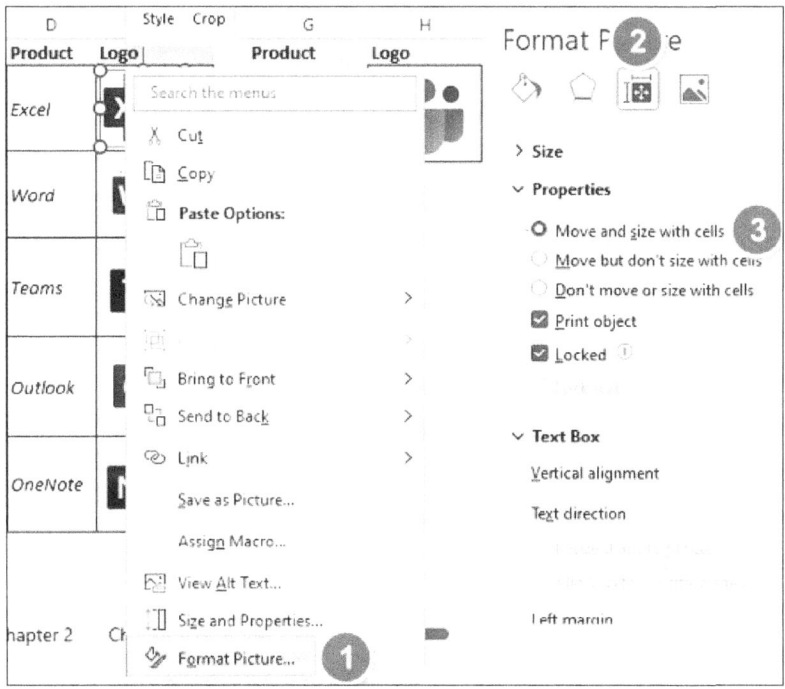

Figure **5.21**: *Locking images to cells*

4. The next steps involve creating a linked image:

    a. Select and copy any cell that has the image. Ensure you copy the cell and not the image.

    b. Right-click on another cell where you want to store the lookup image.

    c. Select **Paste Special** and paste it as a Linked image (see *Figure* 5.22).

    d. The logo in your selected cell will be pasted into that new cell.

Other LOOKUP Methods and Functions 103

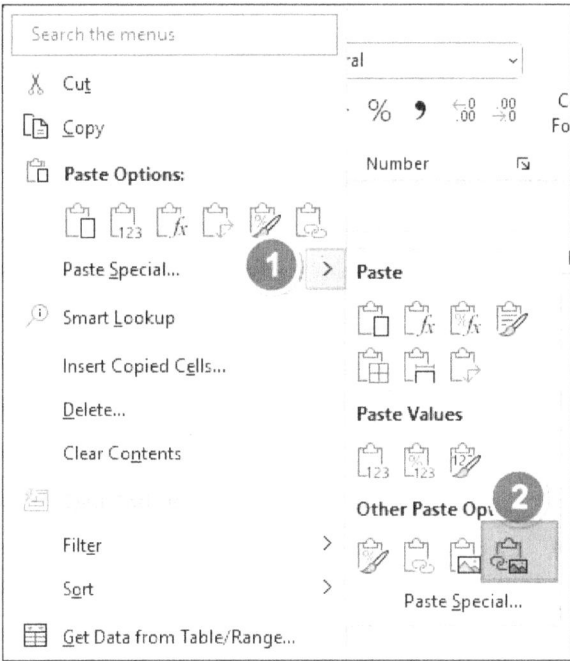

Figure 5.22: Pasting as Linked Picture

5. The next step is to create a named range. This will ensure that the copied logo dynamically changes based on the product name.

   a. Go to the **Formula** tab and select define name.

   b. In the new name dialogue form, write ▶ in the Name Field: **Logos**, and in the refers to: `=INDEX($E$116:$E$120,MATCH($G$116,$D$116:$D$120,0))` (see *Figure* 5.22).

   c. Where `$E$116:$E$120` ▶ Column containing the logo images, `$G$116` ▶ the cell containing the product whose logo image you want to look up, and `$D$116:$D$120` ▶ Column containing product names.

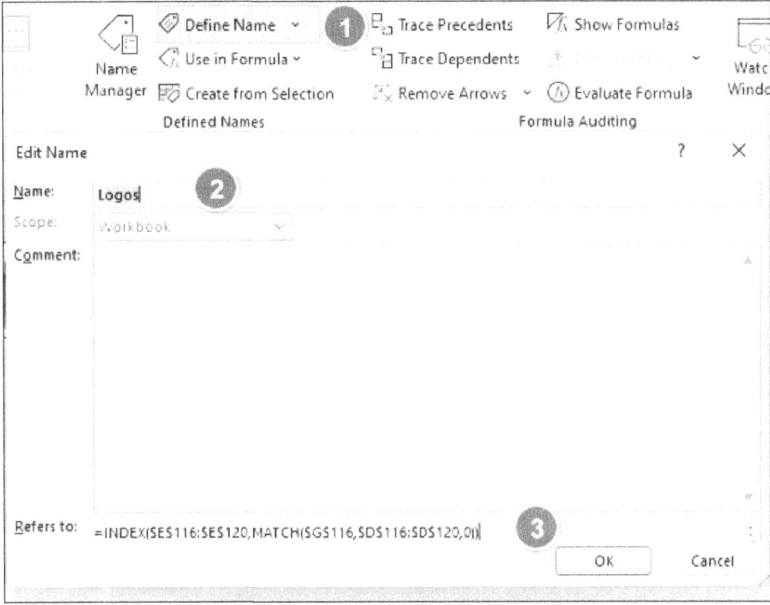

Figure 5.23: Creating name range

6. Finally, select the linked image we created in the previous step and replace its reference with the dynamic reference from the created name range (see *Figure 5.24*):

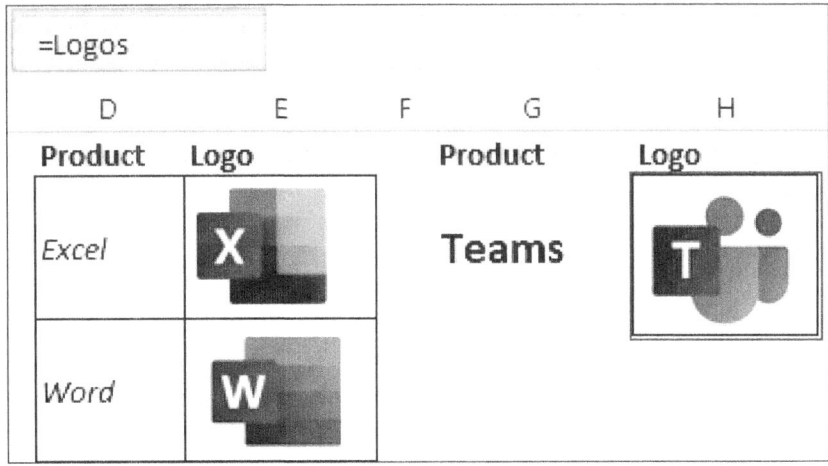

Figure 5.24: Changing the image reference to created name range

Note: The defined name should only return a cell reference, so we use the **INDEX/MATCH** functions. Other functions like **VLOOKUP** will not work since they do not return references.

Other LOOKUP Methods and Functions

Looking up cell addresses

In this section, we will learn how to look up cell addresses using the ADDRESS function.

In general, the **ADDRESS** function will return the cell address given a row number and a column number.

Note that the returned cell address is a text string, not an actual reference. Also, the addresses returned are either relative, mixed, or absolute based on the selected address type.

As shown in *Figure 5.25*, we want to know the last cell address for the crop "**Traka**".

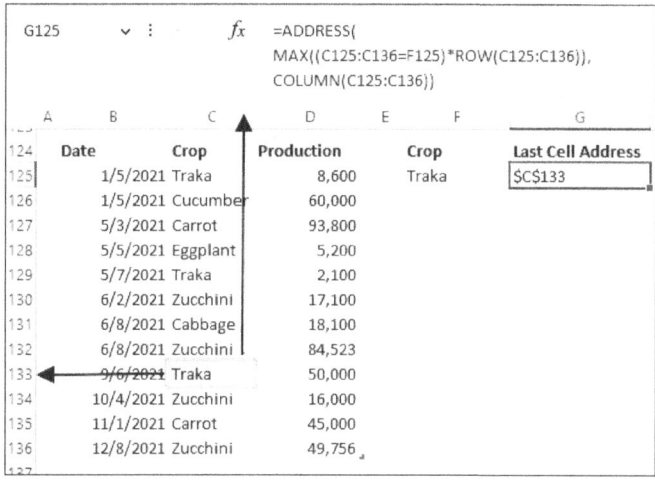

Figure 5.25: *Looking up the last cell address with a criterion*

```
=ADDRESS(
MAX( (C125:C136=F125)*ROW(C125:C136) ),
COLUMN(C125:C136) )
```

Here is how the preceding function works:

1. **C125:C136=F125** returns an array of **TRUE** and **FALSE**, where **TRUE** is the position where the crop meets the criterion; otherwise, **FALSE**.

2. **(C125:C136=F125)*ROW(C125:C136),** Multiply the corresponding Row numbers and the array of **TRUE**s and **FALSE**s. This will return Row numbers for all **TRUE**s and zeros for all **FALSE**s.

3. **MAX** function returns the largest row number from the preceding array.

4. **COLUMN(C125:C136)** returns the column number for all the crops.

5. The **ADDRESS** function returns the absolute cell reference given the row and column numbers.

Note: By default, the **ADDRESS** function returns an absolute cell reference. If you want to return a mixed or relative address, select the options as shown in *Figure 5.26*.

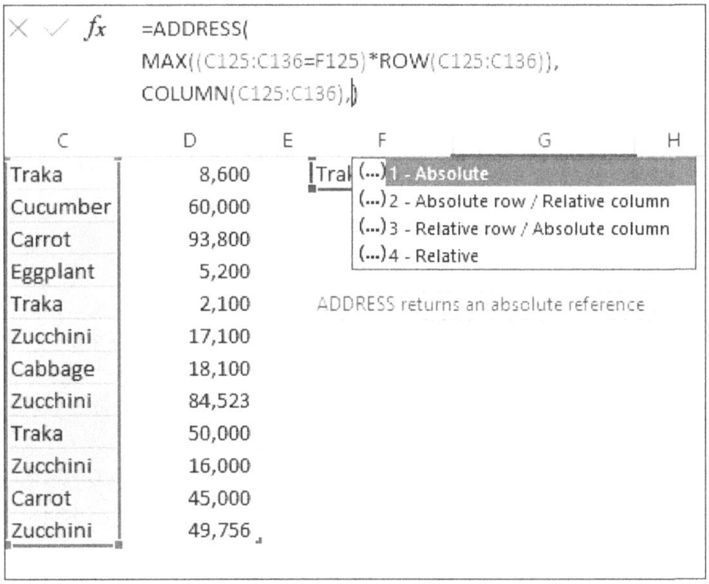

Figure 5.26: Returning relative or mixed references in the ADDRESS function

Using Pivot Table to lookup unique items in a list

A pivot table allows you to summarize and analyze large amounts of data quickly and easily. It helps you make sense of your data by organizing it meaningfully.

It can also be used to look up unique items in a list as shown in *Figure 5.27*:

Other LOOKUP Methods and Functions   107

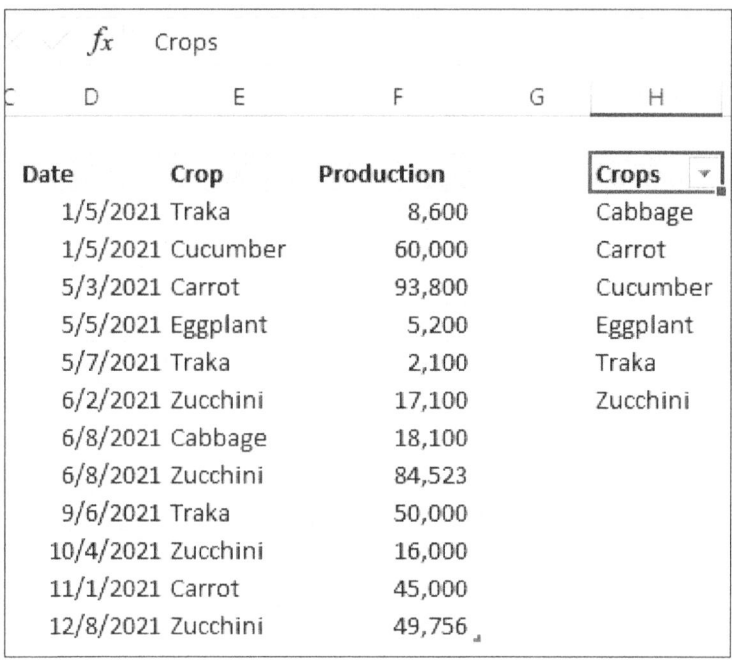

Figure 5.27: *Looking up Unique Items Using a Pivot Table*

Here are the steps to follow:

1. Convert your range into a table, click anywhere on your Excel table, go to **Table Design** tab, and click Summarize with PivotTable (see *Figure 5.28*):

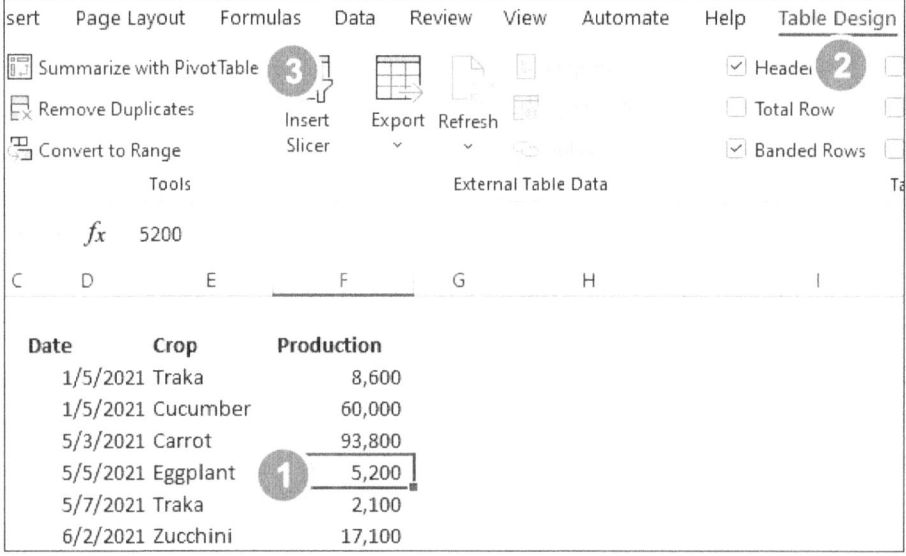

Figure 5.28: *Creating a Pivot Table*

2. On the pop-up window, click the existing worksheet, then under location, select a cell to place the Pivot Table (see *Figure 5.29*):

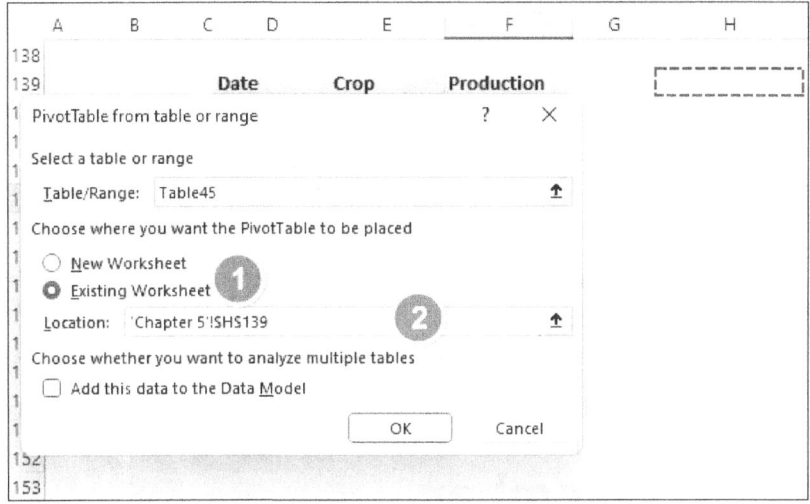

Figure 5.29: *Select where to place the pivot table*

3. Tick the **Crop** field among the pivotable fields or drop the field in the rows area. This populates a list of unique fields (see *Figure 5.30*):

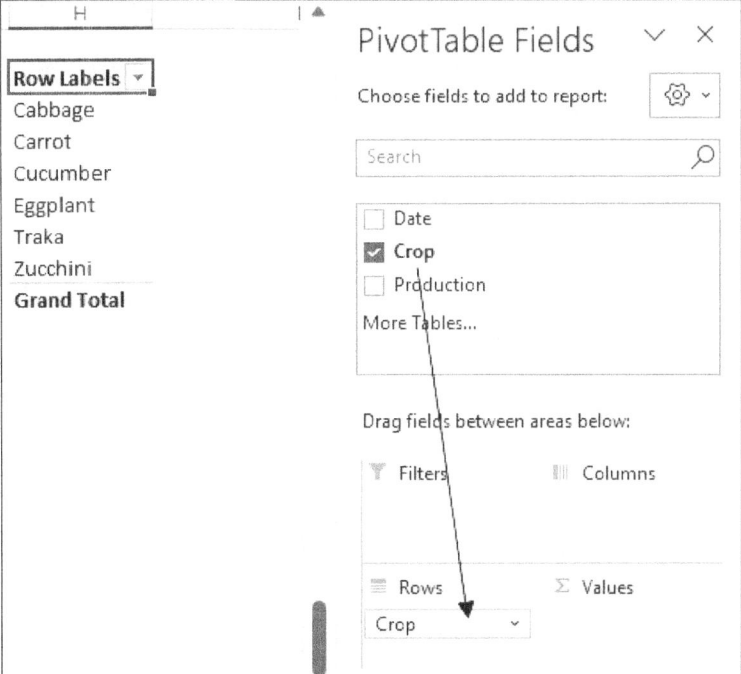

Figure 5.30: *Select the Pivot table fields*

Conclusion

In this chapter, we learned that Excel offers multiple ways to look up data. By learning different approaches, you gain flexibility in choosing the best method.

Some of these alternative methods are more efficient or faster than the known lookup functions, depending on the size of your data set or the complexity of the task. For example, the `DSUM` function can accommodate more complex criteria and calculates faster than the `VLOOKUP` function on numeric data.

In summary, learning alternative ways of looking up data in Excel provides you with a broader skill set, increased efficiency, adaptability, and problem-solving capabilities.

In the next chapter, we will start learning dynamic array lookup functions.

Points to remember

- Learning alternative ways of solving problems in Excel enhances your problem-solving skills. It encourages you to think critically, consider different approaches, and explore creative solutions. These skills are transferable and valuable beyond Excel, benefiting you in other areas of work or life.
- Excel is widely used across various industries and professions. Expanding your knowledge of alternative techniques makes you better equipped to handle diverse problems and adapt to evolving requirements or limitations.

CHAPTER 6
XLOOKUP

Introduction

In this chapter, we will introduce the first dynamic array lookup function — **XLOOKUP**.

When introduced in 2019, it was hailed as the "Functions Killer", "Ultimate Lookup Function", "Single Most Important function", and so on. It was supposed to replace the `LOOKUP`, `VLOOKUP`, `HLOOKUP`, and `INDEX/MATCH` combo.

Let us now explore areas where we can use this function and what advantages it has over the others.

Structure

In this chapter, we will discuss the 15 reasons why **XLOOKUP** is a far better option than the previously discussed functions:

- Defaults to exact match
- Easily return multiple adjacent and non-adjacent columns
- Easily lookup to the left or right
- Easily accommodates column insertion/deletion
- Easily lookup vertically or horizontally
- Easily lookup from the bottom up
- Easily integrates wildcards in the lookup
- Returns a cell reference
- Returns values in case of "No Match"
- Easily two-way or three-way lookup
- Returns non-adjacent columns

- Returns the last empty or non-empty cell
- Lookup non-contiguous array
- Easily returns duplicate lookup values

Exact match default

The following is the basic **XLOOKUP** syntax:

=XLOOKUP(lookup_value, lookup_array, return_array, [match_mode], [search_mode])

Where:

- **lookup_value:** We want to search for this value in the lookup_array. It can be a cell reference or a constant value.
- **lookup_array:** This is the range or array where we search the above value. It can be a single column or row or a two-dimensional range.
- **return_array:** This is the range or array from which we want to retrieve the result. It can be a single column or row or a two-dimensional range.
- **match_mode (optional):** This parameter determines how the function matches the lookup_value with the values in the lookup_array. It can be specified as 0 (exact match), -1 (exact or next smaller), 1 (exact or next larger), or 2 (wild character match). If omitted, **XLOOKUP** will default to an exact match.
- **search_mode (optional):** This parameter determines the search behavior of the function, that is, 1 (first to last), -1 (last to first), or 2 (binary search). If omitted, **XLOOKUP** will default to 1 (first to last).

This default to an exact match makes **XLOOKUP** less prone to errors present when using the **VLOOKUP** function.

Also, unlike the complicated **VLOOKUP** function syntax, where you will be required to count columns, the **XLOOKUP** function parameters are self-explanatory – easy to read and understand.

For example, in *Figure 6.1*, we are looking up the amount sold on 15th January:

```
fx  =XLOOKUP(H3,SalesTable[[ Date]],SalesTable[Amount])
```

Customer	Date	Amount	Date	Amount	
Barry French	1/8/2010	16,000	1/15/2010	84,523	XLOOKUP
Carl Jackson	1/5/2010	45,000		18,100	VLOOKUP
Carl Jackson	1/14/2010	18,100			
Carl Jackson	1/24/2010	49,756			
Carlos Daly	1/20/2010	55,200			
Carlos Daly	1/21/2010	28,600			
Carlos Soltero	1/11/2010	53,800			
Carlos Soltero	1/12/2010	50,000			
Clay Rozendal	1/10/2010	60,000			
Clay Rozendal	1/15/2010	84,523			
Neola Seider	1/17/2010	77,100			
Neola Seider	1/18/2010	32,100			

Figure 6.1: XLOOKUP exact match default

=XLOOKUP(H3,SalesTable[[Date]],SalesTable[Amount])

With **XLOOKUP**, all we need is three arguments: Lookup Value (H3), Lookup Array (Dates), and Return Array (**Amounts**). Furthermore, unlike **VLOOKUP**, data does not need to be sorted.

The result must be corrected with **VLOOKUP**, as shown in *Figure 6.2*, since the lookup array is not sorted, and we have skipped the match mode.

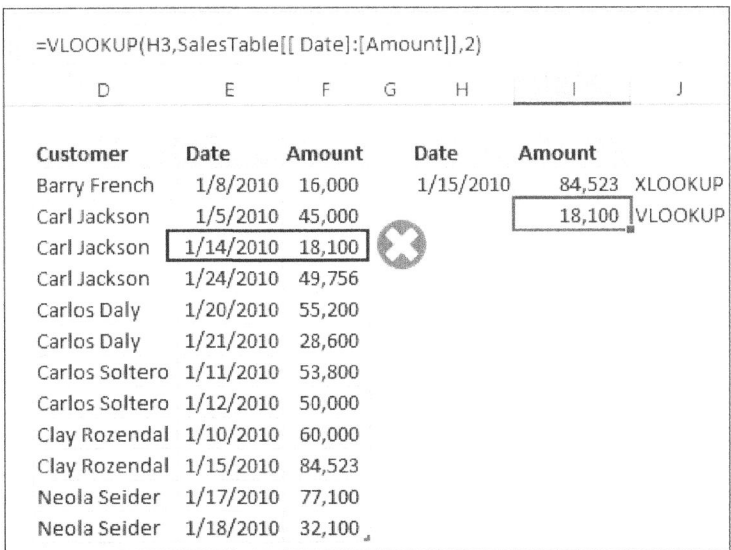

Figure 6.2: VLOOKUP approximate match default

```
=VLOOKUP(H3,SalesTable[[ Date]:[Amount]],2)
```

Easily returns multiple adjacent and non-adjacent columns

XLOOKUP belongs to the new Dynamic array formulas in Excel, allowing one to return multiple results to a range of cells. This range is known as Spill Range, which can be multiple rows/columns or a table.

Dynamic array functions are designed to accommodate their output by automatically populating adjacent cells with results. This spill behavior allows the functions to return multiple values or an array of values rather than a single result.

The size of the spill range depends on the number of values returned by the function.

If we use a legacy array function like **VLOOKUP**, we must manually select adjacent cells and use the **Ctrl + Shift + Enter** to commit it. This is the only way it can populate adjacent cells.

As shown in *Figure 6.3*, we are looking up the sales date and amount for customer "Luke Daly."

```
=XLOOKUP(H3, SalesTable[Customer], SalesTable[[ Date]:[Amount]] )
```

The only trick with returning multiple columns is ensuring that you select them as a return array. In the preceding example, we have selected both the date and amount columns: `SalesTable[[ Date]:[Amount]]`

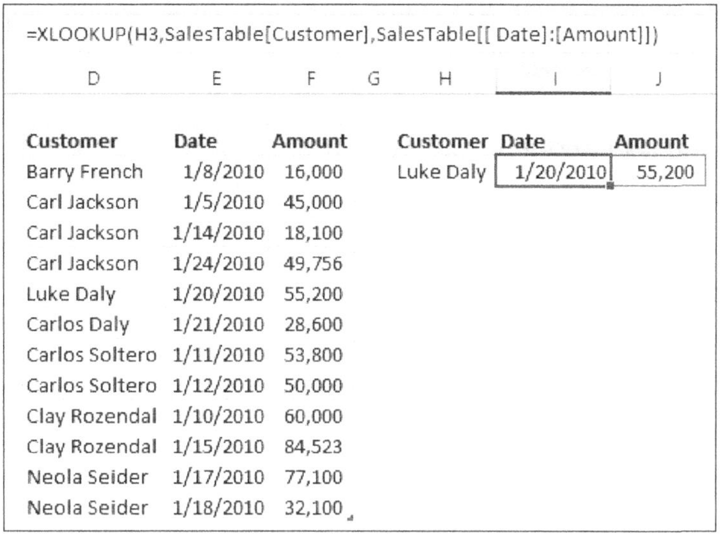

```
=XLOOKUP(H3,SalesTable[Customer],SalesTable[[ Date]:[Amount]])
```

Customer	Date	Amount	Customer	Date	Amount
Barry French	1/8/2010	16,000	Luke Daly	1/20/2010	55,200
Carl Jackson	1/5/2010	45,000			
Carl Jackson	1/14/2010	18,100			
Carl Jackson	1/24/2010	49,756			
Luke Daly	1/20/2010	55,200			
Carlos Daly	1/21/2010	28,600			
Carlos Soltero	1/11/2010	53,800			
Carlos Soltero	1/12/2010	50,000			
Clay Rozendal	1/10/2010	60,000			
Clay Rozendal	1/15/2010	84,523			
Neola Seider	1/17/2010	77,100			
Neola Seider	1/18/2010	32,100			

Figure 6.3: XLOOKUP returns multiple adjacent columns

To return multiple non-adjacent columns, we need to use the CHOOSECOLS functions in the return array argument to return the selected columns (see *Figure 6.4*):

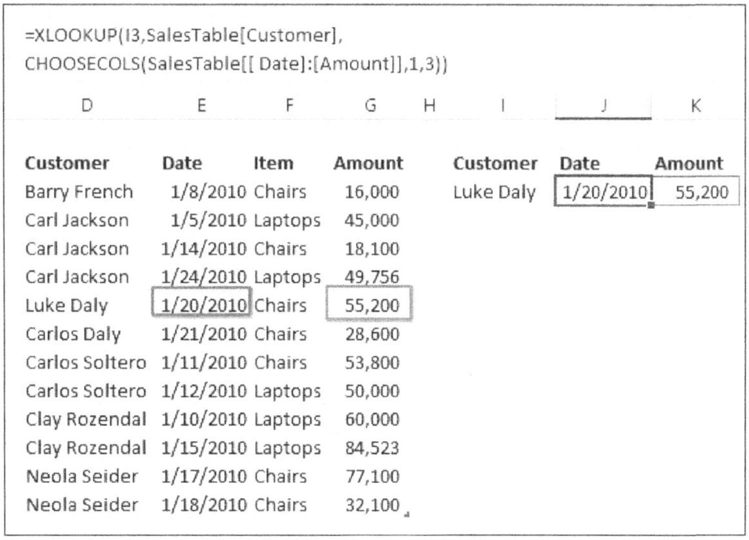

```
=XLOOKUP(I3,SalesTable[Customer],
CHOOSECOLS(SalesTable[[ Date]:[Amount]],1,3))
```

Customer	Date	Item	Amount	Customer	Date	Amount
Barry French	1/8/2010	Chairs	16,000	Luke Daly	1/20/2010	55,200
Carl Jackson	1/5/2010	Laptops	45,000			
Carl Jackson	1/14/2010	Chairs	18,100			
Carl Jackson	1/24/2010	Laptops	49,756			
Luke Daly	1/20/2010	Chairs	55,200			
Carlos Daly	1/21/2010	Chairs	28,600			
Carlos Soltero	1/11/2010	Chairs	53,800			
Carlos Soltero	1/12/2010	Laptops	50,000			
Clay Rozendal	1/10/2010	Laptops	60,000			
Clay Rozendal	1/15/2010	Laptops	84,523			
Neola Seider	1/17/2010	Chairs	77,100			
Neola Seider	1/18/2010	Chairs	32,100			

Figure 6.4: XLOOKUP returns multiple non-adjacent columns

```
=XLOOKUP(I3,SalesTable[Customer],CHOOSECOLS(SalesTable[[
Date]:[Amount]],1,3))
```

In this example, we select three columns: date, item, and amount. Using

CHOOSECOLS(SalesTable[[Date]:[Amount]],1,3), the choose column returns only the first and third columns.

The only thing to remember is that we can use the CHOOSECOLS function to return selected non-adjacent columns in one array.

Easily lookup data to the left or right

Unlike the VLOOKUP function, the XLOOKUP function easily looks up data from the left.

In *Figure* 6.5, we are looking for the date of the sale for the customer Luke.

```
=XLOOKUP(I3,SalesTable[Customer],SalesTable[Date])
```

Date	Customer	Item	Amount		Customer	Date	
1/8/2010	Emily	Chairs	16,000		Luke	1/12/2010	XLOOKUP
1/5/2010	Theodore	Laptops	45,000			1/12/2010	VLOOKUP
1/14/2010	Luna	Chairs	18,100				
1/24/2010	Penelope	Laptops	49,756				
1/20/2010	Austin	Chairs	55,200				
1/21/2010	Joshua	Chairs	28,600				
1/11/2010	Ruby	Chairs	53,800				
1/12/2010	Luke	Laptops	50,000				
1/10/2010	Easton	Laptops	60,000				
1/15/2010	Gupta	Laptops	84,523				
1/17/2010	Barnes	Chairs	77,100				
1/18/2010	Martin	Chairs	32,100				

Figure **6.5**: XLOOKUP lookup to the left

=XLOOKUP(I3,SalesTable[Customer],SalesTable[Date])

Even though the dates are stored on the left side of the customer data, XLOOKUP still uses its simple three arguments, unlike VLOOKUP, which requires nesting of the IF function (see *Figure* 6.6):

=VLOOKUP(I3, IF({1,0},SalesTable[Customer],SalesTable[Date]) , 2 , 0)

With VLOOKUP, you must create a custom table array using the IF function, as we saw in the previous chapter.

```
=VLOOKUP(I3,IF({1,0},SalesTable[Customer],SalesTable[Date]),2,0)
```

```
   D         E        F        G        H     I        J        K
  Date    Customer   Item   Amount         Customer   Date
  1/8/2010  Emily    Chairs   16,000        Luke      1/12/2010 XLOOKUP
  1/5/2010  Theodore Laptops  45,000                  1/12/2010 VLOOKUP
  1/14/2010 Luna     Chairs   18,100
  1/24/2010 Penelope Laptops  49,756
  1/20/2010 Austin   Chairs   55,200
  1/21/2010 Joshua   Chairs   28,600
  1/11/2010 Ruby     Chairs   53,800
  1/12/2010 Luke     Laptops  50,000
  1/10/2010 Easton   Laptops  60,000
  1/15/2010 Gupta    Laptops  84,523
  1/17/2010 Barnes   Chairs   77,100
  1/18/2010 Martin   Chairs   32,100
```

Figure 6.6: VLOOKUP *lookup to the left*

Easily accommodates column insertion/deletion

Unlike the VLOOKUP function, XLOOKUP can handle the insertion and deletion of columns in a table.

For example, *Figure* 6.7 shows the two functions' results before inserting a new column.

```
=VLOOKUP(I3,SalesTable,4,0)
```

```
   D         E        F        G        H     I        J        K
  Date    Customer   Item   Amount         Customer   Amount
  1/8/2010  Emily    Chairs   16,000        1/5/2010   45,000 XLOOKUP
  1/5/2010  Theodore Laptops  45,000                   45,000 VLOOKUP
  1/14/2010 Luna     Chairs   18,100
  1/24/2010 Penelope Laptops  49,756
  1/20/2010 Austin   Chairs   55,200
  1/21/2010 Joshua   Chairs   28,600
  1/11/2010 Ruby     Chairs   53,800
  1/12/2010 Luke     Laptops  50,000
  1/10/2010 Easton   Laptops  60,000
  1/15/2010 Gupta    Laptops  84,523
  1/17/2010 Barnes   Chairs   77,100
  1/18/2010 Martin   Chairs   32,100
```

Figure 6.7: VLOOKUP *and* XLOOKUP *functions before column insertion*

When you insert a column in the table, **VLOOKUP** returns the wrong values, but **XLOOKUP** can dynamically handle the insertion (see *Figure 6.8*):

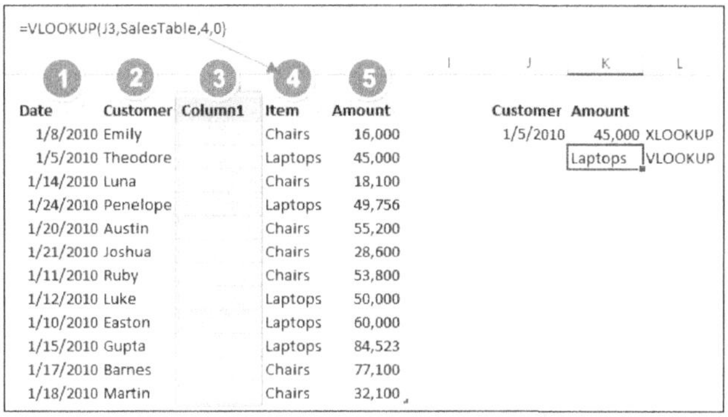

Figure 6.8: VLOOKUP and XLOOKUP functions after column insertion

Note: The **VLOOKUP** cannot handle the insertion because we have a hard-coded lookup column, that is, column 4.

As we learned in *Chapter 2, VLOOKUP IS DEAD: Or is it?* You can overcome this by nesting the **MATCH** function in **VLOOKUP** as follows:

`=VLOOKUP(J3, SalesTable,MATCH(K2,SalesTable[#Headers],0),0)`

When you delete a column, the **VLOOKUP** function returns an error, but **XLOOKUP** can dynamically handle the deletion. Refer to *Figure 6.9* after we have deleted the items column.

The **VLOOKUP** function returns an error because it cannot find the return column, that is, column 4.

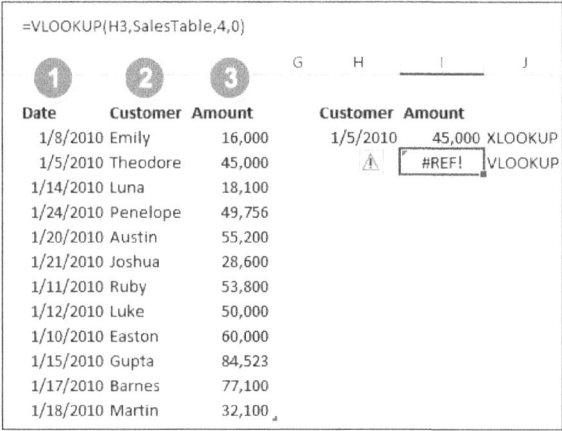

Figure 6.9: VLOOKUP and XLOOKUP functions after column deletion

Easily looks up data vertically or horizontally

With the **XLOOKUP** function, we no longer need the **HLOOKUP** or modified **VLOOKUP** function to lookup data horizontally.

In *Figure* 6.10, we look up the supplier with the lowest quoted price:

	D	E	F	G	H	I
					VLOOKUP	XLOOKUP
					Lowest	Lowest
	Item	Luna	Ruby	Gupta	Quote	Quote
	Chairs	70,000	50,000	45,000	Gupta	Gupta
	Laptops	45,000	43,000	46,000	Ruby	Ruby
	Cabinets	43,800	53,800	60,000	Luna	Luna
	Books	42,683	49,756	35,200	Gupta	Gupta
	Desktops	77,100	47,100	50,000	Ruby	Ruby
	Pens	95,200	55,200	18,100	Gupta	Gupta
	CCTV	32,100	35,100	84,523	Luna	Luna
	Printers	60,600	60,000	77,100	Ruby	Ruby

Formula bar: `=XLOOKUP(MIN(E67:G67),E67:G67,$E$66:$G$66)`

Figure **6.10**: VLOOKUP and XLOOKUP *function after column deletion*

```
=VLOOKUP(MIN(E67:G67),TRANSPOSE(IF({1;0},E67:G67,Reps)), 2,0)
=XLOOKUP(MIN(E67:G67),E67:G67,$E$66:$G$66)
```

As we can see from the preceding functions, **XLOOKUP** is easy to write and explain.

Here is how the **XLOOKUP** function works:

- **MIN(E67:G67):** the MIN function returns the smallest quoted price per item. This becomes our lookup value.
- **E67:G67:** This is our lookup array, that is, all the price ranges. This is where we will find the position of the lowest price.
- **$E$66:$G$66:** This is our return array, that is, all the suppliers. We will return the supplier whose position corresponds to the lowest price.

Easily lookup data from the bottom up

By default, the XLOOKUP and VLOOKUP functions lookup data from top to bottom and return the first TRUE value.

XLOOKUP

In *Figure 6.11*, we look up the last date customer "Clay Rozendal" bought from us:

```
=XLOOKUP(H3,SalesTable[Customer],SalesTable[Date],,,-1)
```

Date	Customer	Amount		Customer	Last Buy Date	
1/8/2010	Barry French	16,000		Clay Rozendal	1/17/2010	XLOOKUP
1/5/2010	Clay Rozendal	45,000			1/17/2010	VLOOKUP
1/14/2010	Carl Jackson	18,100				
1/24/2010	Clay Rozendal	49,756				
1/20/2010	Carlos Daly	55,200				
1/21/2010	Carlos Daly	28,600				
1/11/2010	Carlos Soltero	53,800				
1/12/2010	Carlos Soltero	50,000				
1/10/2010	Clay Rozendal	60,000				
1/15/2010	Barry French	84,523				
1/17/2010	Clay Rozendal	77,100				
1/18/2010	Neola Seider	32,100				

Figure 6.11: XLOOKUP function lookup from bottom to top

=XLOOKUP(H3,SalesTable[Customer],SalesTable[Date],,,-1)

The only trick here is to specify the correct search mode in **XLOOKUP**, that is, -1.

This search mode parameter determines the search behavior of the function, that is, 1 (first to last), -1 (last to first), or 2 (binary search). If omitted, **XLOOKUP** will default to 1 (first to last).

We need to use the following function to get the same results using **VLOOKUP**. As shown in *Figure 6.12*, the **VLOOKUP** function is complicated and hard to understand:

=VLOOKUP(

MAX((SalesTable[Customer]=H3)*ROW(SalesTable[Customer])),

IF({1,0},(SalesTable[Customer]=H3)*ROW(SalesTable[Customer]),SalesTable[Date]),

2,0)

```
=VLOOKUP(MAX((SalesTable[Customer]=H3)*ROW(SalesTable[Customer])),
IF({1,0},(SalesTable[Customer]=H3)*ROW(SalesTable[Customer]),SalesTable[Date]),
2,0)
```

Date	Customer	Amount	Customer	Last Buy Date	
1/8/2010	Barry French	16,000	Clay Rozendal	1/17/2010	XLOOKUP
1/5/2010	Clay Rozendal	45,000		1/17/2010	VLOOKUP
1/14/2010	Carl Jackson	18,100			
1/24/2010	Clay Rozendal	49,756			
1/20/2010	Carlos Daly	55,200			
1/21/2010	Carlos Daly	28,600			
1/11/2010	Carlos Soltero	53,800			
1/12/2010	Carlos Soltero	50,000			
1/10/2010	Clay Rozendal	60,000			
1/15/2010	Barry French	84,523			
1/17/2010	Clay Rozendal	77,100			
1/18/2010	Neola Seider	32,100			

Figure 6.12: VLOOKUP function lookup from bottom to top

Refer to *Chapter 2, VLOOKUP Is Dead: Or is it?* for an explanation of how the preceding **VLOOKUP** function works.

Easily integrates wildcards in the lookup

Using the asterisk (*) or the question mark (?) wildcard characters creates a versatile and simpler lookup value.

For example, in *Figure 6.13*, we look up the date for a cost code that contains the letter "P".

```
=XLOOKUP(I3,SalesTable[Cost Code],SalesTable[Date],,2)
```

Date	Customer	Cost Code	Amount	Cost Code Contains P	Date
1/8/2010	Barry French	111-BN-018	16,000	*P*	1/24/2010
1/5/2010	Clay Rozendal	111-CJ-003	45,000		
1/14/2010	Carl Jackson	224-BX-002	18,100	Cost Code	
1/24/2010	Clay Rozendal	224-FP-011	49,756	5th Character is a P	Date
1/20/2010	Carlos Daly	224-MO-204	55,200	????P*	1/11/2010
1/21/2010	Carlos Daly	224-VV-004	28,600		
1/11/2010	Carlos Soltero	220-PU-009	53,800		
1/12/2010	Carlos Soltero	220-SA-001	50,000		
1/10/2010	Clay Rozendal	221-UP-011	60,000		
1/15/2010	Barry French	222-AG-001	84,523		
1/17/2010	Clay Rozendal	222-FE-002	77,100		
1/18/2010	Neola Seider	222-PK-002	32,100		

Figure 6.13: XLOOKUP using the asterisk Wildcards

```
=XLOOKUP(I3,SalesTable[Cost Code],SalesTable[Date],,2)
```

The only trick here is remembering to use 2 as the match mode.

The match mode parameter determines how the function matches the lookup_value with the values in the lookup_array. It can be specified as 0 (exact match), -1 (exact or next smaller), 1 (exact or next larger), or 2 (wild character match). If omitted, XLOOKUP will default to an exact match.

Note: The Asterisk (*) wildcard represents one or more characters in a text string. For example, P* will find any word that starts with the letter P, *P will find any word that ends with the letter P, and *P* will find any word with the letter P.

Also, remember **XLOOKUP** function returns the first **TRUE** value.

We are not limited to using only the asterisk wildcard, but we can combine both, as shown in *Figure 6.14*. In this example, we look up the date for a cost code whose fifth character is a "P".

As discussed, a question mark (?) wildcard represents a single character in a text string. Therefore, a lookup value "????P*" will find any text string whose fifth character is the letter "P" followed by indefinite characters.

	=XLOOKUP(I7,SalesTable[Cost Code],SalesTable[Date],,2)					
D	E	F	G	H	I	J
					Cost Code	
Date	Customer	Cost Code	Amount		Contains P	Date
1/8/2010	Barry French	111-BN-018	16,000		*P*	1/24/2010
1/5/2010	Clay Rozendal	111-CJ-003	45,000			
1/14/2010	Carl Jackson	224-BX-002	18,100		Cost Code	
1/24/2010	Clay Rozendal	224-FP-011	49,756		5th Character is a P	Date
1/20/2010	Carlos Daly	224-MO-204	55,200		????P*	1/11/2010
1/21/2010	Carlos Daly	224-VV-004	28,600			
1/11/2010	Carlos Soltero	220-PU-009	53,800			
1/12/2010	Carlos Soltero	220-SA-001	50,000			
1/10/2010	Clay Rozendal	221-UP-011	60,000			
1/15/2010	Barry French	222-AG-001	84,523			
1/17/2010	Clay Rozendal	222-FE-002	77,100			
1/18/2010	Neola Seider	222-PK-002	32,100			

Figure 6.14: *XLOOKUP using the question mark and asterisk Wildcards*

Returns a cell reference

One of the least known features of the **XLOOKUP** function is that it returns a cell reference, not just values.

Though the cell reference is unseen, unlike the returned value, it can still be used, as shown in *Figure 6.15*:

```
=SUM(XLOOKUP(I95,Customers,XLOOKUP(J95,Regions,Data)):
XLOOKUP(I95,Customers,XLOOKUP(K95,Regions,Data)))
```

	D	E	F	G	H	I	J	K	L
	Customer	Eastern	Western	Southern		Customer	From Region	To Region	Total
	Emily	70,000	50,000	45,000		Joshua	Eastern	Western	150,400
	Theodore	45,000	45,000	16,000					
	Luna	83,800	53,800	60,000					
	Penelope	16,000	16,000	53,800					
	Austin	77,100	77,100	50,000					
	Joshua	95,200	55,200	18,100					
	Ruby	32,100	32,100	84,523					
	Luke	40,600	60,000	77,100					
	Easton	18,100	18,100	32,100					
	Gupta	32,683	49,756	55,200					
	Barnes	28,600	28,600	28,600					
	Martin	24,517	84,523	49,756					

Figure 6.15: XLOOKUP returning cell reference

=SUM(XLOOKUP(I95,Customers,XLOOKUP(J95,Regions,Data)):

XLOOKUP(I95,Customers,XLOOKUP(K95,Regions,Data)))

Here is how the formula works:

- **Step 1**: Create named ranges for the sections to use in the formulas. Select every region, as shown in *Figure 6.16*, go to the Name box, and give it a name.

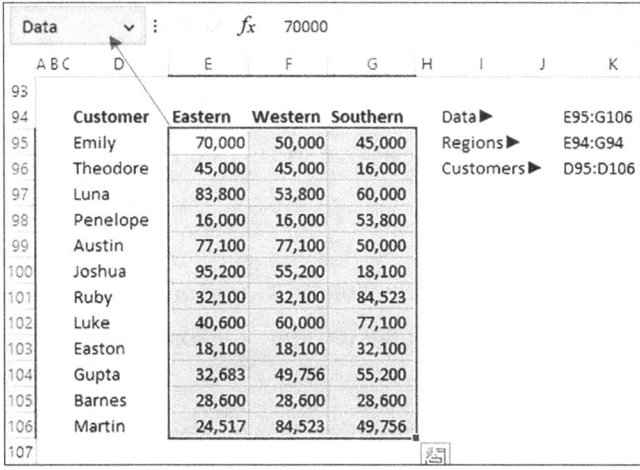

Figure 6.16: Creating Named Ranges

- **Step 2**: Write the nested **XLOOKUP** functions:
  - The nested **XLOOKUP** function, XLOOKUP(J95,Regions,Data), returns the region data. This forms the return array of the main **XLOOKUP** function.
  - Using the nested **XLOOKUP** function results as the return array, lookup the position of the customer:

    XLOOKUP(I95,Customers,XLOOKUP(J95,Regions,Data))

  - To force the **XLOOKUP** functions to return the cell references, use the range operator (:) between the **XLOOKUP** returning the Eastern Region and the one returning the Western region (see *Figure 6.17*):

    XLOOKUP(I95,Customers,XLOOKUP(J95,Regions,Data)):

    XLOOKUP(I95,Customers,XLOOKUP(K95,Regions,Data))

Customer	Eastern	Western	Southern		Customer	From Region	To Region		Total	
Emily	70,000	50,000	45,000		Joshua	Eastern	Western		95,200	55200
Theodore	45,000	45,000	16,000							
Luna	83,800	53,800	60,000							
Penelope	16,000	16,000	53,800							
Austin	77,100	77,100	50,000							
Joshua	95,200	55,200	18,100							
Ruby	32,100	32,100	84,523							
Luke	40,600	60,000	77,100							
Easton	18,100	18,100	32,100							
Gupta	32,683	49,756	55,200							
Barnes	28,600	28,600	28,600							
Martin	24,517	84,523	49,756							

Figure 6.17: XLOOKUP returns cell Ranges

- Step 3: Finally, sum up the above-returned range:

=SUM(

XLOOKUP(I95,Customers,XLOOKUP(J95,Regions,Data)):

XLOOKUP(I95,Customers,XLOOKUP(K95,Regions,Data))

)

Note: The **XLOOKUP** cannot return multiple rows/column references; it is limited to a single-cell reference. For multiple rows/columns references, use multiple **XLOOKUP** separated by a range operator (:)

Returns values in case of No Match

Unlike other lookup functions, which return an error if a match is not found, XLOOKUP has an inbuilt "if no match" found argument.

For example, in *Figure 6.19*, we are only supposed to get a discount for discounted items while returning zero for the rest.

					Product	Discount
	fx	=XLOOKUP([@Product],tblDiscounts[Product],tblDiscounts[Discount],0)				
	XLOOKUP(lookup_value, lookup_array, return_array, [if_not_found], [match_mode], [search_mode])					
Customer	Product	Amount	Discount		Product	Discount
Emily	Tables	50,000	],0)		Books	12%
Theodore	Laptops	45,000	25%		Chairs	23%
Luna	Cabinets	3,800	0%		Laptops	25%

Figure 6.18: XLOOKUP if_not_ found argument

We must use the `if_not_found` argument to capture the zero for non-discounted items, as shown in *Figure 6.18*:

	fx	=XLOOKUP([@Product],tblDiscounts[Product],tblDiscounts[Discount],0)				
	D	E	F	G	H	I	J
Customer	Product	Amount	Discount		Product	Discount
Emily	Tables	50,000	0%		Books	12%
Theodore	Laptops	45,000	25%		Chairs	23%
Luna	Cabinets	3,800	0%		Laptops	25%
Penelope	Books	30,000	12%		Pens	34%
Austin	Desktops	17,100	0%			
Joshua	Pens	5,200	34%			
Ruby	CCTV	2,100	0%			
Luke	Printers	60,000	0%			
Easton	Chairs	18,100	23%			
Gupta	Laptops	49,756	25%			
Barnes	Cabinets	8,600	0%			
Martin	Books	84,523	12%			

Figure 6.19: XLOOKUP Return a value if Match is not found

Easily do a three-way lookup

Unlike the VLOOKUP function, a nested XLOOKUP function easily does a three-way lookup, as shown in *Figure 6.20*:

XLOOKUP

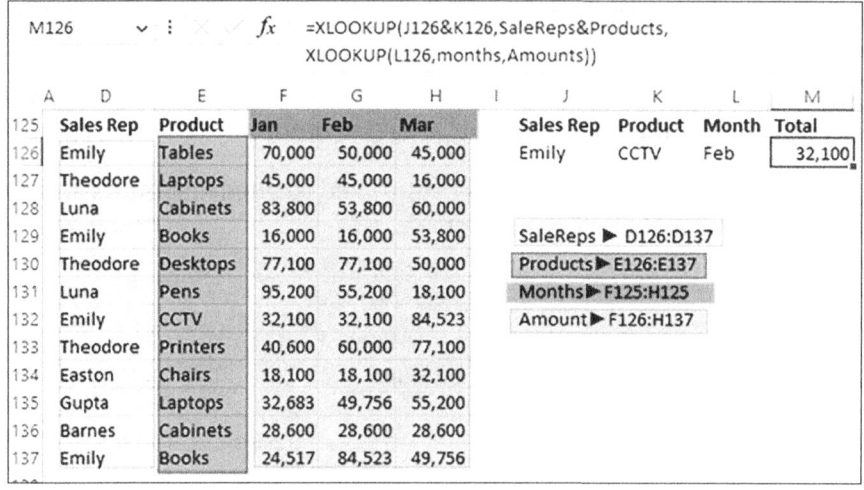

Figure 6.20: XLOOKUP three-way lookup

=XLOOKUP(J126&K126,SaleReps&Products,

XLOOKUP(L126, Months, Amount))

Here is how the function works:

- **Step 1**: Create named ranges for the sections to use in the formulas. Select every region as highlighted in *Figure* 6.20. To create a named range, Highlight the data, go to the Name box, and give it a Name. Finally, press Enter.
- **Step 2**: Write the nested XLOOKUP functions:
  - The nested XLOOKUP function, XLOOKUP(L126, Months, Amount), returns the criterion Month data. This forms the return array of the main XLOOKUP function.
  - As for the main XLOOKUP function, first, create a concatenated criterion – J126&K126. This returns a combination of the sales rep and product criteria. Then create combined Sales reps and Product columns, as shown in *Figure 6.21*:

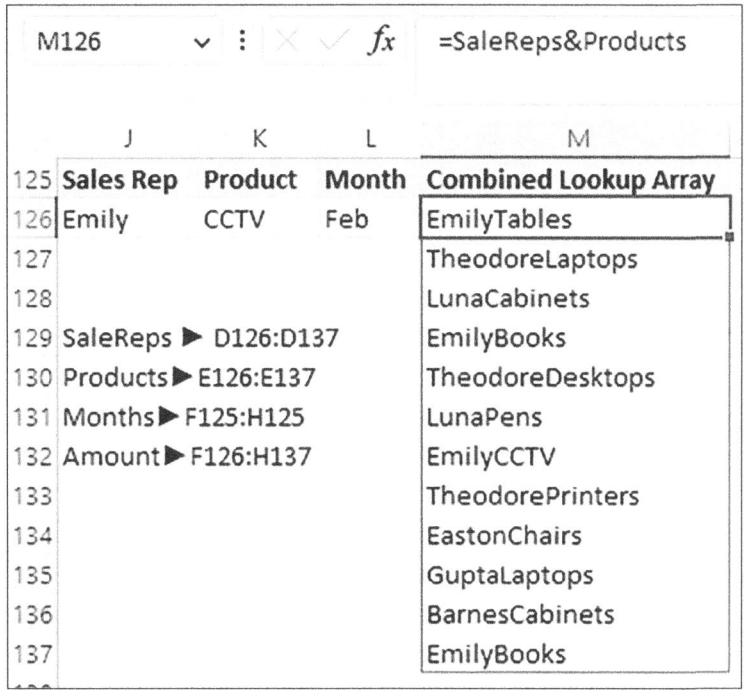

Figure 6.21: XLOOKUP concatenated columns as lookup array

- **Step 3**: Finally, get the position of the combined criteria in the combined columns. Then return the amount in the same position.

Note: The order in which you concatenate the criteria should be the same order for the columns.

For example, if, in the preceding scenario, we created a `SalesRep&Product` combo criterion, then we must create a `SalesRep&Product` combo Lookup array. Any other order will not work.

Easily returns non-adjacent columns

Using the preceding example, let us now use the XLOOKUP function to return the January and March Amounts, as shown in *Figure 6.22*:

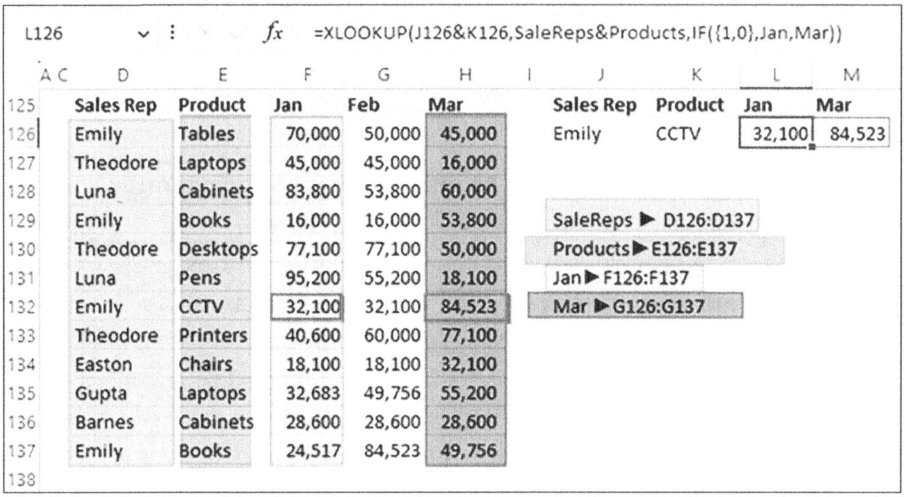

Figure 6.22: XLOOKUP return non-adjacent column values

=XLOOKUP(J126&K126, SaleReps&Products, IF({1,0},Jan,Mar))

Here is how the function works:

- **Step 1**: Create named ranges for the sections to use in the formulas. Select every region as highlighted in *Figure* 6.22. To create a named range, Highlight the data, go to the Name box, and give it a Name. Finally, press Enter.
- **Step 2**: Use the IF function to return non-adjacent columns, as shown in *Figure* 6.23. This is the only trick you need to remember.
- **Step 3**: Create a concatenated criterion – J126&K126. This returns a combination of the sales rep and product criteria. Then create a combined lookup array of Sales reps and Product columns.
- **Step 4**: Finally, get the position of the combined criteria in the combined lookup array columns. Then return the amounts, from the non-adjacent columns, in the same position.

Note: The alternative to the IF function is the CHOOSE function as follows:
=XLOOKUP(J126&K126, SaleReps&Products, CHOOSE({1,2},Jan,Mar))

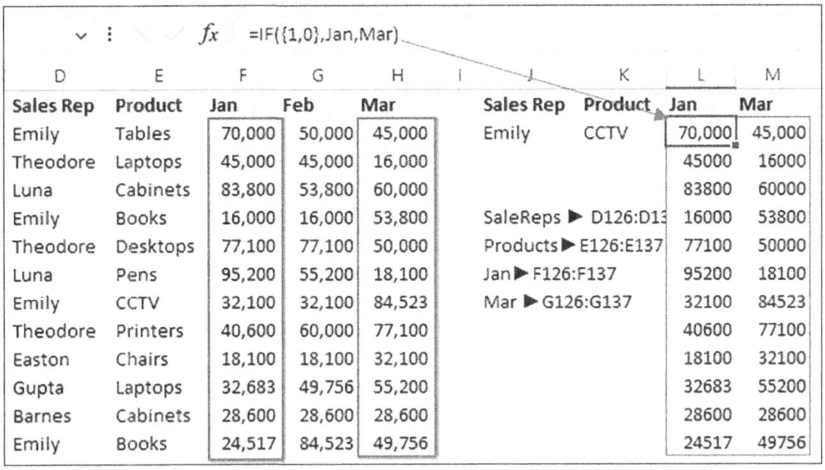

=IF({1,0},Jan,Mar)

Sales Rep	Product	Jan	Feb	Mar		Sales Rep	Product	Jan	Mar
Emily	Tables	70,000	50,000	45,000		Emily	CCTV	70,000	45,000
Theodore	Laptops	45,000	45,000	16,000				45000	16000
Luna	Cabinets	83,800	53,800	60,000				83800	60000
Emily	Books	16,000	16,000	53,800		SaleReps ▶ D126:D13		16000	53800
Theodore	Desktops	77,100	77,100	50,000		Products▶E126:E137		77100	50000
Luna	Pens	95,200	55,200	18,100		Jan▶F126:F137		95200	18100
Emily	CCTV	32,100	32,100	84,523		Mar ▶G126:G137		32100	84523
Theodore	Printers	40,600	60,000	77,100				40600	77100
Easton	Chairs	18,100	18,100	32,100				18100	32100
Gupta	Laptops	32,683	49,756	55,200				32683	55200
Barnes	Cabinets	28,600	28,600	28,600				28600	28600
Emily	Books	24,517	84,523	49,756				24517	49756

Figure 6.23: *IF return non-adjacent columns*

The alternative way is to use the Filter function to return non-adjacent columns as shown in *Figure* 6.24:

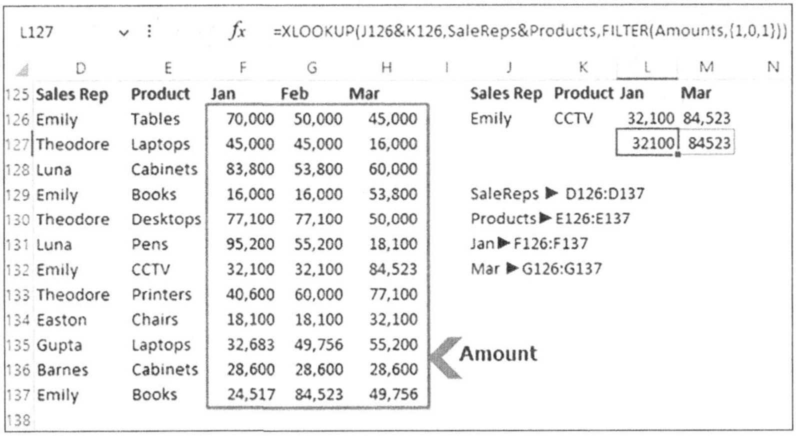

L127 =XLOOKUP(J126&K126,SaleReps&Products,FILTER(Amounts,{1,0,1}))

	D	E	F	G	H	I	J	K	L	M
125	Sales Rep	Product	Jan	Feb	Mar		Sales Rep	Product	Jan	Mar
126	Emily	Tables	70,000	50,000	45,000		Emily	CCTV	32,100	84,523
127	Theodore	Laptops	45,000	45,000	16,000				32100	84523
128	Luna	Cabinets	83,800	53,800	60,000					
129	Emily	Books	16,000	16,000	53,800		SaleReps ▶ D126:D137			
130	Theodore	Desktops	77,100	77,100	50,000		Products▶E126:E137			
131	Luna	Pens	95,200	55,200	18,100		Jan▶F126:F137			
132	Emily	CCTV	32,100	32,100	84,523		Mar ▶G126:G137			
133	Theodore	Printers	40,600	60,000	77,100					
134	Easton	Chairs	18,100	18,100	32,100					
135	Gupta	Laptops	32,683	49,756	55,200	Amount				
136	Barnes	Cabinets	28,600	28,600	28,600					
137	Emily	Books	24,517	84,523	49,756					
138										

Figure 6.24: *FILTER function returns non-adjacent columns*

```
=XLOOKUP(J126&K126, SaleReps&Products,FILTER(Amounts,{1,0,1}))
```

The only trick to learn here is to learn how to use the include parameter to get non-adjacent rows (for more information, please refer to the FILTER function in the next chapter).

The "include" part of a filter function typically refers to the condition that specifies which elements from a given list or array should be included in the filtered result. If a condition is TRUE (1), then it is included; otherwise, it is not included.

Returns the last/first non-empty cell

Other than the **LOOKUP** function, a better alternative to getting the last/first non-empty cell is the **XLOOKUP** function, as shown in *Figure 6.25*:

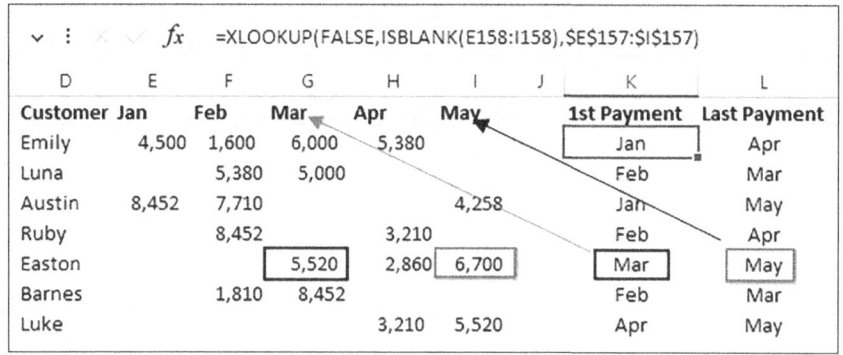

Figure 6.25: XLOOKUP last/first non-empty cells

To get the First payment:

=XLOOKUP(FALSE,ISBLANK(E158:I158),$E$157:$I$157)

To get the Last payment:

=XLOOKUP(FALSE,ISBLANK(E158:I158),$E$157:$I$157,,-1)

Here is how the function works.

- **Step 1**: Check if the cells are blank using the ISBLANK function. This returns an array of TRUE/FALSE values, as shown in *Figure 6.26*:

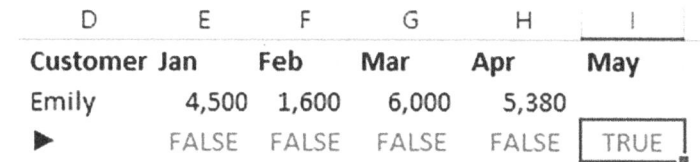

Figure 6.26: ISBLANK array of TRUE/FALSE

- **Step 2**: To get the first Payment, search for the first FALSE value in the array: =**XLOOKUP(FALSE,ISBLANK(E158:I158),$E$157:$I$157)**

- **Step 3**: To get the last Payment, we specify -1 as the search_mode. The XLOOKUP function will match the last FALSE value to the first FALSE value in the range: =**XLOOKUP(FALSE,ISBLANK(E158:I158),$E$157:$I$157,,-1)**

Easily lookup non-contiguous array

A nested XLOOKUP function also easily gets values from the non-contiguous array, as shown in *Figure 6.27*:

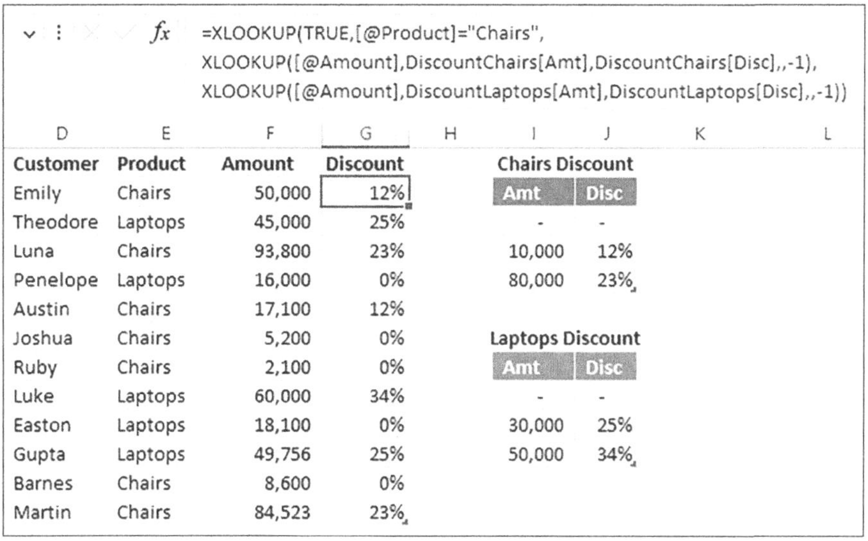

```
=XLOOKUP(TRUE,[@Product]="Chairs",
XLOOKUP([@Amount],DiscountChairs[Amt],DiscountChairs[Disc],,-1),
XLOOKUP([@Amount],DiscountLaptops[Amt],DiscountLaptops[Disc],,-1))
```

Customer	Product	Amount	Discount
Emily	Chairs	50,000	12%
Theodore	Laptops	45,000	25%
Luna	Chairs	93,800	23%
Penelope	Laptops	16,000	0%
Austin	Chairs	17,100	12%
Joshua	Chairs	5,200	0%
Ruby	Chairs	2,100	0%
Luke	Laptops	60,000	34%
Easton	Laptops	18,100	0%
Gupta	Laptops	49,756	25%
Barnes	Chairs	8,600	0%
Martin	Chairs	84,523	23%

Chairs Discount

Amt	Disc
-	-
10,000	12%
80,000	23%

Laptops Discount

Amt	Disc
-	-
30,000	25%
50,000	34%

***Figure 6.27**: XLOOKUP non-contiguous array*

```
=XLOOKUP(TRUE,[@Product]="Chairs",
XLOOKUP([@Amount], DiscountChairs[Amt], DiscountChairs[Disc],,-1),
XLOOKUP([@Amount], DiscountLaptops[Amt], DiscountLaptops[Disc],,-1))
```

Here is how the function works.

- **Step 1**: Check if the product is "Chairs". This returns a TRUE/FALSE value.
- **Step 2**: Since we use "TRUE" as the lookup value, the first nested XLOOKUP is executed if the preceding comparison is TRUE. It gets the discount percentage from the chairs' discount table using an approximate match (we specify -1 as the match_mode for an approximate match lookup).

  ```
  XLOOKUP([@Amount], DiscountChairs[Amt], DiscountChairs
  [Disc],,-1),
  ```

- **Step 3**: If the value is **`FALSE`**, we execute the **`XLOOKUP`** that is in the **"if_not_found"** argument of the **`XLOOKUP`**. This **`XLOOKUP`** gets a discount percentage from the laptops' discount table. Note: this is also an approximate match lookup.

  ```
  XLOOKUP([@Amount], DiscountLaptops[Amt], DiscountLaptops
  [Disc],,-1)
  ```

Easily returns duplicate lookup values

While, by default, the **XLOOKUP** function does not return multiple match values if the lookup_array contains duplicate values, it returns the first **TRUE** value.

However, you can achieve this if you nest the **LARGE** function, as shown in *Figure 6.28*:

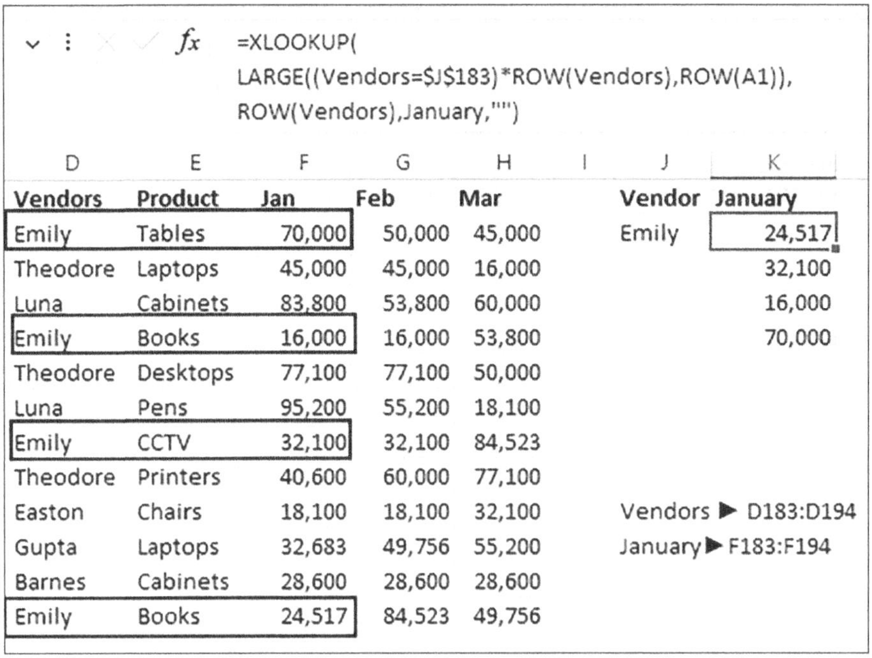

	D	E	F	G	H	I	J	K
	Vendors	**Product**	**Jan**	**Feb**	**Mar**		**Vendor**	**January**
	Emily	Tables	70,000	50,000	45,000		Emily	24,517
	Theodore	Laptops	45,000	45,000	16,000			32,100
	Luna	Cabinets	83,800	53,800	60,000			16,000
	Emily	Books	16,000	16,000	53,800			70,000
	Theodore	Desktops	77,100	77,100	50,000			
	Luna	Pens	95,200	55,200	18,100			
	Emily	CCTV	32,100	32,100	84,523			
	Theodore	Printers	40,600	60,000	77,100			
	Easton	Chairs	18,100	18,100	32,100		Vendors ▶	D183:D194
	Gupta	Laptops	32,683	49,756	55,200		January ▶	F183:F194
	Barnes	Cabinets	28,600	28,600	28,600			
	Emily	Books	24,517	84,523	49,756			

Formula shown: `=XLOOKUP(LARGE((Vendors=$J$183)*ROW(Vendors),ROW(A1)),ROW(Vendors),January,"")`

Figure 6.28: XLOOKUP returns duplicate lookup values.

```
=XLOOKUP(
LARGE((Vendors=$J$183)*ROW(Vendors),ROW(A1)),
ROW(Vendors),January,"")
```

Here is how the function works.

- **(Vendors=$J$183)** checks which Vendor is equal to "Emily" and returns an array of TRUE/FALSE.
- **(Vendors=$J$183)*ROW(Vendors)** multiply the above array of TRUE/FALSE with the row numbers. This returns an array of row numbers for vendor Emily; otherwise, it returns zero (see *Figure 6.29*):

	B(	D	E	F	G	H	I	J	K
182		Vendors	Product	Jan	Feb	Mar		Vendor	January
183		Emily	Tables	70,000	50,000	45,000		Emily	183
184		Theodore	Laptops	45,000	45,000	16,000			0
185		Luna	Cabinets	83,800	53,800	60,000			0
186		Emily	Books	16,000	16,000	53,800			186
187		Theodore	Desktops	77,100	77,100	50,000			0
188		Luna	Pens	95,200	55,200	18,100			0
189		Emily	CCTV	32,100	32,100	84,523			189
190		Theodore	Printers	40,600	60,000	77,100			0
191		Easton	Chairs	18,100	18,100	32,100			0
192		Gupta	Laptops	32,683	49,756	55,200			0
193		Barnes	Cabinets	28,600	28,600	28,600			0
194		Emily	Books	24,517	84,523	49,756			194

Formula bar: K183 fx =(Vendors=$J$183)*ROW(Vendors)

Figure 6.29: *Row numbers for criterion vendor*

- We need to iterate over these row numbers lists and return one at a time as the lookup value for **XLOOKUP**. We use the LARGE function for this task, which returns the row numbers from the Largest to the Smallest. Note ROW(A1) evaluates to 1, and as you drag the function down, it increases until the complete list is iterated. **LARGE((Vendors=$J$183)*ROW(Vendors),ROW(A1)),**
- **XLOOKUP** returns the January Amount for every row number.

Conclusion

In this chapter, we explored the power of the new XLOOKUP dynamic function and observed how easily it makes looking up values.

One of the unique features that sets **XLOOKUP** apart from other functions is its search mode from last to first, unlike functions that search from top to bottom.

Unlike other functions that return errors if the lookup value is not found and we need to nest them in the IFERROR function, this is not the case with XLOOKUP, since it has an **If_not_found** argument where we can return a value or a function.

In the next chapter, we will learn of a better lookup function that can return multiple values if the **lookup_array** contains duplicate values – FILTER Function.

Points to remember
- **XLOOKUP** function returns both value and cell reference.
- **XLOOKUP** is generally faster than traditional lookup functions like **VLOOKUP** or **HLOOKUP**, especially when dealing with large data sets. For values sorted in ascending order, specify 2 to enable binary search_mode and -2 for values sorted in descending order.

Multiple choice questions

1. In an **XLOOKUP** function, what is the `lookup_value`?

    a. The value to be searched for in the lookup range

    b. The range of values to search within

    c. The range of values to return

    d. The criteria used to filter the results

2. What happens if the default **XLOOKUP** function does not find a match for the `lookup_value` in the lookup range?

    a. It returns an error

    b. It returns the closest matching value

    c. It returns a specified default value

    d. It returns the average of the lookup range

3. Which of the following is NOT a valid argument in the XLOOKUP function?

    a. "`lookup_value`"

    b. "`return_array`"

    c. "`criteria_range`"

    d. "`not_found`"

4. What is the purpose of the "`if_not_found`" argument in the **XLOOKUP** function?

    a. To specify the value to return if a match is found

    b. To specify the value to return if no match is found

c. To specify the range to search for a match

   d. To specify the data type of the result

5. Which Excel version introduced the **XLOOKUP** function?

   a. Excel 2007

   b. Excel 2010

   c. Excel 2016

   d. Office 365 Excel

6. What is the formula structure of the **XLOOKUP** function?

   a. `=XLOOKUP(lookup_value, lookup_array, return_array)`

   b. `=XLOOKUP(lookup_array, lookup_value, return_array)`

   c. `=XLOOKUP(return_array, lookup_value, lookup_array)`

   d. `=XLOOKUP(return_array, lookup_array, lookup_value)`

Answers

1	a
2	a
3	c
4	b
5	d
6	a

Chapter 7
FILTER: The Ultimate Lookup Function

Introduction

This chapter will discuss one of the ultimate lookup functions–the Filter function. Unlike the **XLOOKUP** function, the **FILTER** function easily returns an array of all matches, not just the first match. This flexibility to return a subset of data, and not just a single entry, makes the FILTER one of the best functions in creating dynamic reports. Let us now explore the different scenarios where we can use the **FILTER** function to **analyze** data in more **customized** ways without the need for complex formulas.

Structure

This chapter will discuss the following 15 scenarios where the **FILTER** function is best suited:

- Return multiple columns and rows
- Return non-adjacent columns
- Easily use multiple criteria lookup using AND/OR
- Easily lookup all X and not Y items
- Easily lookup top or bottom n items
- Easily lookup X or Y and not both
- Looking up data using wildcards

- Looking up weekday vs. weekend data
- Looking up data that excludes holidays
- Looking up ODD/EVEN numbers
- Looking up items repeated N times
- Looking up items based on time
- Looking up data based on week number, month, year
- Looking up common/uncommon values in two lists
- Return end-of-month date items only

Return multiple columns and rows

The FILTER function has one of the simplest and easiest-to-understand syntaxes—only three parameters.

=FILTER(array, include, [if_empty])

- array is the range/array of data you want to look up. This can be a table or single columns/rows.
- include is an array of **TRUE/FALSE**, where **TRUE** represents the values to return else **FALSE**.

  NB: If the filtered array is in columns, the include MUST be the same length as this array. And if the array is in rows, the include MUST be the same width as this array.

- **[if_empty]**- **[optional]** Value to return when no results are returned.

For example, in *Figure 7.1*, we want to look up all the contributions and corresponding dates for staff "Carl Jackson".

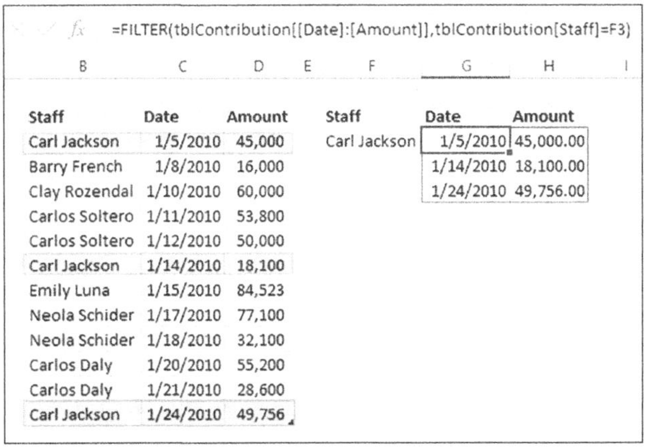

Figure 7.1: *Returning Multiple Rows and Columns*

FILTER: The Ultimate Lookup Function

=FILTER(tblContribution[[Date]:[Amount]],tblContribution[Staff]=F3)

Here is how the preceding function works:

- Select the Columns to filter as our array. Here we are selecting adjacent columns; in the next example, we shall learn how to select non-adjacent columns→ **tblContribution[[Date]:[Amount]]**
- Check all instances where our criterion (Carl Jackson) appears in the staff list→ **tblContribution[Staff]=F3.** This returns a Boolean array (refer to *Figure* 7.2), determining what values to include in the filter.

	fx	=tblContribution[Staff]=F3				
B	C	D	E	F	G	H
Staff	Date	Amount		Staff	Date	Amount
Carl Jackson	1/5/2010	45,000		Carl Jackson	TRUE	
Barry French	1/8/2010	16,000			FALSE	
Clay Rozendal	1/10/2010	60,000			FALSE	
Carlos Soltero	1/11/2010	53,800			FALSE	
Carlos Soltero	1/12/2010	50,000			FALSE	
Carl Jackson	1/14/2010	18,100			TRUE	
Emily Luna	1/15/2010	84,523			FALSE	
Neola Schider	1/17/2010	77,100			FALSE	
Neola Schider	1/18/2010	32,100			FALSE	
Carlos Daly	1/20/2010	55,200			FALSE	
Carlos Daly	1/21/2010	28,600			FALSE	
Carl Jackson	1/24/2010	49,756			TRUE	

Figure 7.2: *Creating the include parameter*

Note: Since the FILTER function spills the results vertically/horizontally or both depending on your filtered array, ensure you have enough empty cells otherwise, you will get a **#SPILL!** Error (refer to *Figure* 7.3).

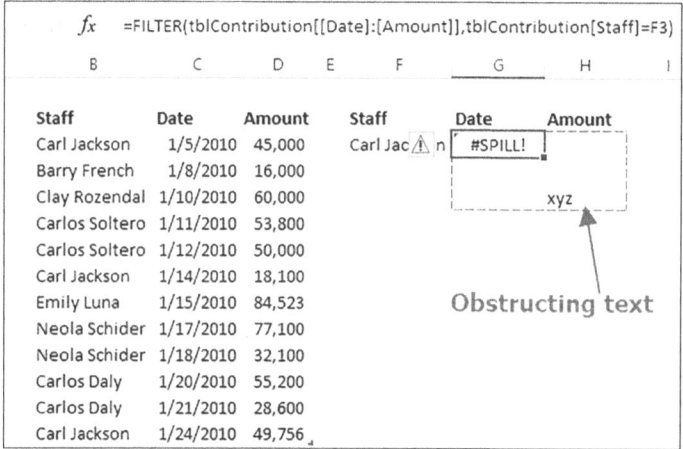

Figure 7.3: *Obstructing text creating a spill error*

Return multiple non-adjacent columns and rows

As shown in *Figure* 7.4, we have adjusted the data in the previous example to include items donated.

In this example, we want to return all donated items and amounts.

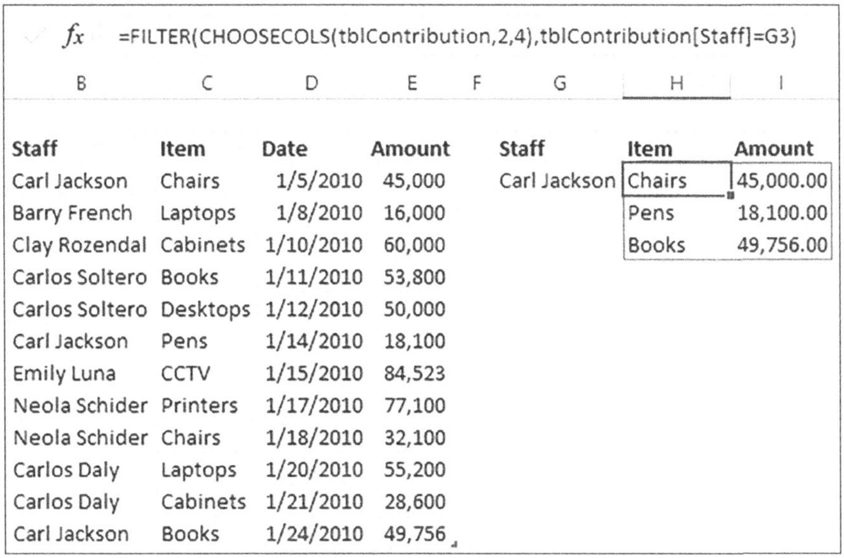

Figure 7.4: *Returning non-adjacent Columns*

=FILTER(CHOOSECOLS(tblContribution,2,4),tblContribution[Staff]=G3)

Here is how the preceding function works:

- To select the non-adjacent columns to filter, we shall use the CHOOSECOLS function. This function requires a table name and required column numbers → **CHOOSECOLS(tblContribution,2,4)**

Note

- If you do not want to hardcode the columns in the **CHOOSECOLS** function, you can use the **XMATCH** function (refer to *Figure* 7.5).
- Check all instances where our criterion (Carl Jackson) appears in the staff list→ **tblContribution[Staff]=F3.** This returns a Boolean array, determining what values to include in the filter.

FILTER: The Ultimate Lookup Function 139

	B	C	D	E	F	G	H	I
	Staff	Item	Date	Amount		Staff	Item	Amount
	Carl Jackson	Chairs	1/5/2010	45,000		Carl Jackson	Chairs	45,000.00
	Barry French	Laptops	1/8/2010	16,000			Laptops	16,000.00
	Clay Rozendal	Cabinets	1/10/2010	60,000			Cabinets	60,000.00
	Carlos Soltero	Books	1/11/2010	53,800			Books	53800
	Carlos Soltero	Desktops	1/12/2010	50,000			Desktops	50000
	Carl Jackson	Pens	1/14/2010	18,100			Pens	18100
	Emily Luna	CCTV	1/15/2010	84,523			CCTV	84523
	Neola Schider	Printers	1/17/2010	77,100			Printers	77100
	Neola Schider	Chairs	1/18/2010	32,100			Chairs	32100
	Carlos Daly	Laptops	1/20/2010	55,200			Laptops	55200
	Carlos Daly	Cabinets	1/21/2010	28,600			Cabinets	28600
	Carl Jackson	Books	1/24/2010	49,756			Books	49756

Formula: =CHOOSECOLS(tblContribution,XMATCH(H2:I2,tblContribution[#Headers]))

Figure 7.5: CHOOSECOLS function dynamically returns non-adjacent columns

Another alternative to return non-adjacent columns is the use of nested **FILTER** functions as follows:

=FILTER(
FILTER(tblContribution,tblContribution[Staff]=G3),
{0,1,0,1})

Here is how the preceding function works:
- **FILTER(tblContribution,tblContribution[Staff]=G3)** This nested FILTER function returns all the columns where the staff is equal to Carl Jackson who is stored in cell G3.
- To get only the 2nd and 4th columns we use another **FILTER** function and specify these columns in the include parameter. As we have learned in the introduction section, the included parameter is an array of **TRUE (1)** /**FALSE (0)**, where TRUE represents the values to return else FALSE. Therefore, {0,1,0,1} will only return the second and fourth columns.

The third alternative to returning non-adjacent columns is nesting the **CHOOSE** function. Just like the **CHOOSECOL** function, you can not only return non-adjacent columns but also rearrange them. Using the below formula, we can return the amount column first and then the date column.

=FILTER(

CHOOSE({1,2},tblContribution[Amount],tblContribution[Date]),tblContribution[Staff]=G51)

Easily use multiple criteria lookups using AND/OR

We are not limited to a single criterion, as shown in the preceding examples. We can use the FILTER function with multiple criteria and different logics (**AND/OR**).

For example, in *Figure 7.6*, we want to look up all donors whose donations were in **ZAR**, **USD**, or **CHF**.

=FILTER(Donors, COUNTIF(List, Currency))

Here is how the preceding function works:

- Select the donor's named range (Donors) as our filter array.
- Use the **COUNTIF** function to count the number of times our list of currency criteria occurs in our database list of currencies. This returns an array of 1/0, as follows, where 1=TRUE, 0= FALSE.
  {0 0 0 0 0 1 0 1 0 0 0 1}

- The **Filter** function returns all the donors corresponding to the 1 values.

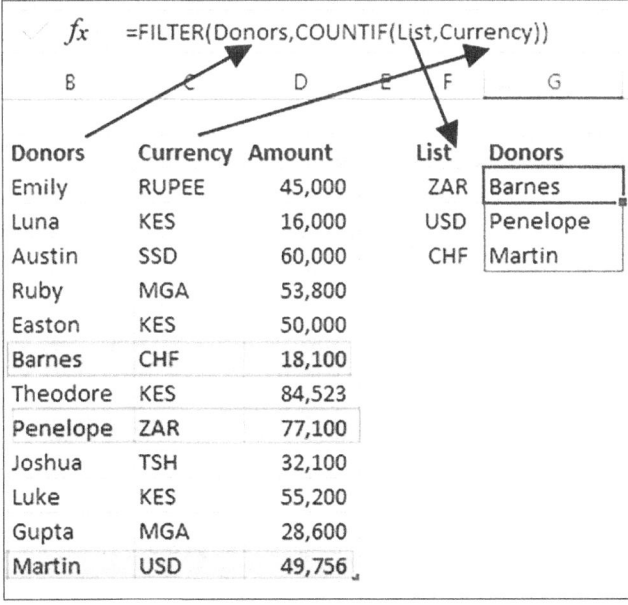

Figure 7.6: *FILTER function Multiple Criteria OR logic using COUNTIF function*

FILTER: The Ultimate Lookup Function   141

The alternative to using the **COUNTIF** function is using the plus sign (+) to represent the OR logic, as shown in *Figure 7.7*.

	A	B	C	D	E	F	G	H	I
H18			fx	=FILTER(Donors, (Currency=F18)+(Currency=F19)+(Currency=F20))					
17		Donors	Currency	Amount		List Donors		Donors	
18		Emily	RUPEE	45,000		ZAR	Barnes	Barnes	
19		Luna	KES	16,000		USD	Penelope	Penelope	
20		Austin	SSD	60,000		CHF	Martin	Martin	
21		Ruby	MGA	53,800					
22		Easton	KES	50,000					
23		Barnes	CHF	18,100					
24		Theodore	KES	84,523					
25		Penelope	ZAR	77,100					
26		Joshua	TSH	32,100					
27		Luke	KES	55,200					
28		Gupta	MGA	28,600					
29		Martin	USD	49,756					

Figure 7.7: FILTER function Multiple Criteria OR logic using Plus sign (+)

In *Figure 7.8*, we want to know when and what amount staff `Carl Jackson` contributed to books.

	A	B	C	D	E	F	G	H	I	J
I3				fx	=FILTER($D$3:$E$14,($B$3:$B$14=G3)*($C$3:$C$14=H3))					
1										
2		Staff	Item	Date	Amount		Staff	Item	Date	Amount
3		Carl Jackson	Chairs	1/5/2010	45,000		Carl Jackson	Books	1/11/2010	53,800.00
4		Barry French	Laptops	1/8/2010	16,000				1/24/2010	49,756.00
5		Clay Rozendal	Cabinets	1/10/2010	60,000					
6		Carl Jackson	Books	1/11/2010	53,800					
7		Carlos Soltero	Desktops	1/12/2010	50,000					
8		Carl Jackson	Pens	1/14/2010	18,100					
9		Emily Luna	CCTV	1/15/2010	84,523					
10		Carl Jackson	Printers	1/17/2010	77,100					
11		Neola Schider	Chairs	1/18/2010	32,100					
12		Carlos Daly	Laptops	1/20/2010	55,200					
13		Carlos Daly	Cabinets	1/21/2010	28,600					
14		Carl Jackson	Books	1/24/2010	49,756					

Figure 7.8: FILTER function Multiple Criteria AND logic

=FILTER($D$3:$E$14,($B$3:$B$14=G3)*($C$3:$C$14=H3))

Here is how the preceding function works:

- Select the filter array (**$D$3:$E$14**).
- Check if the staff equals Carl Jackson (**$B$3:$B$14=G3**) and the items equals Books (**$C$3:$C$14=H3**). These return a Boolean array (**TRUE/FALSE**).
- Since the FILTER function does not accept the nesting of the **AND** function, we use the asterisk (*) to represent the AND logic. When you multiply the preceding two Boolean arrays, we only get a value of 1 where all criteria are met. See *Figure 7.9*.

Staff	Item	Date	Amount	Staff	Item	Date	Amount
Carl Jackson	Chairs	1/5/2010	45,000	Carl Jackson	Books	0	
Barry French	Laptops	1/8/2010	16,000			0	
Clay Rozendal	Cabinets	1/10/2010	60,000			0	
Carl Jackson	Books	1/11/2010	53,800			1	
Carlos Soltero	Desktops	1/12/2010	50,000			0	
Carl Jackson	Pens	1/14/2010	18,100			0	
Emily Luna	CCTV	1/15/2010	84,523			0	
Carl Jackson	Printers	1/17/2010	77,100			0	
Neola Schider	Chairs	1/18/2010	32,100			0	
Carlos Daly	Laptops	1/20/2010	55,200			0	
Carlos Daly	Cabinets	1/21/2010	28,600			0	
Carl Jackson	Books	1/24/2010	49,756			1	

Formula: =($B$3:$B$14=G3)*($C$3:$C$14=H3)

Figure 7.9: Using the asterisk (*) to represent the AND logic

Easily lookup all X and not Y items

In this section, we will learn how to use the NOT comparative operator (<>) in the FILTER function.

As shown in *Figure 7.10*, we want to look up all students who scored a grade of A but not in the English subject.

FILTER: The Ultimate Lookup Function

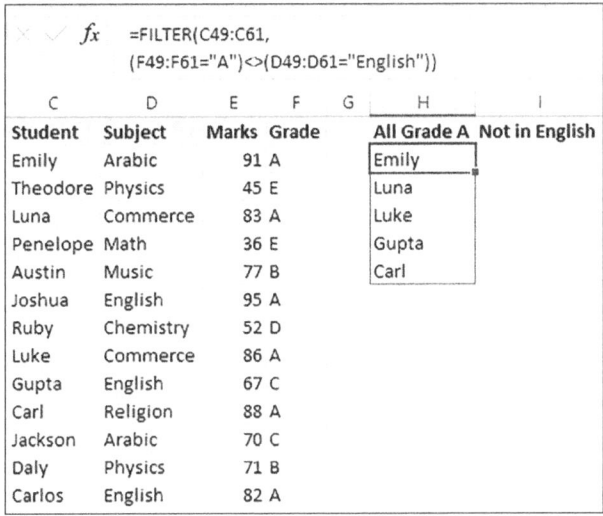

Figure 7.10: Filtering data using the NOT comparative operator (<>)

=FILTER(C49:C61,(F49:F61="A")=(D49:D61<>"English"))

Here is how the preceding function works:

- Select the Students filter array **(C49:C61)**.
- Check if the grade is equal to **A (F49:F61="A")** and if the subject is NOT equal to **English (D49:D61<>English)**. These return a Boolean array—**TRUE** (where both checks are true) and **FALSE** (where one/both tests are false)

The alternative uses the greater-than-comparative operator, as shown in *Figure 7.11*.

```
fx  =FILTER(C49:C61,
     (F49:F61="A")>(D49:D61="English"))
```

C	D	E	F	G	H	I
Student	Subject	Marks	Grade		All Grade A	Not in English
Emily	Arabic	91	A		Emily	
Theodore	Physics	45	E		Luna	
Luna	Commerce	83	A		Luke	
Penelope	Math	36	E		Carl	
Austin	Music	77	B			
Joshua	English	95	A			
Ruby	Chemistry	52	D			
Luke	Commerce	86	A			
Gupta	English	67	C			
Carl	Religion	88	A			
Jackson	Arabic	70	C			
Daly	Physics	71	B			
Carlos	English	82	A			

Figure 7.11: Filtering data using the Greater than (>) comparative operator

```
=FILTER(C49:C61,(F49:F61="A")>(D49:D61="English"))
```

The only trick to learn here is that Excel treats the FALSE value as zero (0) and one (1) as TRUE; then, only in the instances where 1>0 will the result be TRUE. See *Figure 7.12*.

All Grade A	Not in English	TRUE>FALSE
TRUE	FALSE	TRUE
FALSE	FALSE	FALSE
TRUE	FALSE	TRUE
FALSE	FALSE	FALSE
FALSE	FALSE	FALSE
TRUE	TRUE	FALSE
FALSE	FALSE	FALSE
TRUE	FALSE	TRUE
FALSE	TRUE	FALSE
TRUE	FALSE	TRUE
FALSE	FALSE	FALSE
FALSE	FALSE	FALSE
TRUE	TRUE	FALSE

Figure 7.12: Comparing Boolean values

Easily lookup top or bottom n items

Unlike the previously learned Lookup functions, the FILTER function easily returns the top or bottom items, as shown in *Figure 7.13*.

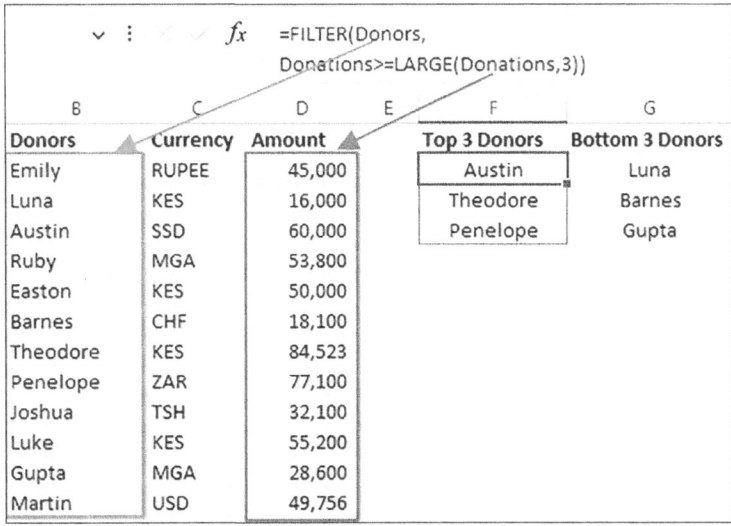

Figure 7.13: Filtering the Top or Bottom items

To Filter the top 3

```
=FILTER(Donors, Donations>=LARGE(Donations,3))
```

To Filter the bottom 3

```
=FILTER(Donors, Donations<=SMALL(Donations,3))
```

Here is how the preceding function works:

- Select the donors' named range filter array.
- Use the LARGE function to return the third largest value (**`LARGE(Donations,3)`**) Or the SMALL function to return the third smallest value (**`SMALL(Donations,3)`**).
- To filter the top items, check the donation amounts that are greater or equal to the third largest **`(Donations>=LARGE(Donations,3))`**. To filter the bottom items, check the donation amounts that are lesser or equal to the 3rd smallest **`(Donations<=SMALL(Donations,3))`**. These return a Boolean array–TRUE (where both checks are true) and FALSE (where one/both tests are false).
- The Filter Function returns all the donors corresponding to the TRUE values.

Easily lookup X or Y and not both

This is not a frequent lookup problem, but it is worth knowing how to solve it.

We need to look up all students who scored Grade A or took English, but not both. See *Figure 7.14*.

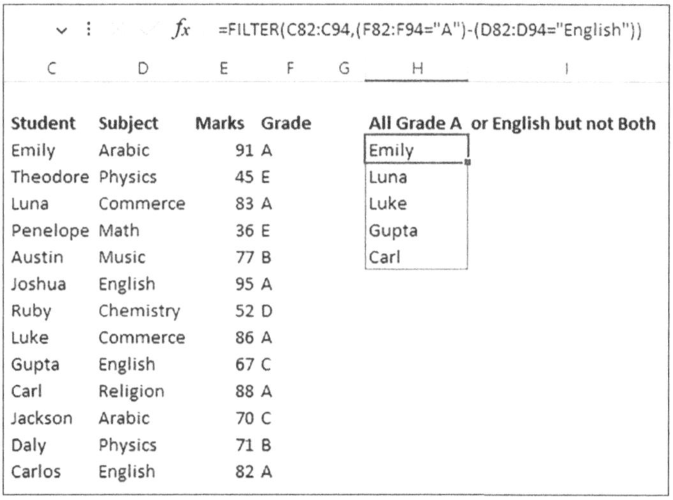

=FILTER(C82:C94,(F82:F94="A")-(D82:D94="English"))

Student	Subject	Marks	Grade		All Grade A or English but not Both
Emily	Arabic	91	A		Emily
Theodore	Physics	45	E		Luna
Luna	Commerce	83	A		Luke
Penelope	Math	36	E		Gupta
Austin	Music	77	B		Carl
Joshua	English	95	A		
Ruby	Chemistry	52	D		
Luke	Commerce	86	A		
Gupta	English	67	C		
Carl	Religion	88	A		
Jackson	Arabic	70	C		
Daly	Physics	71	B		
Carlos	English	82	A		

Figure 7.14: *Filtering all X or Y but not Both*

=FILTER(C82:C94,(F82:F94="A")-(D82:D94="English"))

The only trick to learn is using the minus sign (-) as a comparison operator.

Here is how the comparison works.

If one comparison is TRUE (1) and the other is FALSE (0), then the comparison would be 1-0=1. Thus, Overall will be TRUE. When comparing two FALSE conditions 0-0=0, thus overall FALSE. When comparing two TRUE conditions, 1-1=0, this also would be an overall FALSE. See *Figure 7.15*.

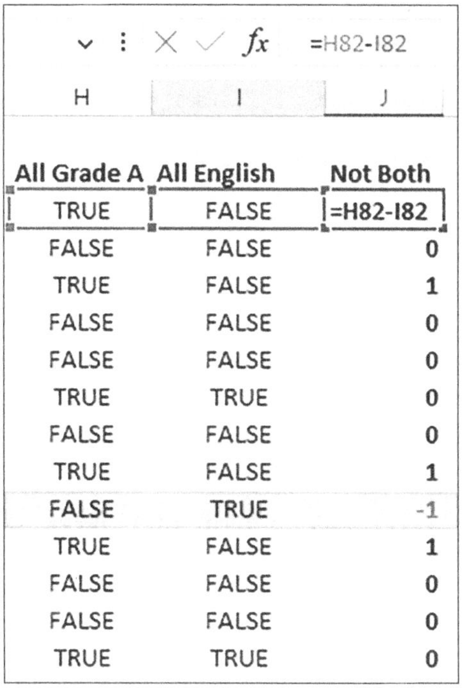

Figure 7.15: *Minus Sign (-) comparison operator*

Note
- In Excel, FALSE equals 0 value, and any other value equals TRUE.
- This is why in *Figure 7.15*, the value of −1 is equal to TRUE.

Looking up data using wildcards

Unfortunately, the two wildcard characters (*?) do not work with the FILTER function.

However, there is a walkaround using a combination of SEARCH and ISNUMBER functions, as shown in *Figure 7.16*.

The task is to filter all producers whose product contains the word "Milk".

Producers	Product	Amount		Milk Producers Only
Luna	Lemon Yoghurt	16,000		Gupta
Barnes	Vanilla Yoghurt	18,100		Martin
Gupta	Long Life Milk	28,600		Luke
Joshua	Probiotic Yoghurt	32,100		Penelope
Emily	Banana Yoghurt	45,000		Theodore
Martin	Flavoured Milk	49,756		
Easton	Tropical Yoghurt	50,000		
Ruby	Berry Yoghurt	53,800		
Luke	Sweetened Milk	55,200		
Austin	Mango Yoghurt	60,000		
Penelope	Premium Milk	77,100		
Theodore	Whole Fresh Milk	84,523		

Formula: `=FILTER(Producers,ISNUMBER(SEARCH("Milk",Product)))`

Figure 7.16: *Filtering data using wildcards*

=FILTER(Producers, ISNUMBER(SEARCH("Milk", Product)))

Here is how the preceding function works:

- The search function returns a number if the product name contains the word "milk", else it returns an error **(SEARCH("Milk", Product))**.
- **ISNUMBER** function returns an array of TRUE/FALSE which will be used as the include criteria in the FILTER function. ISNUMBER returns TRUE if the returned value by the SEARCH function is a number; else, it returns FALSE.

Looking up weekday or weekend data

Analyzing transactions based on the weekday or weekend is required, especially for sales analysts.

This can be easily done using a combination of the FILTER function and the WEEKDAY function, as shown in F*igure 7.17*.

To Filter Weekday sold items:

=FILTER(tblSportSale[Item],WEEKDAY(tblSportSale[Date],2)<6)

To Filter Weekend sold items:

=FILTER(tblSportSale[Item],WEEKDAY(tblSportSale[Date],2)>=6)

Here is how the preceding formula works.

- Given the date of the sale, the `WEEKDAY` function (**`WEEKDAY(tblSportSale[Date],2))`** returns a number between 1 and 7 representing the day of the week. Monday(1) to Sunday(7)
- For the Weekdays dates, these are dates with a day number less than 6, while Weekend dates have a day number greater or equal to 6

fx =FILTER(tblSportSale[Item],WEEKDAY(tblSportSale[Date],2)<6)

B	C	D	E	F	G
Item	**Date**	**Amount**		**Weekday**	**Weekend**
Abdominal Pads	Sunday, March 5, 2023	45,000		Batting Gloves	Abdominal Pads
Batting Legguards	Sunday, January 8, 2023	16,000		Batting Legguards	Batting Legguards
Batting Gloves	Friday, February 10, 2023	60,000		Chest Guard	Caps/Hats
Batting Legguards	Wednesday, January 11, 2023	53,800		Cricket Balls	Cricket Bags
Caps/Hats	Sunday, February 12, 2023	50,000		Elbow Guards	Helmets
Chest Guard	Friday, April 14, 2023	18,100		Inner Gloves	Thigh Pads
Cricket Bags	Sunday, January 15, 2023	84,523		Synthetic Balls	
Cricket Balls	Tuesday, January 17, 2023	77,100		Cricket Shoes	
Elbow Guards	Thursday, May 18, 2023	32,100			
Helmets	Saturday, May 20, 2023	55,200			
Inner Gloves	Wednesday, June 21, 2023	28,600			
Synthetic Balls	Thursday, May 18, 2023	49,756			
Thigh Pads	Saturday, May 20, 2023	48,006			
Cricket Shoes	Wednesday, June 21, 2023	50,643			

***Figure 7.17**: Filtering Weekday or Weekend data*

Looking up data that excludes holidays and weekends

In the previous example, we saw how to look up either weekday or weekend-sold items.

Assuming we have holidays, how do we look up items sold on workdays only? As shown in *Figure* 7.18, you can exclude Holidays and Weekends by using the `po` function.

```
=FILTER(SportSales[Item],WORKDAY(SportSales[Date]-1,1,Holidays)=Sport-
Sales[Date])
```

Here is how the preceding function works:

- **`WORKDAY(SportSales[Date]-1, 1, Holidays)`** will subtract one day from the Sales date to get the initial date, then add one working day to find the next working day after that initial date, while excluding any dates specified in the "Holidays" list. If the Sales date is not a holiday or a weekend, the WORKDAY function will return the same date; otherwise, it will return the next working day.

- Compare the returned working days with the Sales dates, **`WORKDAY(SportSales[Date]-1,1,Holidays)=SportSales[Date].`** This comparison returns **`TRUE`** if the dates are the same otherwise, **`FALSE`**.

The `FILTER` function returns only items corresponding to the `TRUE` values from the preceding array.

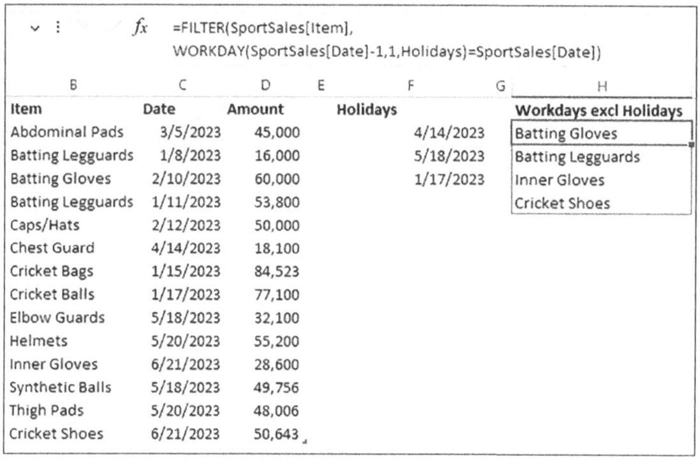

=FILTER(SportSales[Item], WORKDAY(SportSales[Date]-1,1,Holidays)=SportSales[Date])

Item	Date	Amount	Holidays		Workdays excl Holidays
Abdominal Pads	3/5/2023	45,000		4/14/2023	Batting Gloves
Batting Legguards	1/8/2023	16,000		5/18/2023	Batting Legguards
Batting Gloves	2/10/2023	60,000		1/17/2023	Inner Gloves
Batting Legguards	1/11/2023	53,800			Cricket Shoes
Caps/Hats	2/12/2023	50,000			
Chest Guard	4/14/2023	18,100			
Cricket Bags	1/15/2023	84,523			
Cricket Balls	1/17/2023	77,100			
Elbow Guards	5/18/2023	32,100			
Helmets	5/20/2023	55,200			
Inner Gloves	6/21/2023	28,600			
Synthetic Balls	5/18/2023	49,756			
Thigh Pads	5/20/2023	48,006			
Cricket Shoes	6/21/2023	50,643			

Figure 7.18: *Filtering working days data only*

Looking up ODD/EVEN numbers

Let us assume that you are an auditor and want to extract only Even numbered invoices, as shown in *Figure* 7.19.

Here is the formula you can use for this task.

```
=FILTER(B147:B158,ISEVEN(0+B147:B158))
```

Here is how the preceding function works:

- **`ISEVEN(0+B147:B158)`** `ISEVEN` function returns an array of `TRUE/FALSE.` TRUE for all even numbered invoices else, `FALSE`.

Note

- To force the `ISEVEN` function to evaluate the entire range as an array, you must add a zero in your referenced range else the function will return a `#VALUE` error.
- The FILTER function returns only Invoices that correspond to the TRUE values of the array returned earlier.
- To filter the ODD numbered invoices, change the formula as follows:

```
=FILTER(B147:B158,ISODD(0+B147:B158))
```

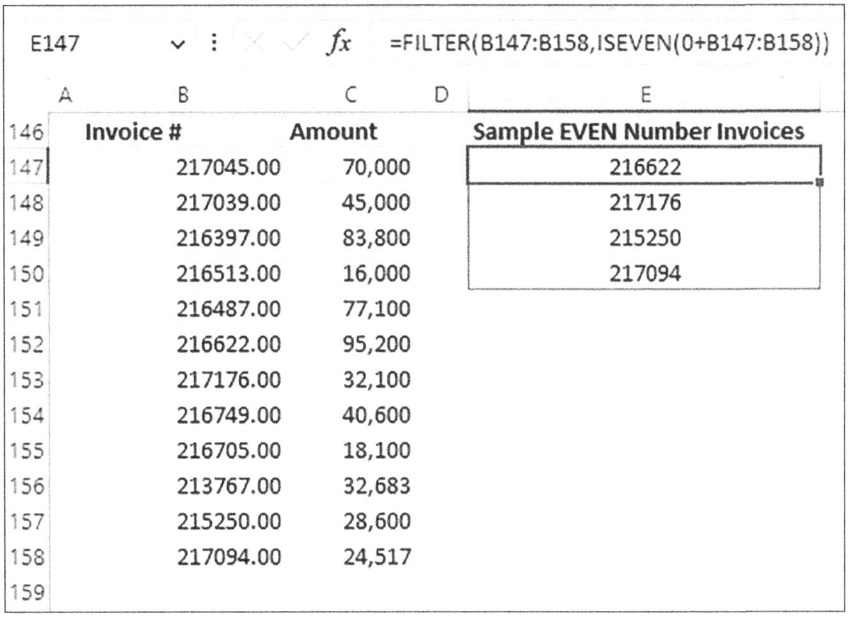

	Invoice #	Amount		Sample EVEN Number Invoices
146	**Invoice #**	**Amount**		**Sample EVEN Number Invoices**
147	217045.00	70,000		216622
148	217039.00	45,000		217176
149	216397.00	83,800		215250
150	216513.00	16,000		217094
151	216487.00	77,100		
152	216622.00	95,200		
153	217176.00	32,100		
154	216749.00	40,600		
155	216705.00	18,100		
156	213767.00	32,683		
157	215250.00	28,600		
158	217094.00	24,517		

Cell E147: `=FILTER(B147:B158,ISEVEN(0+B147:B158))`

Figure 7.19: Filtering Even values only

Looking up items repeated N times

Using the previous data on contributions, let us see how to filter all staff who have donated more than two times, as shown in *Figure 7.20*:

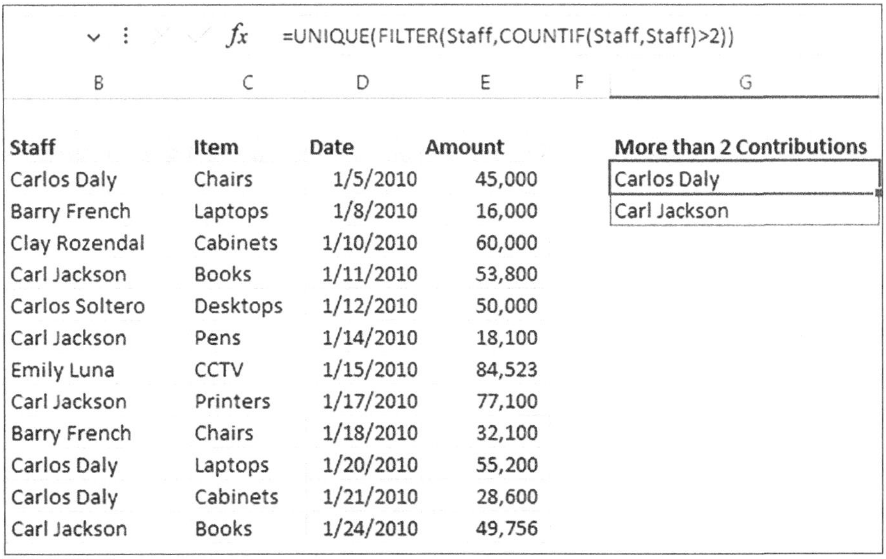

Formula: `=UNIQUE(FILTER(Staff,COUNTIF(Staff,Staff)>2))`

Staff	Item	Date	Amount		More than 2 Contributions
Carlos Daly	Chairs	1/5/2010	45,000		Carlos Daly
Barry French	Laptops	1/8/2010	16,000		Carl Jackson
Clay Rozendal	Cabinets	1/10/2010	60,000		
Carl Jackson	Books	1/11/2010	53,800		
Carlos Soltero	Desktops	1/12/2010	50,000		
Carl Jackson	Pens	1/14/2010	18,100		
Emily Luna	CCTV	1/15/2010	84,523		
Carl Jackson	Printers	1/17/2010	77,100		
Barry French	Chairs	1/18/2010	32,100		
Carlos Daly	Laptops	1/20/2010	55,200		
Carlos Daly	Cabinets	1/21/2010	28,600		
Carl Jackson	Books	1/24/2010	49,756		

Figure 7.20: Filtering Items Repeated n times

FILTER: The Ultimate Lookup Function   151

```
=UNIQUE(FILTER(Staff, COUNTIF(Staff, Staff)>2))
```

Here is how the preceding function works:

- **COUNTIF(Staff, Staff)** COUNTIF function returns an array of the number of times a staff is repeated in the list. Refer to *Figure 7.21*.

Staff	Item	Date	Amount	More than 2 Contributions
Carlos Daly	Chairs	1/5/2010	45,000	3
Barry French	Laptops	1/8/2010	16,000	2
Clay Rozendal	Cabinets	1/10/2010	60,000	1
Carl Jackson	Books	1/11/2010	53,800	4
Carlos Soltero	Desktops	1/12/2010	50,000	1
Carl Jackson	Pens	1/14/2010	18,100	4
Emily Luna	CCTV	1/15/2010	84,523	1
Carl Jackson	Printers	1/17/2010	77,100	4
Barry French	Chairs	1/18/2010	32,100	2
Carlos Daly	Laptops	1/20/2010	55,200	3
Carlos Daly	Cabinets	1/21/2010	28,600	3
Carl Jackson	Books	1/24/2010	49,756	4

Figure 7.21: COUNTIF function showing repeats per item

- Next, we check which items have been repeated more than two times **COUNTIF(Staff, Staff)>2**. This returns an array of TRUE/FALSE.
- The FILTER function only includes staff corresponding to the TRUE value, as shown in *Figure 7.22*.

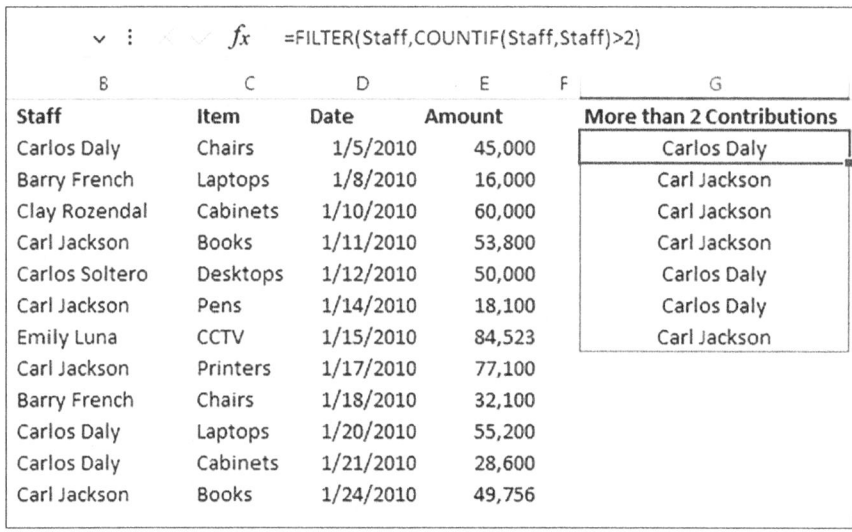

Staff	Item	Date	Amount	More than 2 Contributions
Carlos Daly	Chairs	1/5/2010	45,000	Carlos Daly
Barry French	Laptops	1/8/2010	16,000	Carl Jackson
Clay Rozendal	Cabinets	1/10/2010	60,000	Carl Jackson
Carl Jackson	Books	1/11/2010	53,800	Carl Jackson
Carlos Soltero	Desktops	1/12/2010	50,000	Carlos Daly
Carl Jackson	Pens	1/14/2010	18,100	Carlos Daly
Emily Luna	CCTV	1/15/2010	84,523	Carl Jackson
Carl Jackson	Printers	1/17/2010	77,100	
Barry French	Chairs	1/18/2010	32,100	
Carlos Daly	Laptops	1/20/2010	55,200	
Carlos Daly	Cabinets	1/21/2010	28,600	
Carl Jackson	Books	1/24/2010	49,756	

Figure 7.22: Filtered duplicate values

- To eliminate duplicate values, we use the **`UNIQUE`** **`function`** **`UNIQUE(FILTER(Staff, COUNTIF(Staff, Staff)>2))`**

Looking up items based on time

Most of the attendance data is collected in DateTime format, as shown in *Figure* 7.23. Yet we are required to look up that data using the time portion of the DateTime only.

When faced with such a problem, the only thing to remember is that the time value is always stored as a fraction of 24 hours while the Date is stored as a serial number.

Therefore, time will be the value after the decimal in a DateTime serial number.

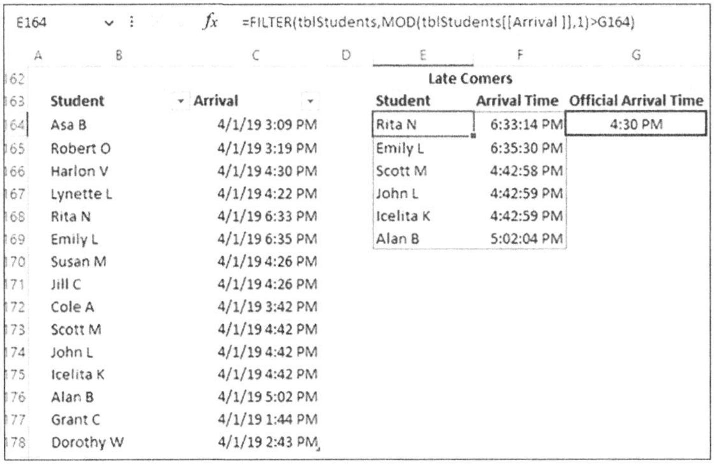
E164 fx =FILTER(tblStudents,MOD(tblStudents[[Arrival]],1)>G164)

	A	B	C	D	E	F	G
162					Late Comers		
163		Student	Arrival		Student	Arrival Time	Official Arrival Time
164		Asa B	4/1/19 3:09 PM		Rita N	6:33:14 PM	4:30 PM
165		Robert O	4/1/19 3:19 PM		Emily L	6:35:30 PM	
166		Harlon V	4/1/19 4:30 PM		Scott M	4:42:58 PM	
167		Lynette L	4/1/19 4:22 PM		John L	4:42:59 PM	
168		Rita N	4/1/19 6:33 PM		Icelita K	4:42:59 PM	
169		Emily L	4/1/19 6:35 PM		Alan B	5:02:04 PM	
170		Susan M	4/1/19 4:26 PM				
171		Jill C	4/1/19 4:26 PM				
172		Cole A	4/1/19 3:42 PM				
173		Scott M	4/1/19 4:42 PM				
174		John L	4/1/19 4:42 PM				
175		Icelita K	4/1/19 4:42 PM				
176		Alan B	4/1/19 5:02 PM				
177		Grant C	4/1/19 1:44 PM				
178		Dorothy W	4/1/19 2:43 PM				

***Figure* 7.23**: *Filtered based on time*

```
=FILTER(tblStudents,MOD(tblStudents[[Arrival ]],1)>G164)
```

Here is how the preceding function works:

- **`MOD(tblStudents[[Arrival ]],1)`** When used with a divisor of 1, the MOD function always returns the fractional part of a number.
- **`MOD(tblStudents[[Arrival ]],1)>G164`** This condition checks whether the calculated fractional part of the **`Arrival`** time (**`MOD`** result) is greater than the value in cell G164. This is essentially checking if the minutes' portion of the arrival time is greater than the value in G164.
- The FILTER function is used to retrieve rows from the **`tblStudents`** table based on a certain condition. In this case, it filters the rows where the calculated fractional part of the **`Arrival`** time is greater

than the value in cell G164.

Looking up data based on week number, month, and year

In the previous section, we learned how to filter data based on a weekday or weekend. In this section, we shall learn how to look up data based on Week number, Month, and Year.

In *Figure 7.24*, we are looking up all items sold in Week 3.

Item	Date	Amount		Week 3 Items	
Abdominal Pads	3/5/2023	45,000		Cricket Bags	
Batting Legguards	1/8/2023	16,000		Cricket Balls	
Batting Gloves	2/10/2023	60,000		Thigh Pads	
Batting Legguards	1/11/2023	53,800			
Caps/Hats	2/12/2023	50,000			
Chest Guard	4/14/2023	18,100			
Cricket Bags	1/15/2023	84,523			
Cricket Balls	1/17/2023	77,100			
Elbow Guards	5/18/2023	32,100			
Helmets	5/20/2023	55,200			
Inner Gloves	6/21/2023	28,600			
Synthetic Balls	5/18/2023	49,756			
Thigh Pads	1/19/2023	48,006			
Cricket Shoes	6/21/2023	50,643			

Figure 7.24: *Filtered based on a Week number*

`=FILTER(SportSales[Item],WEEKNUM(SportSales[Date]+0)=3)`

Note:

- The WEEKNUM function does not accept a range of data. It returns the **#VALUE** error. We, however, can force it by adding a zero **(SportSales[Date]+0)** to the range.
- The WEEKNUM function returns an array of week numbers (Refer to *Figure 7.25*).
- When we compare the calculated week numbers (from the preceding step) to the value, we return an array of TRUE and FALSE.
- The FILTER function is used to filter the rows where the values from the preceding step are TRUE.

```
                    fx  =WEEKNUM(SportSales[Date]+0)
```

Item	Date	Amount		Week numbers
Abdominal Pads	3/5/2023	45,000		10
Batting Legguards	1/8/2023	16,000		2
Batting Gloves	2/10/2023	60,000		6
Batting Legguards	1/11/2023	53,800		2
Caps/Hats	2/12/2023	50,000		7
Chest Guard	4/14/2023	18,100		15
Cricket Bags	1/15/2023	84,523		3
Cricket Balls	1/17/2023	77,100		3
Elbow Guards	5/18/2023	32,100		20
Helmets	5/20/2023	55,200		20
Inner Gloves	6/21/2023	28,600		25
Synthetic Balls	5/18/2023	49,756		20
Thigh Pads	1/19/2023	48,006		3
Cricket Shoes	6/21/2023	50,643		25

Figure 7.25: WEEKNUM *returning an array of Week numbers*

To filter specific months' data, use the month function as shown in *Figure 7.26*.

```
                    fx  =FILTER(SportSales[Item],MONTH(SportSales[Date])=6)
```

Item	Date	Amount		Week 3 Items
Abdominal Pads	3/5/2023	45,000		Cricket Bags
Batting Legguards	1/8/2023	16,000		Cricket Balls
Batting Gloves	2/10/2023	60,000		Thigh Pads
Batting Legguards	1/11/2023	53,800		
Caps/Hats	2/12/2023	50,000		June Sold Items
Chest Guard	4/14/2023	18,100		Inner Gloves
Cricket Bags	1/15/2023	84,523		Cricket Shoes
Cricket Balls	1/17/2023	77,100		
Elbow Guards	5/18/2023	32,100		
Helmets	5/20/2023	55,200		
Inner Gloves	6/21/2023	28,600		
Synthetic Balls	5/18/2023	49,756		
Thigh Pads	1/19/2023	48,006		
Cricket Shoes	6/21/2023	50,643		

Figure 7.26: *Filtered based on a Month*

`=FILTER(SportSales[Item],MONTH(SportSales[Date])=6)`

The only thing to note here is that the MONTH function returns an array of month numbers. Everything else is as explained in the WEEKNUM function.

Finally, *Figure 7.27* shows how to filter data using years values.

FILTER: The Ultimate Lookup Function   155

Figure 7.27: Filtered based on a Year

=FILTER(SportSales[Item],YEAR(SportSales[Date])=2022)

The only thing to note here is that the YEAR function returns an array of year numbers. Everything else is as explained in the preceding functions.

Lookup common/uncommon items in two lists

Comparing values in a list is a common activity in Excel. For example, in *Figure 7.28*, we look up common and new customers between two lists.

To get new (uncommon) customers

=FILTER(Current_Customers, COUNTIF(LastYear_Customers,Current_Customers)=0)

To get old(common) customers

=FILTER(Current_Customers, COUNTIF(LastYear_Customers,Current_Customers)=0)

The only trick with the function is the use of the **COUNTIF** function to count how many times items in the new list are repeated on the old list.

▶**COUNTIF(LastYear_Customers, Current_Customers)** count the number of customers who appeared both in the **LastYear_Customers** range and the **Current_Customers** range. It returns an array of 1 and 0. Where 1= common in both and 0=uncommon.

```
fx    =FILTER(Current_Customers,
         COUNTIF(LastYear_Customers,Current_Customers)=0)
```

Last Year Customers	Current Customers	New Customers
Alan B	Acelita K	Acelita K
Asa B	Alan B	Easton B
Cole A	Asa B	Emily W
Dorothy W	Dorothy W	Joshua K
Emily L	Easton B	Martin G
Grant C	Emily W	
Harlon V	Grant C	**Common Customers**
Icelita K	Harlon V	Alan B
Jill C	John L	Asa B
John L	Joshua K	Dorothy W
Lynette L	Martin G	Grant C
Rita N	Robert O	Harlon V
Robert O		John L
Scott M		Robert O
Susan M		

Figure 7.28: *Filtered common/uncommon items between lists*

Return end-of-the-month date items only

When you want to return what was sold on the last date of any month, as shown in *Figure 7.29*, you must use the **EOMONTH** function.

```
=FILTER(Sport_Sales[Item],
   EOMONTH(Sport_Sales[Date]+0,0)=Sport_Sales[Date])
```

Item	Customer	Date	Amount	End of the Month Sales
Batting Legguards	Asa B	3/30/2023	16,000	Chest Guard
Chest Guard	Asa B	1/31/2022	18,100	Cricket Shoes
Inner Gloves	Joshua K	2/10/2023	28,600	Helmets
Elbow Guards	Emily W	1/11/2023	32,100	
Abdominal Pads	Alan B	2/12/2023	45,000	
Thigh Pads	Robert O	8/30/2022	48,006	
Synthetic Balls	Martin G	1/15/2023	49,756	
Caps/Hats	Alan B	1/17/2023	50,000	
Cricket Shoes	Robert O	5/31/2023	50,643	
Batting Legguards	Dorothy W	5/20/2023	53,800	
Helmets	Grant C	6/30/2023	55,200	

Figure 7.29: *Filtered items sold on the last day of the month*

```
=FILTER(Sport_Sales[Item], EOMONTH(Sport_Sales[Date]+0,0)=Sport_Sales[Date])
```

Note:

- **EOMONTH** function does not accept a range of data. It returns the **#VALUE** error. We, however, can force it by adding a zero (SportSales[Date]+0) to the range.
- The **EOMONTH** function returns an array of the last day of a month given a date (refer to *Figure 7.30*).

Item	Customer	Date	Amount	End of the Months
Batting Legguards	Asa B	3/30/2023	16,000	3/31/2023
Chest Guard	Asa B	1/31/2022	18,100	1/31/2022
Inner Gloves	Joshua K	2/10/2023	28,600	2/28/2023
Elbow Guards	Emily W	1/11/2023	32,100	1/31/2023
Abdominal Pads	Alan B	2/12/2023	45,000	2/28/2023
Thigh Pads	Robert O	8/30/2022	48,006	8/31/2022
Synthetic Balls	Martin G	1/15/2023	49,756	1/31/2023
Caps/Hats	Alan B	1/17/2023	50,000	1/31/2023
Cricket Shoes	Robert O	5/31/2023	50,643	5/31/2023
Batting Legguards	Dorothy W	5/20/2023	53,800	5/31/2023
Helmets	Grant C	6/30/2023	55,200	6/30/2023

Formula: =EOMONTH(Sport_Sales[Date]+0,0)

Figure 7.30: EOMONTH *return an array of the last date in months*

- When we compare the calculated end-of-month dates (from the preceding step) to the sales dates, we return an array of **TRUE** and **FALSE**.
- The **FILTER** function is used to filter the rows where the values from the preceding step are **TRUE**.

Conclusion

In this chapter, we learned one of the easiest-to-understand and use lookup functions in Excel—the **FILTER** function. It is mostly recommended when you want to return multiple values.

The **FILTER** function stands as a powerful tool within the Excel arsenal, providing users with a dynamic and efficient means of extracting specific data subsets from extensive datasets. Through this chapter, we have explored the intricacies of the **FILTER** function, delving into its syntax, parameters, and real-world applications.

By harnessing the capabilities of the **FILTER** function, Excel users can streamline their data analysis processes, enhancing both accuracy and efficiency. This function empowers users to effortlessly retrieve relevant information based on complex criteria, enabling informed decision-making, and facilitating comprehensive insights into their data.

In the next chapter, we shall learn about Power Query.

Points to remember

- The `FILTER` function works seamlessly with other Excel dynamic arrays functions like `SORT`, `UNIQUE`, and `TRANSPOSE`, allowing you to create complex data manipulation workflows.
- The FILTER function is non-volatile. Unlike some other functions that recalculate every time you make a change, the `FILTER` function recalculates only when the underlying data or criteria change, improving overall worksheet performance.
- The FILTER function does not accommodate the AND/OR functions. So, in case of multiple criteria use an asterisk (*) to invoke the AND operation and a Plus sign (+) to invoke an OR operation.
- The FILTER function can handle various data types, including numbers, text, dates, and more, making it suitable for a wide range of data analysis tasks.

Quiz

1. Which parameter of the `FILTER` function is used to display a custom message or value when no matching results are found?

    a. array

    b. criteria

    c. `[if_empty]`

    d. `[include]`

2. Which of the following is NOT a benefit of using the `FILTER` function over traditional filtering techniques?

    a. Dynamic array spill

    b. Compatibility with other dynamic array functions

    c. Volatile recalculations

    d. Simplified multiple criteria handling

3. What Excel error is returned by the FILTER function if no matching results are found based on the criteria?

   a. **#REF!**

   b. **#VALUE!**

   c. **#CALC!**

   d. **#NUM!**

4. What Excel function can be used to re-order the results Column of the **FILTER** function?

   a. **SORT**

   b. **SUM**

   c. **VLOOKUP**

   d. **CHOOSE**

5. Which of the following formulas uses the FILTER function to extract rows from a table where the "**Region**" column is equal to "**East**"?

   a. **=FILTER(Table1, "Region", "East")**

   b. **=FILTER(Table1, "Region"="East")**

   c. **=FILTER(Table1, Table1[Region]="East")**

   d. **=FILTER(Table1, "East", "Region")**

Answers

1. **[if_empty]**

2. Volatile recalculations

3. **#CALC!**

4. **CHOOSE**

5. **=FILTER(Table1, Table1[Region]="East")**

CHAPTER 8

Power Query: One-Stop Solution

Introduction

This chapter will discuss one of the game-changing tools in Excel that promises to revolutionize the way we handle data retrieval and transformation – Power Query.

Often hailed as the *one-stop solution* for data lookup, Power Query empowers users to seamlessly connect, reshape, and cleanse data from various sources, transforming raw information into valuable insights with remarkable efficiency and ease.

Like the FILTER function, Power Query has the flexibility to return a subset of data, not just a single entry, which is important for creating dynamic reports.

In Excel 2010 and Excel 2013 versions, the Power Query feature is not integrated by default. You need to download and install the Power Query add-in, which can be found on the add-in on the Microsoft Download Center. Once installed, you'll find the Power Query option in the **Power Query** tab on the Excel ribbon.

Structure

In this chapter, we will discuss the 15 scenarios where we can Power Query:

- Installing the Power Query add-in for Excel 2010 and Excel 2013
- Exact Lookup
- Return multiple results and Multiple columns.
- Approximate Lookup
- Lookup using table joins.
- Looking up the top or bottom n items
- Lookup using the List function.
- Looking up Weekday vs. Weekend data
- Looking up Data that excludes Holidays.
- Looking up Items repeated N times.
- Return end of Month date items Only
- Fuzzy Lookup

Installing the Power Query add-in for Excel 2010 and Excel 2013

Here's a guide on how to do it:

For Excel 2010:

- Download the Power Query Add-in:
    - Go to the Microsoft Download Center.
    - Search for "Power Query for Excel 2010" and download the appropriate version (32-bit or 64-bit) based on your Excel version and system architecture.
- Install the Add-in:
    - Run the downloaded installer.
    - Follow the on-screen instructions to install the Power Query add-in. Make sure Excel is closed during this process.
    - After installation, open Excel 2010.
- Enable the Add-in:
    - Click File tab in Excel.

- Select Options.
  - In the Excel Options dialog box, click Add-Ins on the left sidebar.
  - In the Manage box at the bottom, select COM Add-ins and click Go.
  - Check the Microsoft Office Power Query for the Excel option.
  - Click OK to enable the add-in.

For Excel 2013:

Power Query is already integrated, but you might need to enable it.

Here is how to enable Power Query:
- Click File tab in Excel.
- Select Options.
- In the Excel Options dialog box, click Add-Ins on the left sidebar.
- In the Manage box at the bottom, select COM Add-ins and click Go.
- Check the Microsoft Office Power Query option.
- Click OK to enable Power Query.
- With Power Query enabled, you can access it from the Data tab in the Ribbon. You'll see options like Get & Transform and Get Data there.

The first step in using Power Query is importing data into its editor. There are two ways of importing data as follows:
- If your data is in the Excel workbook, go to the "Data" tab and select "From Table/Range" if your data is in a structured table.
- If your data is in a different workbook or different format (CSV, text file, database, web source, and more), go to the "Data" tab, select "Get Data," and choose the appropriate source.

Note:
- If you're connecting to a different data source, a Navigator window will appear. Navigate to the specific file or database, select the table or query you want, and click `Load` or `Transform Data` to open the Power Query Editor.

Exact Lookup

To use Power Query to do an exact lookup, we need to have both the criteria and lookup data in tables.

For example, in *Figure* 8.1, we want to get the date for any debtor in cell E2:

Power Query: One-Stop Solution

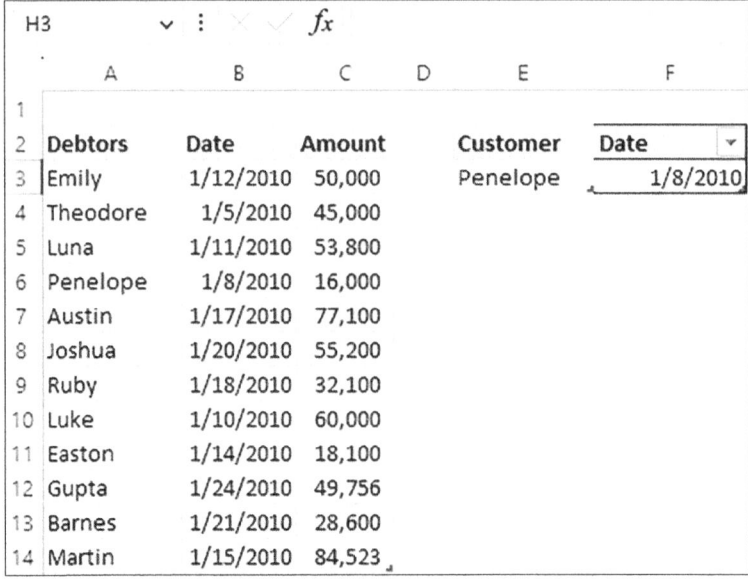

Figure 8.1: *Power Query exact match lookup*

Here are the steps to follow:

1. Convert the cells containing the criterion to a table. Name the table criteria as shown in *Figure 8.2*:

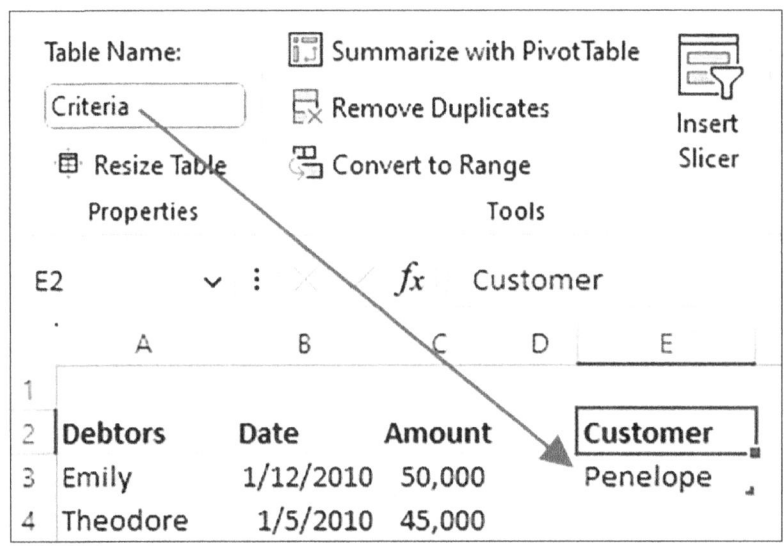

Figure 8.2: *Create a Criterion table*

2. Convert the data to look up into a table as well and name it `tblDebtors`, as shown in *Figure 8.3*:

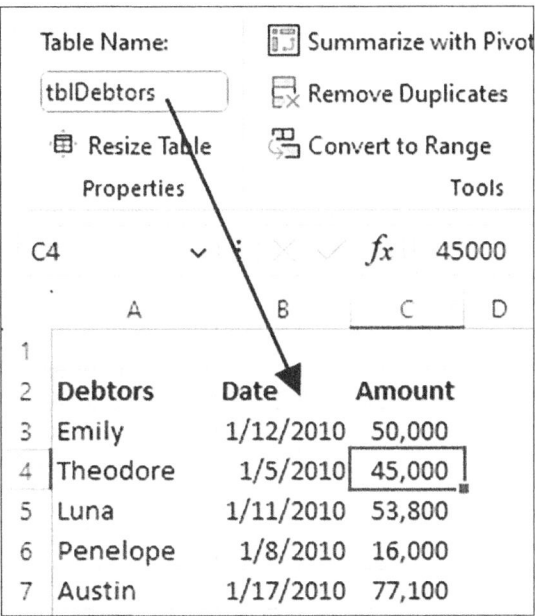

Figure 8.3: *Create a Lookup data table*

3. Load the criterion table to Power Query first. To do this, click anywhere on the table ▶ Go to the **Data** tab ▶ Click **From Table/Range** (see *Figure 8.4*):

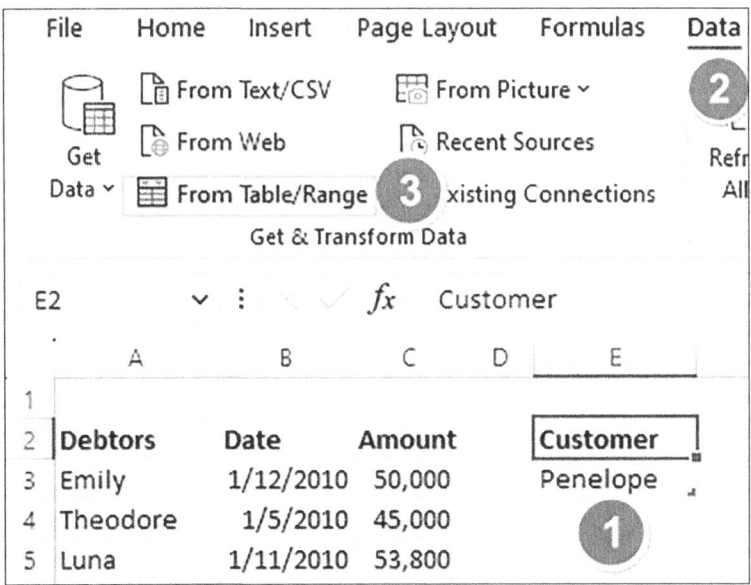

Figure 8.4: *Loading the Criterion Table to Power Query Editor*

4. Go to the `Power Query Editor` and load out the criteria table as a connection only, as shown in *Figure 8.5*:

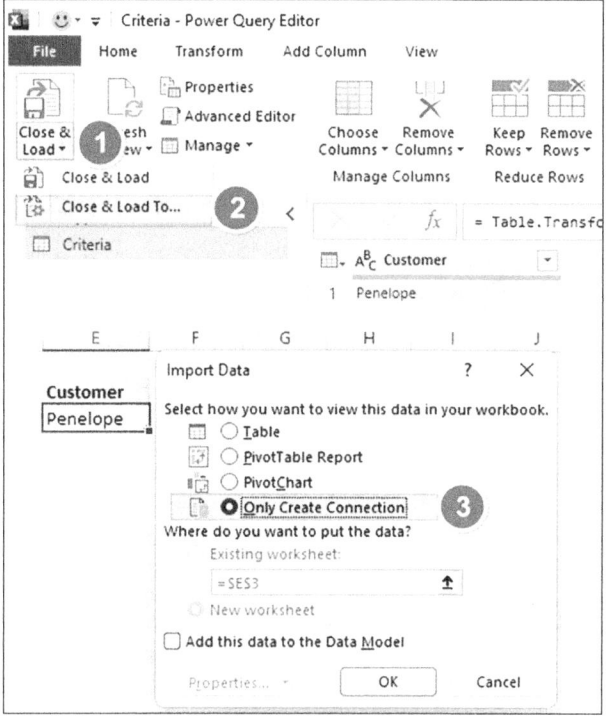

Figure 8.5: Loading Out the Criterion Table as a connection only

5. Follow the same procedure as outlined in Step 3 to load the data table in Power Query. By now, you should see the `Criteria` and Lookup Table in Power Query Editor, as shown in *Figure 8.6*:

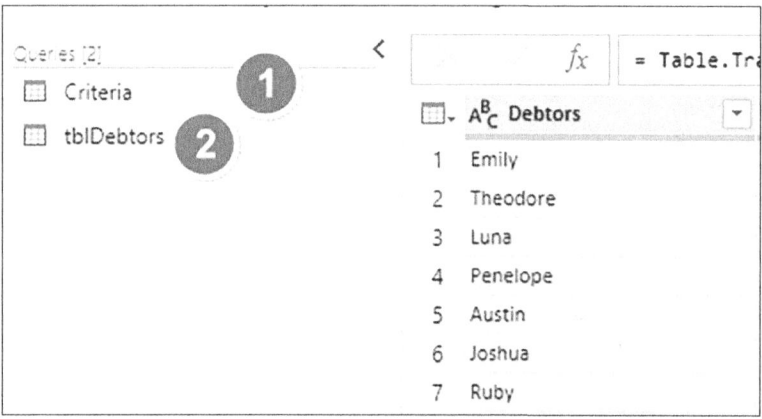

Figure 8.6: Criteria and Lookup Table in Power Query Editor

6. Go to the **Debtors**' table and filter with the first debtor, as shown in *Figure 8.7*:

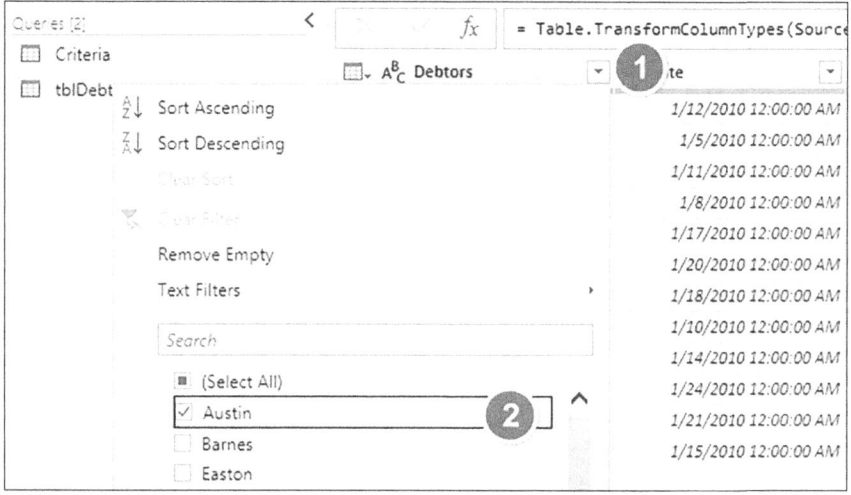

Figure 8.7: Apply Filter on the Lookup table

7. Convert the criterion table into a value by right-clicking the Value and Drilling down, as shown in *Figure 8.8*:

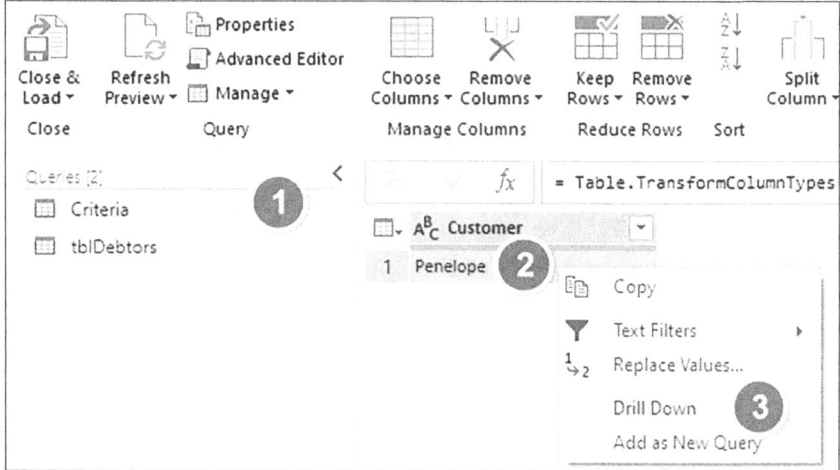

Figure 8.8: Convert the Criteria table to a Value

8. Replace the Filtered value in Step 6 above with the criteria value, as shown in *Figure 8.9*:

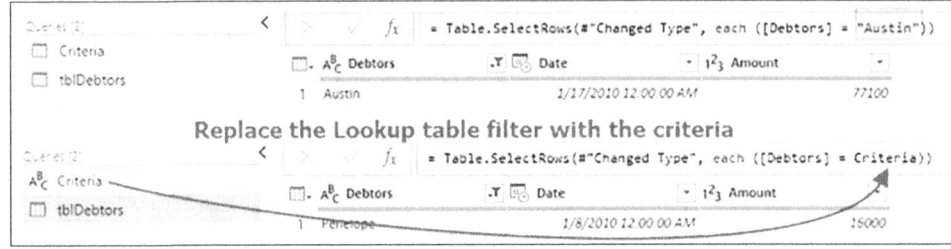

Figure 8.9: Replace Filtered Value with Criterion Value

9. Since we want to return the date value, we should select and remove other columns, as shown in Figure 8.10:

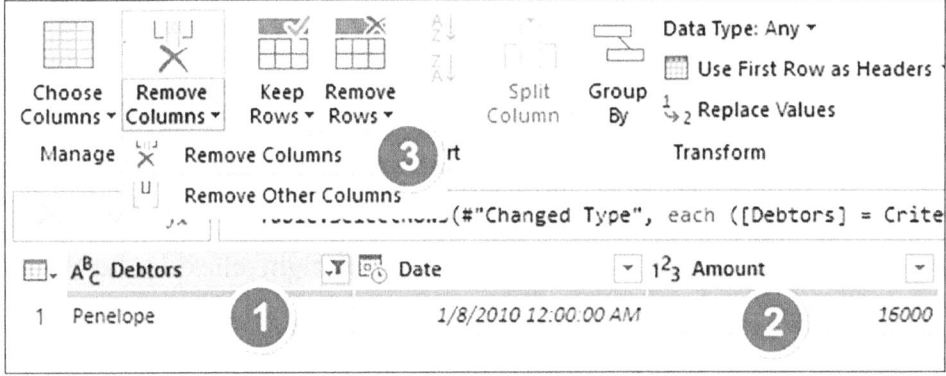

Figure 8.10: Replace Filtered Value with Criterion Value

10. Close and load the retrieved date (see *Figure 8.11*):

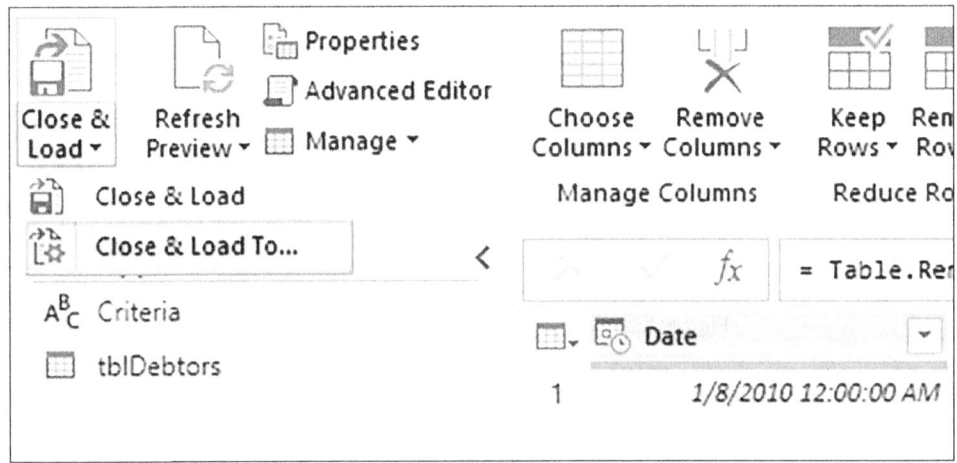

Figure 8.11: Load out the returned data

11. The final step is to load out the filtered Customer/debtor's date not as a connection but to an existing worksheet (see *Figure 8.12*):

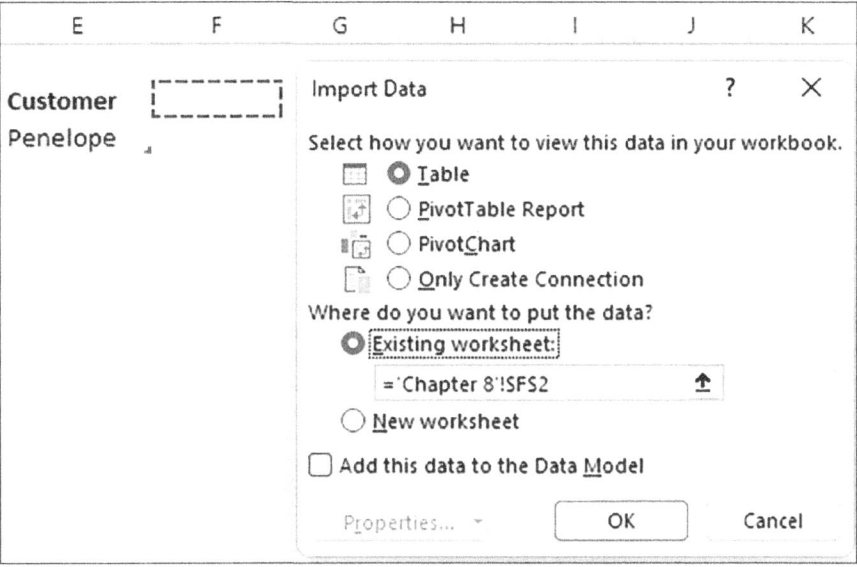

Figure 8.12: Load data to an existing worksheet

Note:

- To look up another customer/debtor's date, just replace the name. Then, go to the Data tab. In the queries and connection group, click Refresh All.
- Power Query stores and remembers all the steps, so there's no need to repeat them when the criteria change.

Return multiple results and multiple columns

Now, let us assume that we have multiple transactions for the debtors, and we want to return all transactions and multiple columns, as shown in *Figure 8.13*:

Power Query: One-Stop Solution

	A	B	C	D	E	F	G	H	I
2	Debtors	Date	Items	Amount		Debtor	Date	Items	Amount
3	Emily	1/12/2010	Chairs	50,000		Penelope	1/5/2010	Laptops	45,000
4	Penelope	1/5/2010	Laptops	45,000			1/8/2010	Books	16,000
5	Luna	1/11/2010	Cabinets	53,800			1/14/2010	Chairs	18,100
6	Penelope	1/8/2010	Books	16,000					
7	Austin	1/17/2010	Desktops	77,100					
8	Joshua	1/20/2010	Pens	55,200					
9	Ruby	1/18/2010	CCTV	32,100					
10	Luke	1/10/2010	Printers	60,000					
11	Penelope	1/14/2010	Chairs	18,100					
12	Gupta	1/24/2010	Laptops	49,756					
13	Barnes	1/21/2010	Cabinets	28,600					
14	Martin	1/15/2010	Books	84,523					
15									

Figure 8.13: *Power Query returns Multiple items and multiple Columns*

Here are the steps to follow:

You will follow the same steps as outlined earlier, except for a small change in Step 9.

In Step 9, where we were removing unwanted columns, this time, we will only remove the debtor's column, as shown in *Figure 8.14*:

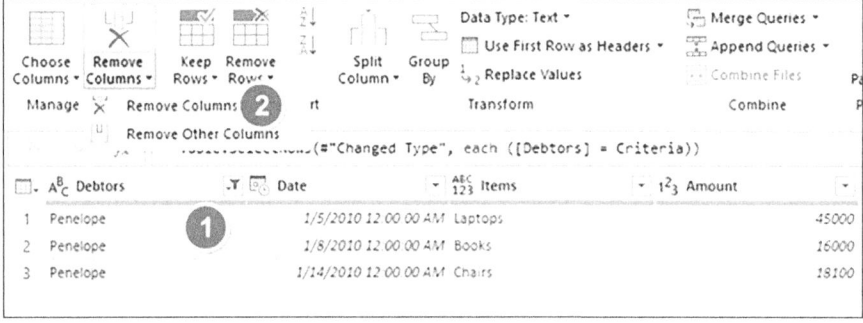

Figure 8.14: *Allowing multiple columns to be returned*

Steps 10 and 11 in the previous section remains unchanged.

Approximate Lookup

Unlike in Excel, Power Query does not have a VLOOKUP or XLOOKUP function that can do an approximate lookup.

In this section, we will learn the steps to use to lookup grades using an approximate lookup, as shown in *Figure 8.15*. Please note your grades table needs to be sorted in ascending order:

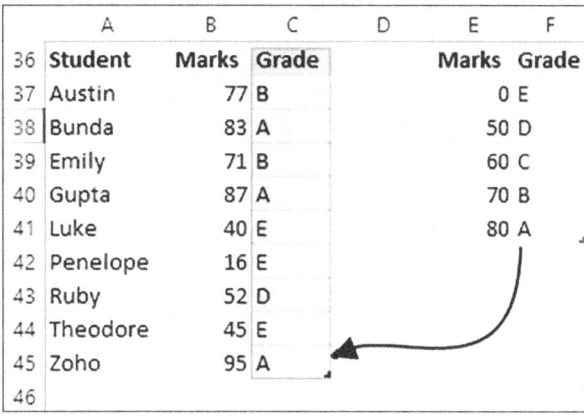

Figure 8.15: Power Query Approximate Match

Here are the steps to follow:

1. Load the grades table (**tblGrade**) as a connection only and then load the exams table (**tblExams**). Then, follow Steps 3–5 outlined in the preceding section (see *Figure 8.16*):

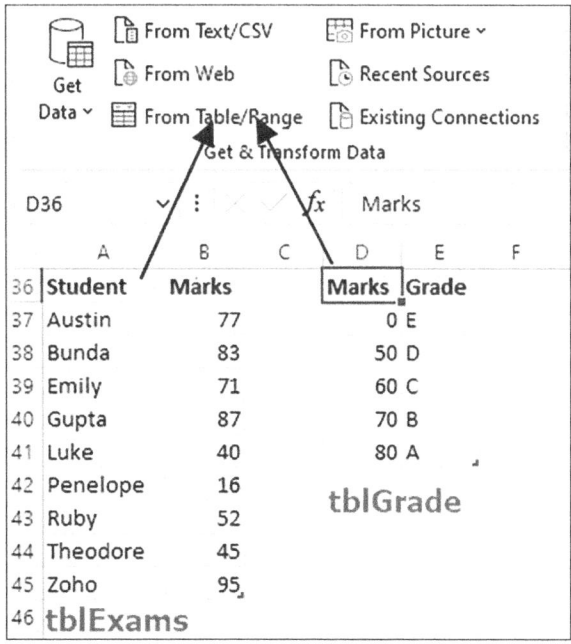

Figure 8.16: Name the tables and load them to Power Query

2. Click exams table, go to the Combine tab, and append queries as new (see *Figure 8.17*):

Power Query: One-Stop Solution   171

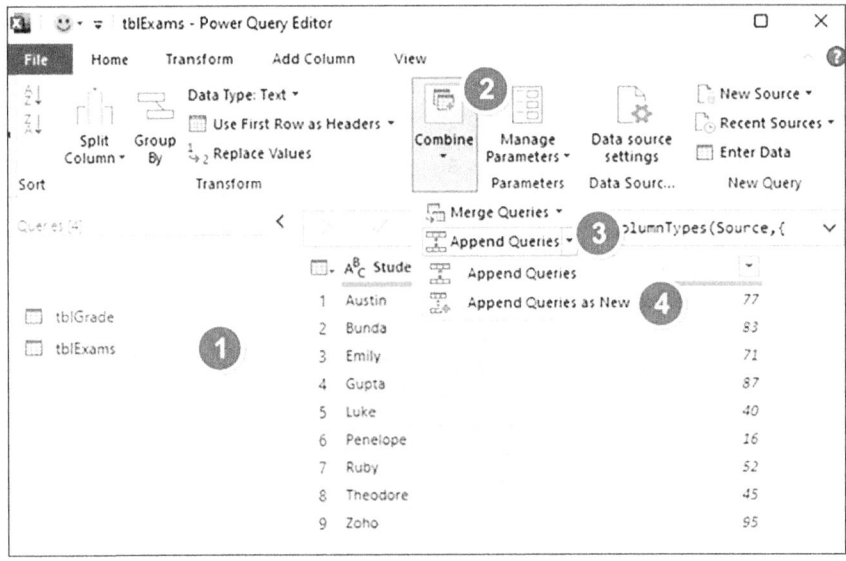

Figure 8.17: Appending Queries in Power Query

3. Append the exams table (**tblExams**) and grade tables (**tblGrade**) (see Figure 8.18):

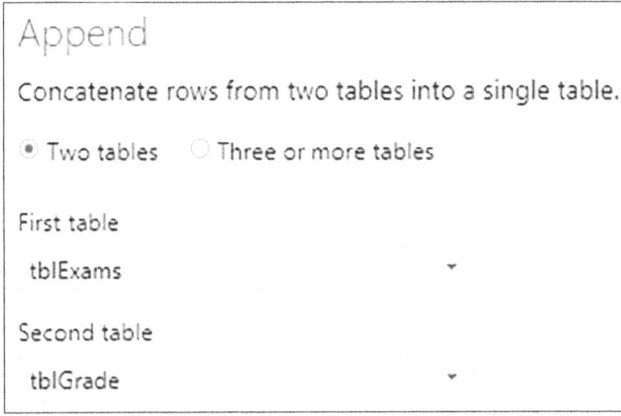

Figure 8.18: Appending two tables

4. On the appended query, go to the **Add Column** tab and add an **Index Column**. We will use this to sort the data later (see Figure 8.19):

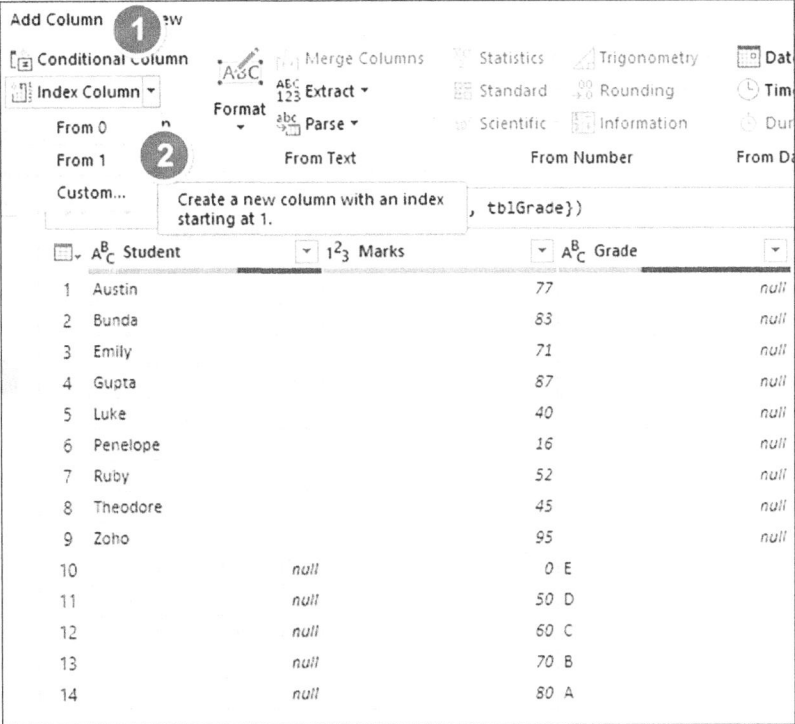

Figure 8.19: Adding an Index Column to Appended Query

5. Sort the marks in ascending order (see Figure 8.20):

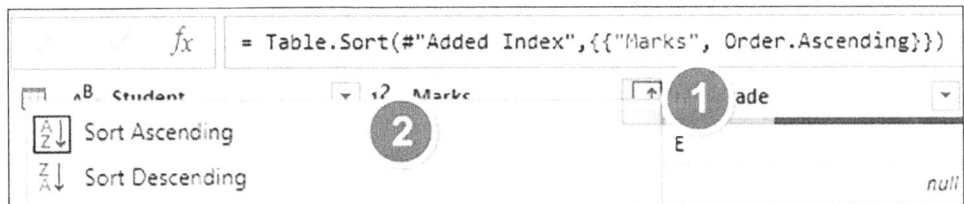

Figure 8.20: Sort the marks in Ascending order

6. Click Grade Column, go to the **Transform** tab, then in the Fill options, and click Down (see Figure 8.21):

Power Query: One-Stop Solution

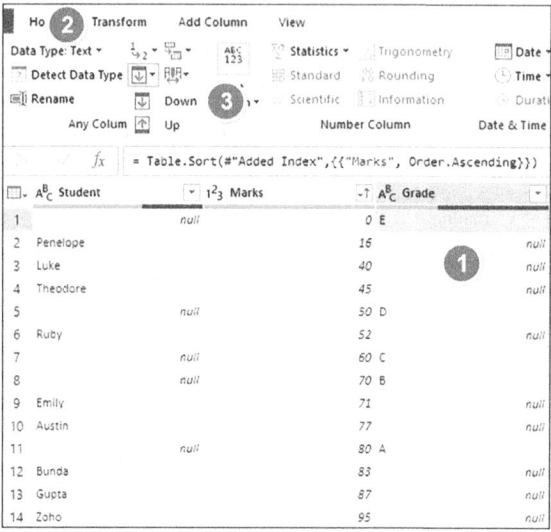

Figure 8.21: Fill down the grades

7. Go to the Students Column and Filter out the null values. Just untick the null values.

8. Go to the Index column and sort it in ascending order.

9. Highlight the Grades table, then go to the **Home** tab, under the Remove columns options, and click Remove other columns.

10. Click appended query, go to the **Home** tab, and then under the Close and Load options, click **Close & Load To** (see *Figure 8.22*):

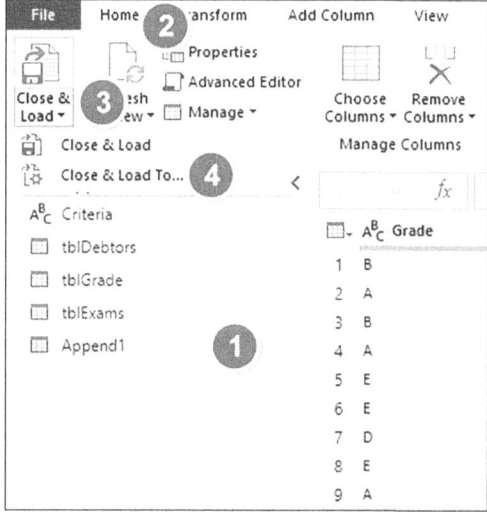

Figure 8.22: Load the grades from the Approximate Lookup

11. Load the grades as a table next to the exams table (see *Figure 8.23*):

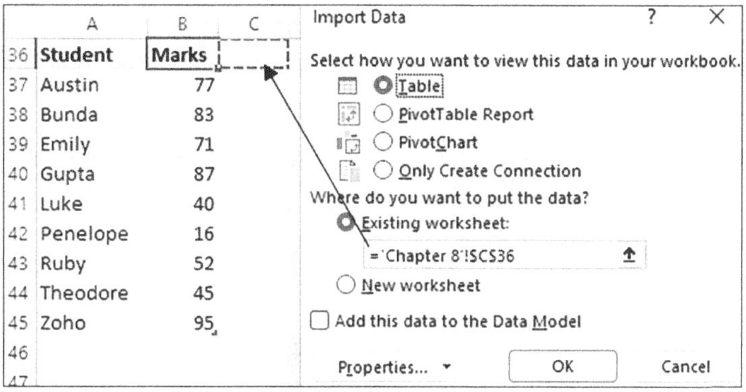

Figure 8.23: *Load the grades next to the exams table*

Lookup using table joins

In Power Query, one of the most important things to learn is the different forms of table joins. In this example, we are going to use only two joins:

- **Inner Join**: Only the rows with matching values in both tables are included in the result.
- **Left Anti-join**: Only rows from the left (or first) table are included in the result.

In the following example, see *Figure 8.24*, we want to look up from the `tblCars`, the customers whose cars were serviced (`tblServiced`) (happy customers) and those with un-serviced cars (unhappy customers):

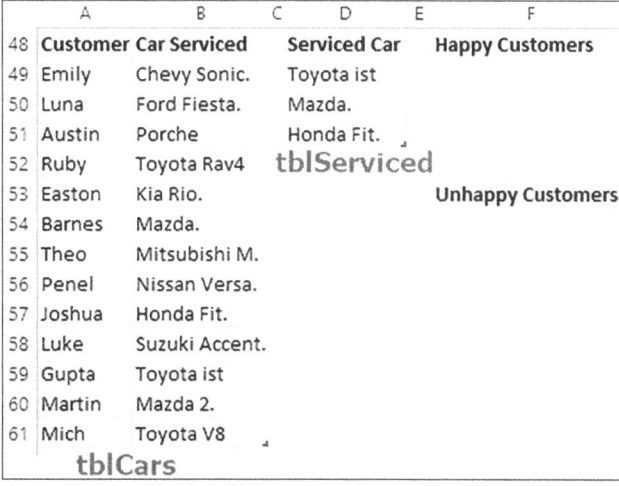

Figure 8.24: *Looking up data using table joins*

Power Query: One-Stop Solution

Here are the steps to follow:

1. Load the Cars table (**tblCars**) and Serviced tables (**tblServiced**) as a connection only. Follow Steps 3–5 in the Exact Lookup section previously mentioned.

2. Click Cars table and go to the **Home** tab. Under the **Combine** group, select Merge queries, and then select **Merge Queries** as New (see *Figure 8.25*):

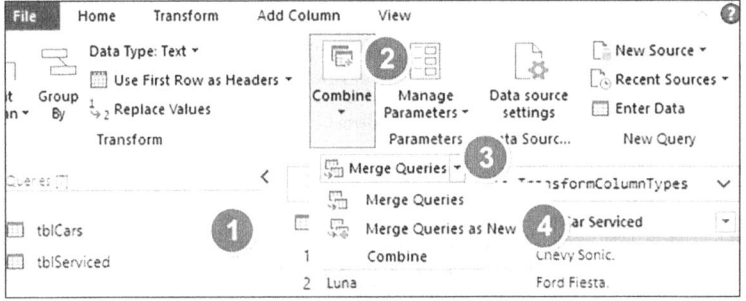

Figure 8.25: Merging Queries

3. In the Merge pop-up Table, Select **tblServiced** from the second dropdown menu. Then select the **Car Serviced** column from the **tblCars** and the **Serviced Cars** column from the **tblServiced** table. Finally, from the Join kind, select Inner Join. This will only result in happy customers' data (see *Figure 8.26*):

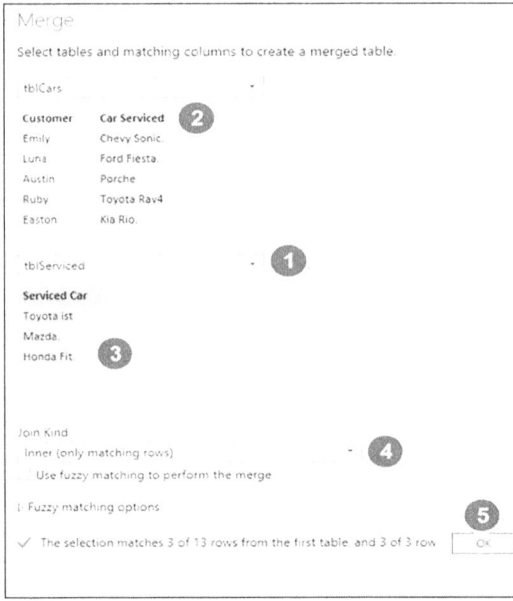

Figure 8.26: Inner Join table merge

4. Rename the query to **HappyCustomers**, select the customer column, and click remove other columns (see Figure 8.27):

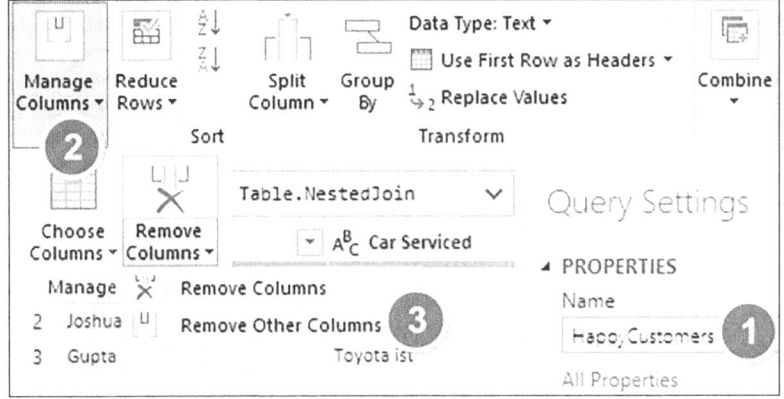

Figure 8.27: Renaming queries

5. Repeat the preceding Steps 1–3 to create a new merged query. This time instead of selecting an inner join, select a Left Anti-join. This will only result in unhappy customers' data whose cars were not serviced (see Figure 8.28):

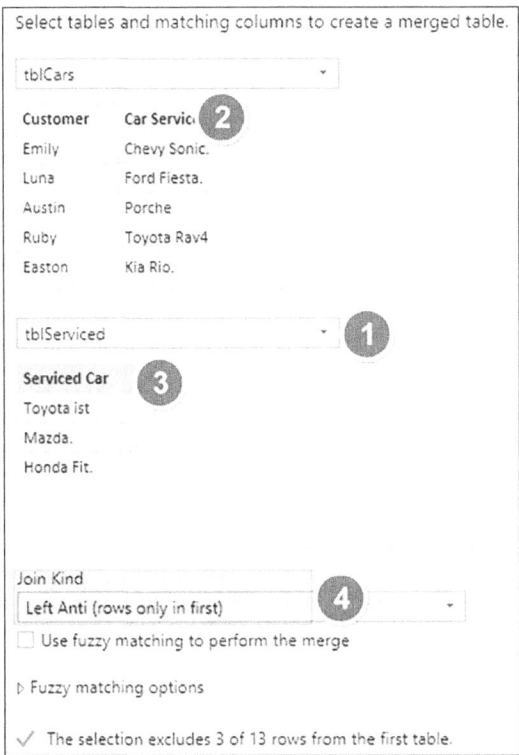

Figure 8.28: Left Anti-Join table merge

6. Rename the query to **UnhappyCustomers**, select the customer column, and click Remove other columns.

7. Lastly, load the two new queries as tables to an existing worksheet.

Looking up the top or bottom n items

To look up the top/bottom n items dynamically, we will use almost the same steps as those used in the Exact lookup section with a slight change.

For example, *Figure 8.29* shows how to look up the top five creditors:

	A	B	C	D	E
64	Creditors	Date	Amount		Top
65	Austin	1/12/2010	50,000		5
66	Barnes	1/5/2010	45,000		tblTop
67	Easton	1/11/2010	53,800		
68	Gupta	1/8/2010	16,000		
69	Luke	1/17/2010	77,100		
70	Luke	1/20/2010	55,200		
71	Luke	1/18/2010	32,100		
72	Luna	1/10/2010	60,000		
73	Martin	1/14/2010	18,100		
74	Penelope	1/24/2010	49,756		
75	Ruby	1/21/2010	28,600		
76	Theodore	1/15/2010	84,523		
77	tblCreditors				

Figure 8.29: Lookup top five creditors

Here are the steps to follow:

1. Load the Top 5 table (**tblTop**) as a connection only, and then load the creditors table (**tblCreditors**). Follow Steps 3–5 in the Exact Lookup section previously mentioned.

2. Convert the **tblTop** table into a value by right-clicking the value and then drilling down. Refer to Step 7 in the Exact Lookup section previously mentioned.

3. Click creditors table, go to the **Home** tab, and under the Keep Rows options, select Keep Top Rows. In the pop-up window, type 5 under the number of rows (see *Figure 8.30*):

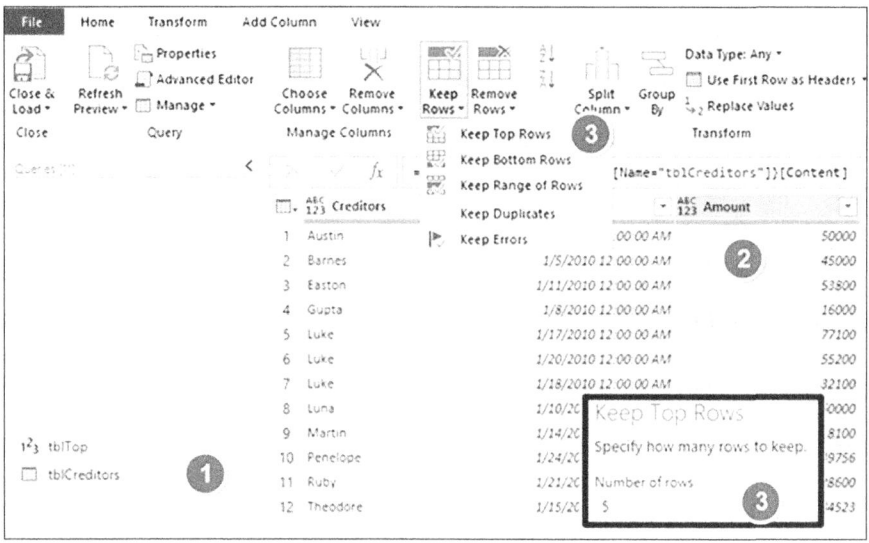

Figure 8.30: Keep the top five rows

4. Go to the **View** tab and click **Advanced Editor** (see Figure 8.31). The reason for this step is to replace the hardcoded five rows with our criteria in the **tblTop** table:

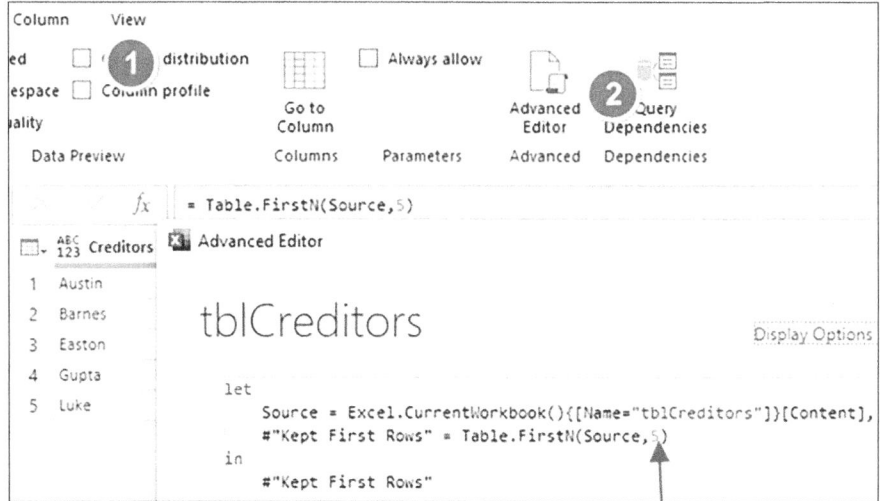

Figure 8.31: Invoke the Advanced Editor

5. Replace the hardcoded 5 with our dynamic criteria in the "tblTop" table (see Figure 8.32):

Power Query: One-Stop Solution

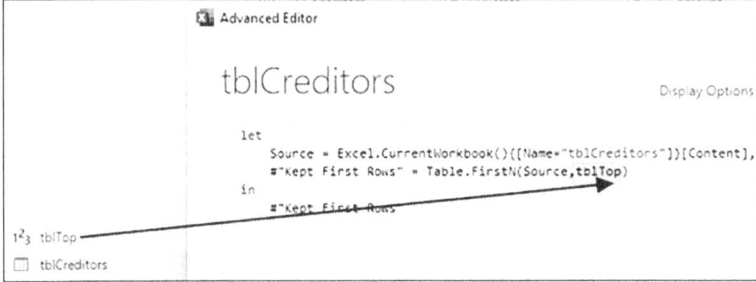

Figure 8.32: Replace hardcoded criteria with dynamic one

6. Load the filtered creditors as a table in the existing worksheet.
7. To test if the dynamic Filter is working, change the top 5–7 and refresh the query.

Note: *To lookup the bottom n items, follow the same steps as mentioned previously, but in step 3, select "Keep the bottom rows"*

Lookup using the List function

There are over 45 list-related functions in Power Query. Let us learn how to use a few to look up data.

We are going to look up the Grades and tutor tables, as shown in *Figure 8.33*:

Student	Marks	Subject		Marks	Grade
		tblClass			**Grades**
Austin	77	English		0	E
Bunda	83	Math		50	D
Emily	71	English		60	C
Gupta	87	Physics		70	B
Luke	40	Physics		80	A
Penelope	16	Math			**tblTutor**
Ruby	52	English		Subject	Tutor
Theodore	45	Physics		English	Aiden
Zoho	95	English		Physics	Adrian
				Math	Amani

Figure 8.33: *Approximate and Exact functions using List function*

Here are the steps to follow:

1. Load all the three tables as a connection only.

2. Select the Class table (**tblClass**), go to the **Add Column** tab, and click **Custom Column** (see *Figure 8.34*):

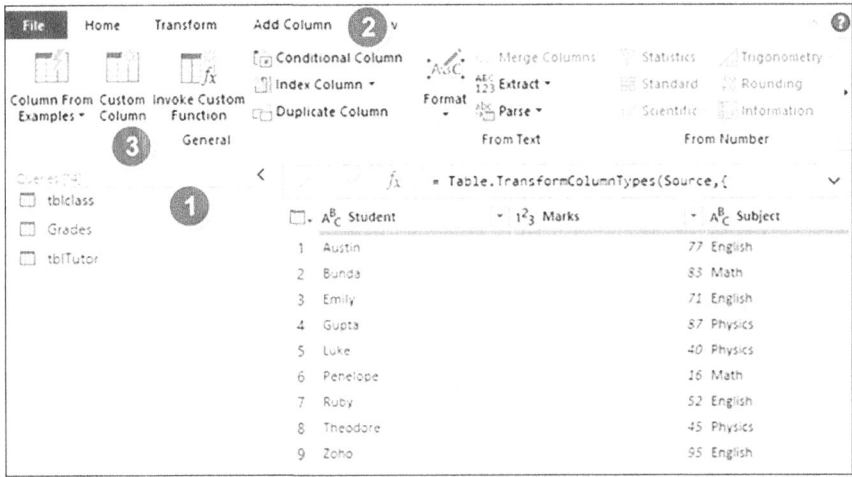

Figure 8.34: Create a Custom Column

3. Rename your column **Tutor** and write the function, as shown in *Figure 8.35*:

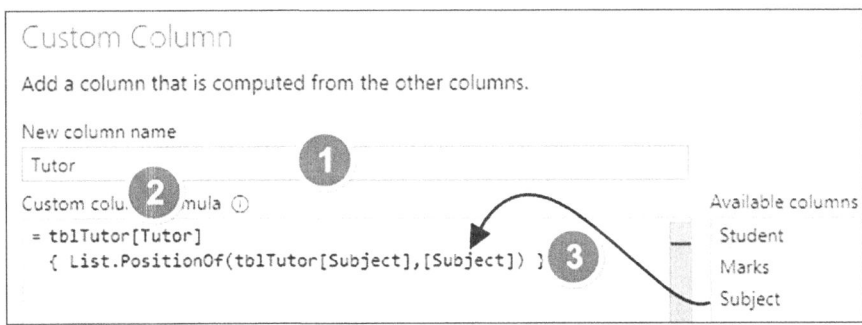

Figure 8.35: Exact Lookup using List.PositionOf function

tblTutor[Tutor]
{ List.PositionOf(tblTutor[Subject],[Subject]) }

Here is how the function works:
- **tblTutor[Tutor]** ▶ returns a list of all the tutors in the lookup **tblTutor** table. In Power Query, you can access the columns of a table using the square bracket notation (**[ColumnName]**).

- After retrieving the column, we need to use the position index operator, that is, the curly braces ({}) to return the row number where the subject in the **tblclass** matches the subject in **tblTutor**
- **List.PositionOf(tblTutor[Subject],[Subject])** ▶ To dynamically return the row per subject, we use the function List.PositionOf. This function is used to find the position of the current value ([Subject]) within the list of values in the **Subject** column (tblTutor[Subject]) of the table. It returns the position (index) of the value within the list.
- This expression works like the INDEX and MATCH combo function we learned in *Chapter 3, Index and Match*. We are looking up the column first from the **tblTutor** and then the row where the subject in the **tblclass** matches the subject in the **tblTutor**

Now, let us see how to do an approximate match by looking up the grades.

Here are the steps to follow:

1. Create another custom column and rename it grades.

2. Write the following functions as shown in *Figure 8.36*:

List.Last(
Table.SelectRows(Grades,(IT)=> IT[Marks]<=[Marks])[Grade])

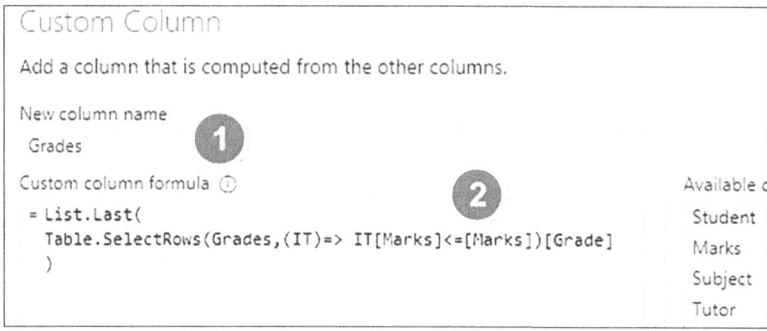

Figure 8.36: *Approximate Lookup using Table.SelectRows and List.Last*

Here is how the function works:

- **Table.SelectRows(Grades, (IT)=> IT[Marks]<=[Marks])** ▶ This function filters the rows of the "Grades" table based on a condition. The second argument, **(IT) => IT[Marks] <= [Marks]**, is an inline function (also called a lambda function) that specifies the filtering condition.

Here's what's happening:
- **(IT)** is the custom variable to represent the Internal table "Grades", which we shall be filtering inside the "tblClass" table.
- **IT[Marks]** refers to the value in the "Marks" column of the internal table.
- **[Marks]** refers to the value of the marks in the "tblClass" per row.

So, the filtering condition checks whether the values in the "Marks" column of the "Grades" table (IT[Marks]) are less than or equal to the value of the "Marks" in "tblClass" and returns a table of those Marks and corresponding Grades.

- `Table.SelectRows(Grades,(IT)=> IT[Marks]<=[Marks])[Grade]` ► Since we are only interested in the grades, we use the field column operator ([]) to get a grades list.
- Finally, we look up the last grade in the list using the **List.Last** function.

Looking up Weekday versus Weekend data

To look up weekend or weekday data in Power Query, we use the **Date.DayOfWeek** function.

For example, using data shown in *Figure 8.37*, let us see how to look up whom we gave credit on the weekends and weekdays.

	A	B	C	D	E	F
64	Creditors	Date	Amount		Weekend	Weekday
65	Austin	1/12/2010	50,000			
66	Barnes	1/5/2010	45,000			
67	Easton	1/11/2010	53,800			
68	Gupta	1/8/2010	16,000			
69	Luke	1/17/2010	77,100			
70	Luke	1/20/2010	55,200			
71	Luke	1/18/2010	32,100			
72	Luna	1/10/2010	60,000			
73	Martin	1/14/2010	18,100			
74	Penelope	1/24/2010	49,756			
75	Ruby	1/21/2010	28,600			
76	Theodore	1/15/2010	84,523			

Figure 8.37: Lookup the Weekday and Weekend data

Here are the steps to follow:

1. Load the table to Power Query.
2. To look up Weekday data, go to the View tab, click Advanced Editor, and write the following function:

let
    Source = Excel.CurrentWorkbook(){[Name="tblCreditors"]}[Content],
    #"Filtered Rows" =
Table.SelectRows(
Source, each Date.DayOfWeek([Date])>=1 and Date.DayOfWeek([Date])<6
)
in
    #"Filtered Rows"

Here is how the function works:

- The **let** clause is used to define a set of named steps, each of which represents a specific transformation or calculation.
- **Source = Excel.CurrentWorkbook(){[Name="tblCreditors"]}[Content]** ▸ assigns the contents of a table named "tblCreditors" from the current Excel workbook to the variable "Source."
- Define a new "Filtered Rows" step using the **Table.SelectRows** function to filter the rows of the "Source" table based on a specific condition involving the day of the week.
- **Date.DayOfWeek([Date]) > 1 and Date.DayOfWeek([Date]) < 6** checks if the day of the week of the "Date" column is greater or equal to 1 (Monday) and less than 6 (Friday). This effectively filters out rows corresponding to weekends (Saturday and Sunday).
- **in #"Filtered Rows"** ▸ The in keyword indicates the output of the script. This line specifies the result of the script, which is the table generated by the "Filtered Rows" step.

Note

- **Date.DayOfWeek** function returns a number (from 0 to 6) indicating the day of the week of the provided Date.
- It treats Sunday as the first day of the week.
- Therefore, to look up only weekend data, replace the previously provided **Table.SelectRows** function with the following function, which returns

only the day of the week of the **Date** equal to 0 or 1, that is (Sunday and Saturday):

```
Table.SelectRows(Source, each Date.DayOfWeek([Date])=0 or Date.DayOfWeek([Date])=6)
```

Looking up date that excludes holidays

Assuming we have the following harvest data and holiday dates, as shown in *Figure* 8.38. Let us learn how to look up harvested data excluding holidays.

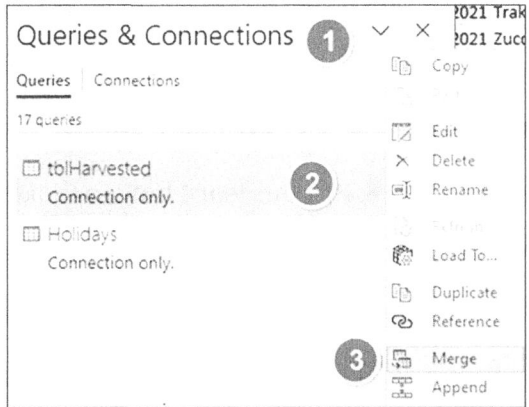

Figure 8.38: *Lookup dates excluding holidays*

Here are the steps to follow:

1. Load the two tables as a connection only.
2. Go to Queries and Connections, right-click the harvested table, and click **Merge** (see *Figure* 8.39):

Figure 8.39: *Merging Queries*

3. On the Merge pop-up window, select the Holidays table in the second drop-down menu. Then, select the Date column in the harvested table and holidays. Finally, select the Left Anti-join to exclude the holidays from the harvested table (see *Figure 8.40*):

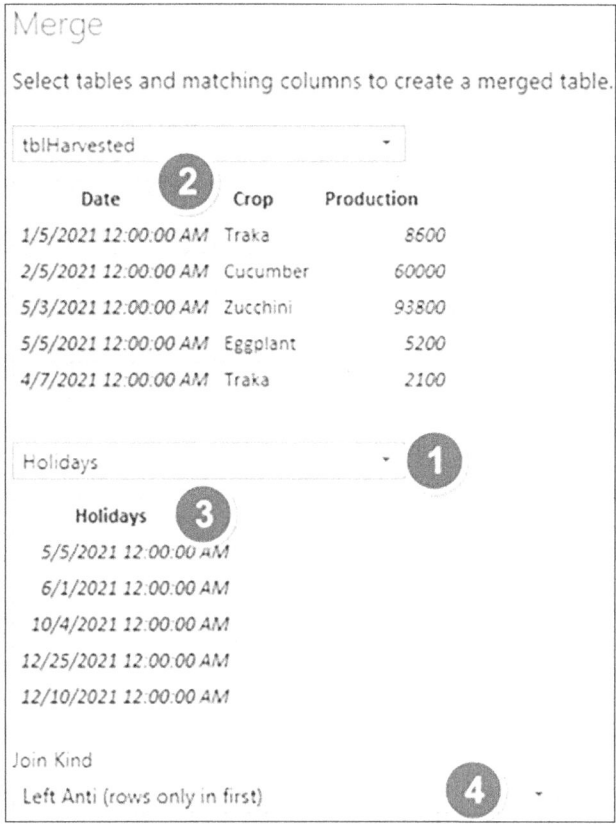

Figure 8.40: *Merging Queries*

4. Finally, delete the holidays column and load out the data.

Looking up items repeated N times

Using the data shown in *Figure 8.41*, let us learn how to lookup the items repeated two times from the **Sports Sale** table.

Please note that we want a solution where we can replace the 2 with any number, and Power Query will look up the items.

186 Ultimate Excel with Power Query and ChatGPT

	A	B	C	D	E
107	**Item**	**Date**	**Amount**		**Items Repeated**
108	Helmets	3/5/2023	45,000		2
109	Batting Legguards	1/8/2022	16,000		
110	Batting Gloves	2/10/2023	60,000		**RepeatN**
111	Batting Legguards	1/11/2023	53,800		
112	Cricket Balls	2/12/2023	50,000		
113	Chest Guard	4/14/2022	18,100		
114	Cricket Bags	1/15/2023	84,523		
115	Cricket Balls	1/17/2023	77,100		
116	Elbow Guards	5/18/2023	32,100		
117	Helmets	5/20/2023	55,200		
118	Inner Gloves	6/21/2023	28,600		
119	Synthetic Balls	5/18/2022	49,756		
120	Thigh Pads	1/19/2023	48,006		
121	Cricket Shoes	6/21/2023	50,643		

SportSales

Figure 8.41: Lookup items repeated 2 times

Here are the steps to follow:

1. Load the two tables as a connection only.

2. Convert the **RepeatN** table to a value ▶ Right-click the value and drill down (see *Figure 8.42*):

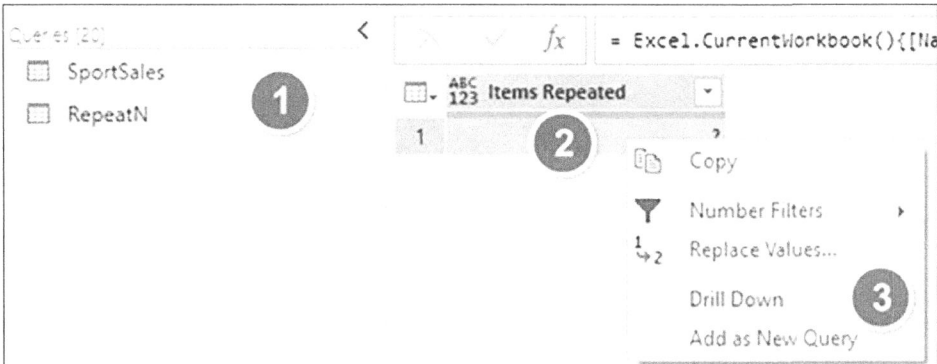

Figure 8.42: Convert table to value

3. Go to the **SportSales** table and select the Items column. Then, go to the Transfo+rm tab and click **GroupBy**. Under the Operation, select **CountRows** and click **OK** (see *Figure 8.43*):

Power Query: One-Stop Solution

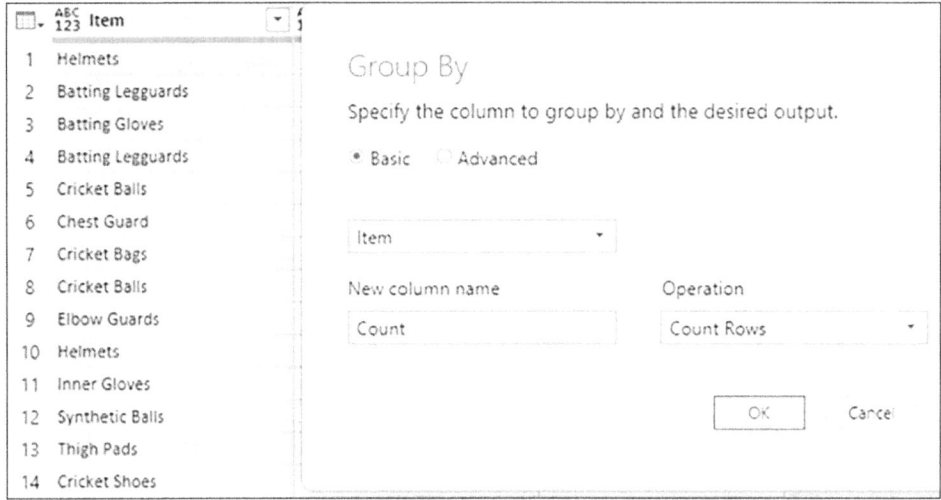

Figure 8.43: Group By Items

4. Go to the new count column and filter by 1 (see *Figure 8.44*):

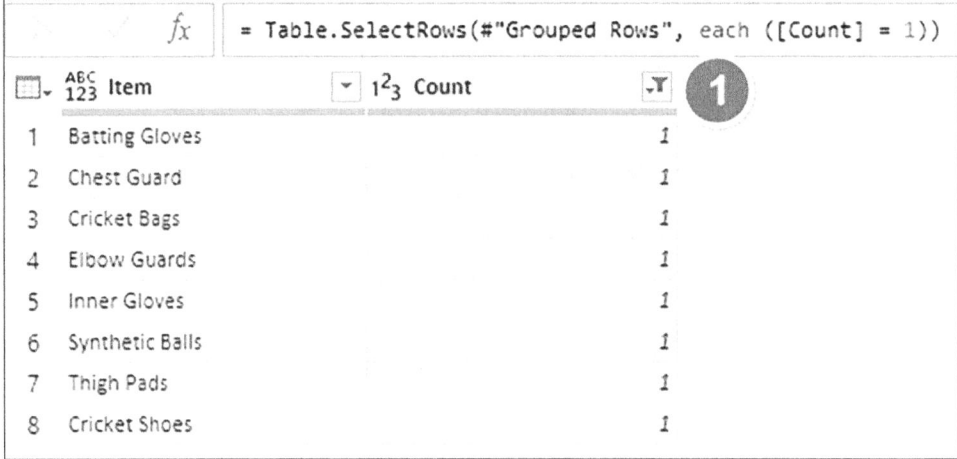

Figure 8.44: Filter by any Count

5. Replace the hardcoded filter criteria with our **RepeatN** value. Go to the View tab and click **Advanced Editor**. Delete the hardcoded filter (1) and type **RepeatN** (see *Figure 8.45*):

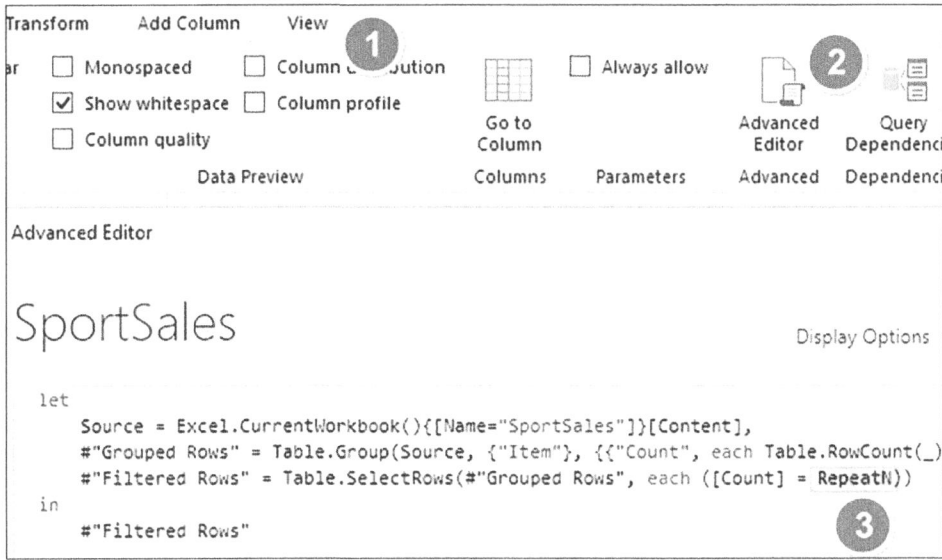

Figure 8.45: Filter by any Count

6. Delete the **Count** column and load the data (see *Figure 8.46*):

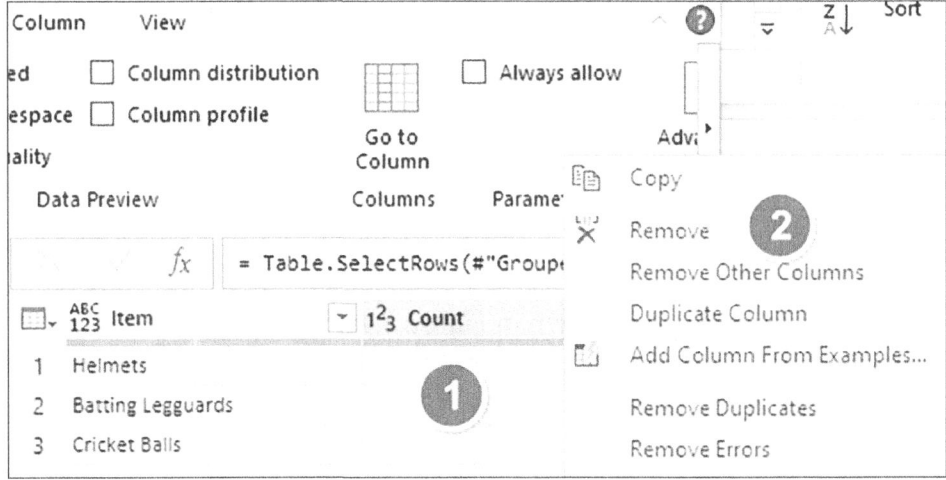

Figure 8.46: Delete the count column and load the data

Return end-of-month date items only

In the previous chapter on the **FILTER** function, we learned how to look up transactions occurring at any end of the month. Now, let us see how we can implement the same using Power Query.

Power Query: One-Stop Solution   189

Using the data shown in *Figure* 8.47, return only the creditors paid at any end of the month:

	A	B	C	D	E
126	Creditors	Paid Date	Amount		End Month Payments
127	Asa B	3/5/2023	45,000		
128	Robert O	1/31/2022	16,000		
129	Harlon V	2/10/2023	60,000		
130	Lynette L	1/11/2023	53,800		
131	Rita N	2/12/2023	50,000		
132	Emily L	4/30/2022	18,100		
133	Susan M	1/15/2023	84,523		
134	Jill C	1/17/2023	77,100		
135	Cole A	5/18/2023	32,100		
136	Scott M	5/20/2023	55,200		
137	John L	6/30/2023	28,600		
138	Icelita K	5/18/2022	49,756		
139	Alan B	1/19/2023	45,020		
140	Grant C	12/31/2023	44,041		

***Figure* 8.47**: *Lookup End of the Month transactions*

Here are the steps to follow:

1. Load the creditors' table in Power Query.
2. Go to the **View** tab and click Advanced Editor.
3. Write the function as shown in *Figure* 8.48:

```
let
    Source = Excel.CurrentWorkbook(){[Name="Creditors"]}[Content],
    #"Filtered Rows" =
    Table.SelectRows(Source,
        each Date.Day([Paid Date])=Date.DaysInMonth([Paid Date]))
in
    #"Filtered Rows"
```

***Figure* 8.48**: *M Code for Selecting End of the Month items*

Here is how the function works:

- The **let** clause is used to define a set of named steps, each of which represents a specific transformation or calculation.

- `Source = Excel.CurrentWorkbook(){[Name="Creditors"]}[Content]` assigns the contents of a table named "Creditors" from the current Excel workbook to the variable "Source".
- Define a new "Filtered Rows" step using the `Table.SelectRows` function to filter the rows of the "Source" table based on a specific condition.
- `Date.Day([Paid Date])` returns the day part of the "Paid Date" column, while `Date.DaysInMonth([Paid Date])` returns a number from 28 to 31 indicating the number of days in the month.
- `Date.Day([Paid Date]) = Date.DaysInMonth([Paid Date])` check if the day of the paid date is equal to the total number of days in that month. If they are equal, the expression will return TRUE, indicating that the payment date falls on the last day of the month.
- `Table.SelectRows` function only returns rows where the preceding condition is TRUE.

4. Load out the filtered table to an existing worksheet.

Fuzzy Lookup

Performing a fuzzy match in Power Query is easier and far more intuitive than using functions.

Fuzzy matching refers to the technique of comparing non-identical text strings based on their similarity. Instead of exact matches, fuzzy matching evaluates the resemblance between strings, allowing for the identification of similar or closely related terms within datasets.

For example, how do we lookup the staff in **tblDirty** using the **Lookup Company** column in the **tblClean**, as shown in *Figure* 8.49:

	A	B	C	D	E
141	tblDirty			tblClean	
142	Company	Staff		Lookup Company	Staff
143	Acme Corp	Anderson, Bob		XYZ Corporation	
144	Electrical Co	Janes, Mary		ABC Incorporated	
145	Electric Limited	Joan, Eric		Acme Corporation	
146	ABC Inc	Johnson, Alice		Electric Company	
147	XYZ Corp	Smith, John		Mega Corporation Ltd	
148	MegaCorp Ltd	Smoth, John		Electric Ltd	
149					
150					

Figure 8.49: *Fuzzy Lookup*

Here are the steps to follow:

1. Load the two tables as a connection only.
2. Click **tblDirty** and click Merge.
3. Select the **tblClean**, and then select the columns to Match, as shown in *Figure 8.50*.
4. Click **Use Fuzzy Matching to perform the merge** and expand the fuzzy matching options. These allow you to fine-tune the matching process. A lower similarity threshold lowers the strictness of the fuzzy matching algorithm.

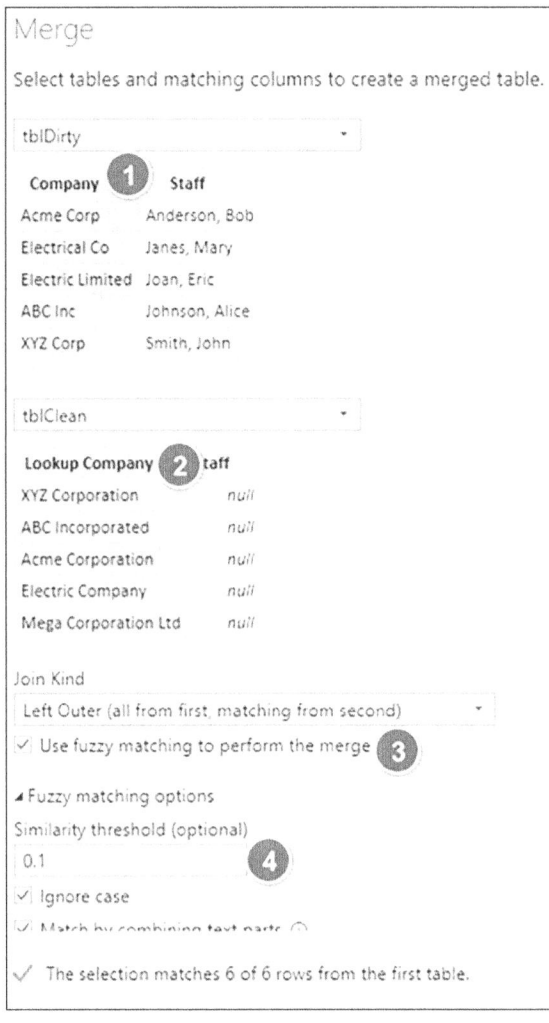

Figure 8.50: Left Outer Fuzzy Lookup

5. Expand the Merged table (see *Figure 8.51*) and select the lookup column only.

Company	Staff	tblClean
1 Acme Corp	Anderson, Bob	Table
2 Electrical Co	Janes, Mary	Table
3 Electric Limited	Joan, Eric	Table
4 ABC Inc	Johnson, Alice	Table
5 XYZ Corp	Smith, John	Table
6 MegaCorp Ltd	Smoth, John	Table

Figure 8.51: *Expand the Merged table*

6. Delete the Dirty column and load out the table.

Conclusion

In this chapter, we learned how to solve different lookup problems using a powerful data transformation and preparation tool – Power Query. It is mainly recommended when handling large data sets.

One of the setbacks is that creating Power Query queries and connections may take more time upfront than using simple Excel formulas. As we have learned, it involves many steps.

Another setback is that, unlike the formulas that recalculate in real-time and provide instant results as you edit the spreadsheet, Power Query requires you to refresh your queries in case your data changes. You can set the queries to refresh after a specific time, but it would be a waste of resources if you have complex queries.

In the next Chapter, we are going to learn how we can leverage the use of AI in Mastering Excel.

Points to remember

- If you're working with a relatively small dataset and need to perform simple lookups, Excel formulas are usually faster to set up and use. However, as the dataset size and complexity increase or when extensive data transformation is required, Power Query becomes a more efficient and scalable option.

- While there are many steps involved, Power Query provides a visual, user-friendly interface that allows users to interact with data transformation. The steps are more intuitive than complex formulas.
- You can create reusable Power Query queries that can be applied to different datasets or shared across teams, ensuring consistency in data preparation and lookup processes.

Multiple choice questions

1. What is the primary purpose of Power Query?

    a. Data Visualization

    b. Data Transformation and Preparation

    c. Statistical Analysis

    d. Data Backup and Recovery

2. Which of the following is NOT a step you can perform in Power Query?

    a. Filtering rows

    b. Creating pivot tables

    c. Merging tables

    d. Removing duplicates

3. Which tab in Excel allows you to access Power Query?

    a. Data

    b. Insert

    c. Format

    d. Home

4. Which operation in Power Query allows you to combine data from multiple tables based on a common column?

    a. Merge

    b. Concatenate

    c. Append

    d. Group By

5. Which of the following is a valid data source for Power Query?

    a. Only Excel files

    b. Only CSV files

    c. Excel files, CSV files, Databases, Web sources, and more

    d. Only Word documents

6. What does the term "Fuzzy Matching" mean in Power Query?

    a. Matching identical strings

    b. Matching non-identical text based on similarity

    c. Matching case-sensitive text

    d. Matching numerical values

Answers

1	b
2	b
3	a
4	a
5	c
6	b

CHAPTER 9
ChatGPT: Using ChatGPT to solve lookup issues

Introduction

In this chapter, we will discuss how we can incorporate artificial intelligence (AI) into solving lookup problems in Excel.

Before we learn about external artificial intelligence, we want to acknowledge some of the inbuilt AI features like Flash Fill (which uses pattern recognition), Column by Example Option in Power Query (also uses pattern recognition and writes a reusable M Code function), Analyze Data Option (creates charts and analysis), Recommended Charts (shows an array of charts you can create from data), and Recommended Pivot Tables (shows an array of pivot table analysis you can create from your data).

ChatGPT represents a cutting-edge development in language generation pioneered by OpenAI. It falls under the GPT (Generative Pre-trained Transformer) family of models. Utilizing a transformer architecture, GPT models can comprehend and generate text resembling human language, drawing upon the input they are provided with.

The most critical skill when using ChatGPT is prompting. A prompt is a text you provide to start a chat or ask for a specific response from the model. When you interact with ChatGPT, you start the conversation with a prompt – a question, a statement, or any text conveying your intent.

The quality and specificity of your prompt often influence the usefulness and relevance of the responses you receive from ChatGPT. Providing clear and detailed prompts can result in more accurate and helpful answers.

Structure

In this chapter, we will discuss the following five ways to make better use of ChatGPT:

- Setting up ChatGPT for optimal results
- Mastering the Perfect ChatGPT Prompt
- Increasing Accuracy of ChatGPT Prompts
- Tips and tricks to advanced ChatGPT usage
- Beyond ChatGPT

Setting up ChatGPT for optimal results

The first step in getting the best out of ChatGPT is creating custom instructions, which helps avoid repeating preferences in every prompt.

Here are the steps to follow:

1. To access your custom instruction setting, click on your profile and then custom instructions, as shown in *Figure 9.1*:

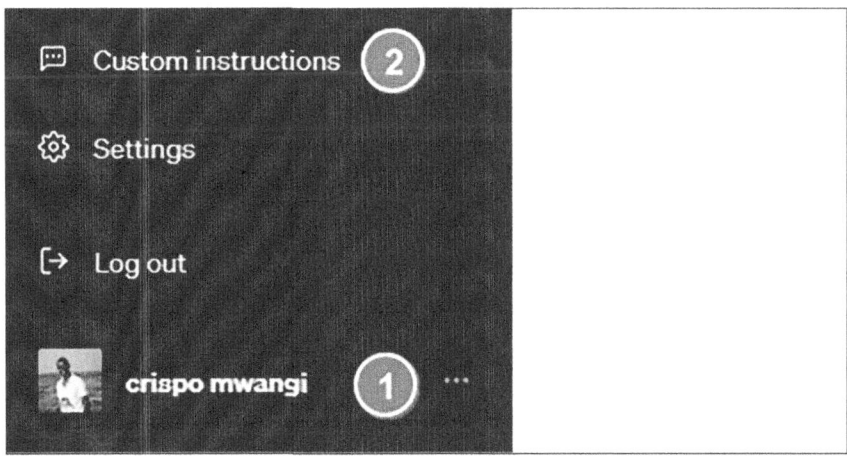

Figure 9.1: Accessing Custom Instructions

2. Tell ChatGPT something about yourself. This helps ChatGPT to give responses more relevant to your work/goals/interests. For example, see my example in *Figure 9.2*:

ChatGPT: Using ChatGPT to solve lookup issues   197

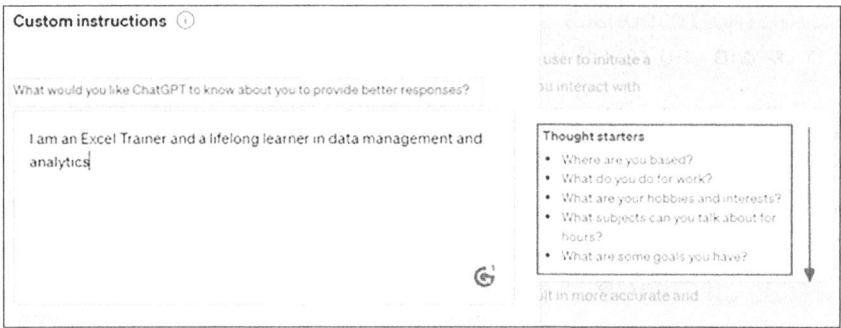

Figure 9.2: Provide ChatGPT with a context of who you are

3. The next step is to tell ChatGPT how you would like it to respond. Would the responses be formal/casual, long/short, neutral/opinionated? For example, see my example in *Figure 9.3*:

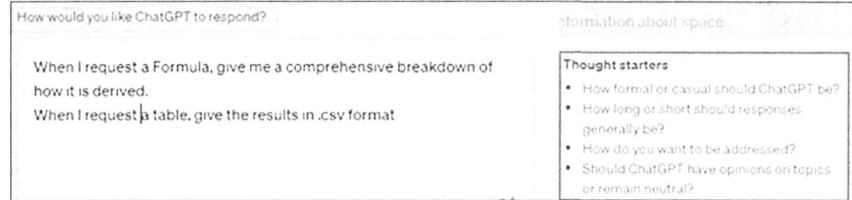

Figure 9.3: Provide ChatGPT with instructions on how you would like your responses to be

4. Save and close, and now you can start prompting. But before then, let us learn how to create the instructions.

Note:

- ChatGPT is known for proving the wrong responses from time to time. As a novice in the field, you may not notice these immediately, but you can reduce the chances of wrong responses by asking it to include the confidence levels and source URL.
- Verify the response by cross-referencing it with reliable sources (URL).

See *Figure 9.4* on configuring the confidence level and URL setting in ChatGPT.

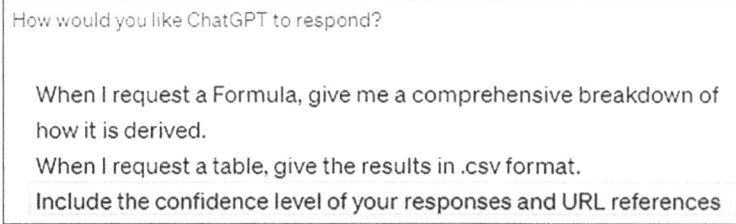

Figure 9.4: Ask for confidence level and factual URLs

Mastering the perfect ChatGPT prompt

As we have learned in the introduction, the quality and specificity of your prompt determine the usefulness and relevance of the response.

Let us now learn the four building blocks that make up a good prompt, that is, Task, Context, Exemplar, and Persona.

1. **Task**

    It is mandatory to have a task in your prompt. This is indicated by starting your prompt with an action verb.

    For example, "Generate a list of Excel inbuilt lookup functions that can use multiple criteria to get data."

    The preceding prompt will list all lookup functions and an example syntax on how you can use it to do a multiple criteria lookup.

    The only problem with the preceding prompt is that it will give only functions in Excel and not Power Query because that is the context we have given it. So, what is the context?

2. **Context**

    ChatGPT can give an infinite amount of information, which may not be what you are looking for. Therefore, you need to limit the endless possibilities.

    One way that ChatGPT limits the possibilities is by looking at the custom instructions we set up in the previous section.

    Additionally, you need to indicate the Environment as a linting factor.

    For example, if you need Power Query Lookup functions, then the prompt would be: "Generate a list of Power Query lookup functions that can use multiple criteria to get data."

    The environment can be narrowed to a specific function. For example, "Generate a list of ways the FILTER function in Excel can use multiple criteria to get data."

    Another way of fine-tuning your context is to tell ChatGPT the user's background. For example, "Write the easiest way for a novice to get data using multiple criteria in Power Query". By indicating the user is a novice, ChatGPT will limit the responses given.

3. **Exemplar**

   These are nothing more than examples in which ChatGPT can learn more about the required response. Including examples in your prompt significantly leads to more accurate results.

   For example, if you want the formula to include the plus sign (+) instead of the OR function (as we learned the **FILTER** function in *Chapter 7, FILTER: The Ultimate Lookup Function*), then the prompt would be "Write a multiple criteria **INDEX/MATCH** function using the plus sign instead of the OR function."

4. **Persona**

   This is who you want the AI to be when executing a task. Think of a famous person whose work is available online and can be easily accessed by ChatGPT. Personas provide ChatGPT with the writing style, domain, and expertise level required when responding to a prompt.

   For example, in Excel, the persona can be a famous Microsoft MVP (most valuable professional).

   Here is an example of a prompt including personas:

   Write a Power Query approximate lookup function. Write it as the famous Excel Expert Bill Jellen, aka "Mr. Excel", or Mike Girvin, aka "Excel is Fun".

   As shown in *Figure 9.5*, ChatGPT will ensure that the response is relevant and consistent with the writing styles of the persona(s) provided.

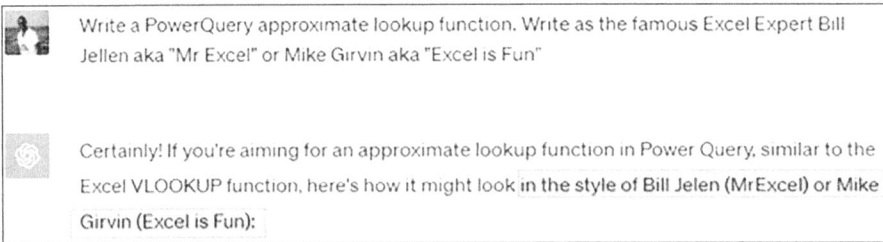

Figure 9.5: Provide ChatGPT with Persona

Note

- It is **mandatory** to have a task in your prompt.
- It is **important** to include a relevant context and exemplar.
- It is **good to have** a persona.

Increasing Accuracy of ChatGPT Prompts

As we have learned in the previous section on setting up ChatGPT, accuracy is not guaranteed, and this tends to frustrate novices who are unable to troubleshoot the responses.

Other than requesting for confidence level and URL in the responses, let us investigate four more ways to increase accuracy:

1. **Self-Critic**

    Ask ChatGPT to critique itself and optimize its response for accuracy.

    For example, in the previous section of Mastering prompt, we asked for an approximate Lookup M code using Bill Jellen or Mike Girvin's style. Assuming we are new to M Code, we want ChatGPT to help us troubleshoot the code before we use it.

    Here is a follow-up self-critic question we can ask, as shown in *Figure 9.6*:

    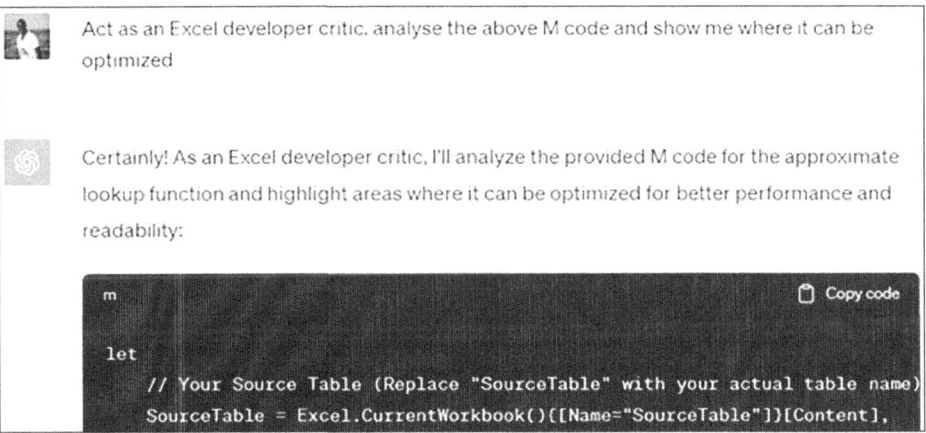

    Figure 9.6: Ask follow-up self-critic questions

2. **Crisp and Concise**

    Forcing the ChatGPT to revise the response and limit it to specific steps or words can help increase its response accuracy.

    While still working on the M Code function for approximate Lookup, we can further ask about the steps reduced to three, as shown in *Figure 9.7*:

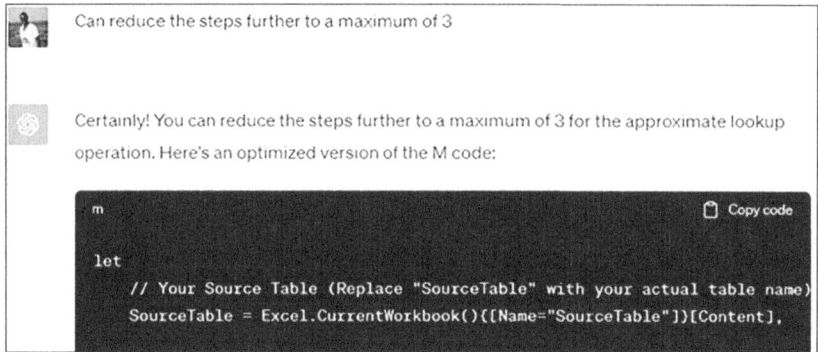

Figure 9.7: Limit the steps or words of the response

Note: The more constraint you give ChatGPT, generally the more creative the response will be. Try to add a constraint every time and test your functions to see which one will be optimized for speed and accuracy.

3. **Ask ChatGPT to self-prompt**

    One of the ways to get the best out of ChatGPT is by allowing it to self-prompt. This ensures it optimizes its prompts and leads to richer responses.

    For example, how can ChatGPT assist you in mastering the lookup functionality in Excel? (see *Figure 9.8*):

Figure 9.8: Self-prompting in ChatGPT

Note: Whether you are a student or a trainer, the above self-prompting and follow-up questions can help you create productive strategies for mastering any concept in Excel.

4. **Understand ChatGPT Limitations**

    Knowing the current weaknesses and their walk-around will drastically increase your accuracy of responses.

Here is a list of limitations:
- Understand that the accessible version of ChatGPT's knowledge is based on its training data up until the last update in September 2021. It might not have access to real-time data or recent events.
- While ChatGPT has been trained on diverse topics, it might not be as specialized as an expert in a specific field. Its responses should be verified with domain-specific sources for accuracy.
- ChatGPT suffers from "AI Hallucination", that is, the tendency to generate answers that sound correct but are factually wrong or biased.
- The free version is limited to text only. It can't view, interpret, or analyze images, charts, or non-textual data.

Tips and tricks to advanced ChatGPT usage

As we have learned so far in this chapter – Prompting is the ultimate skill you need to develop to maximize the use of ChatGPT.

Here are some of the helpful ways to advance your skills:

1. Set a period per day to learn prompting. Start from this free website: https://learnprompting.org/docs/intro

2. Start applying prompts frequently. This can be done by identifying a frequent manual task and then creating and optimizing a prompt to automate it. For example, if you are required to consolidate data from multiple worksheets daily, create a prompt that will generate an M code for you that will automate this.

3. Create a database of valuable prompts you have created or found online. Organize the prompts by the problems they will help resolve instead of functions for easy access and use. For example, store prompts under the header "How to return multiple items in a lookup" instead of "INDEX/MATCH prompts."

4. Set a daily reading period where ChatGPT is solving real-world cases. See the example in the following link:

    https://blog.enterprisedna.co/chat-gpt-for-excel-a-beginners-guide-with-examples/

ChatGPT: Using ChatGPT to solve lookup issues   203

5. Join a Newsletter to be kept up to date with the latest developments in AI. The Big Brains Newsletter is a recommended option. For more information, please visit the following link:

   https://www.bigbraindaily.com/

Beyond ChatGPT

Apart from ChatGPT, a few AI tools and why they are better alternatives are worth mentioning, as follows:

1. Bing Chat (https://www.bing.com/search?q=Bing+AI&showconv=1)

   Unlike the free version of ChatGPT 3.5, the accessible version of Bing Chat provides a way to upload a screenshot of your data and ask AI to analyze it.

   With the uploaded image, you can point to the AI your data cell references and where you want to return the results.

Figure 9.9: Uploading Screenshot of Data in Bing

2. AI Excel Bot (https://aiexcelbot.com/?anchor=features)

   This is a freemium service with an addon in your Excel workbook.

3. Formula Bot (https://formulabot.com/)

   The advantage is that it has an addon and can upload the workbook for quicker analysis. Its current limitation is that it can only execute Python Code and not Excel functions.

4. Install AI addon to Excel.

   For our case, we will install the AI-aided Formula Editor. Here are the steps:

- Go to the **Insert** tab and click **Get Add-ins**.
- Search for the **AI-aided Formula Editor** and click **Add**.

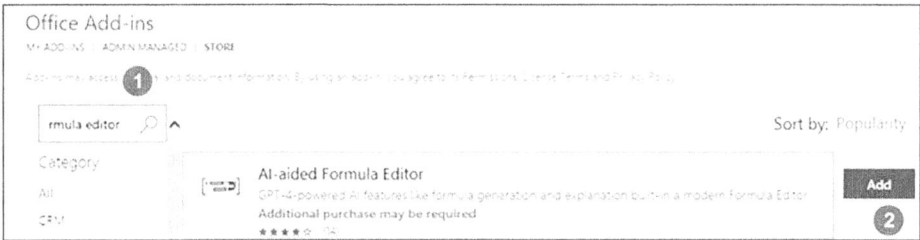

Figure 9.10: Adding AI-aided formula editor

- Sign in using your Gmail, and you are ready to start using it.
- You can upgrade to a premium subscription or use the limited free version to generate a formula or explain a formula.

Conclusion

In this chapter, we explored the integration of artificial intelligence, specifically ChatGPT, to tackle lookup challenges in Excel. Understanding the nuances of prompting and leveraging ChatGPT effectively is pivotal for accurate and tailored responses.

The chapter introduced us to ChatGPT's capabilities, emphasizing the importance of crafting precise prompts to yield accurate responses. Noteworthy mentions of built-in AI features like Flash Fill and Power Query options provided a contextual backdrop for our exploration.

Your journey with ChatGPT doesn't end here; it's only the beginning. Readers are invited to share their experiences or pose questions in Excel forums. Let this be a two-way conversation. Ask the experts to share how they have applied ChatGPT to Excel tasks and what challenges they faced. Their insights can enrich your learning and that of others in the community. Ask questions, share your successes, and let's learn from each other.

Lastly, readers are encouraged to embark on their learning odyssey. They can explore reputable online resources, join forums, or participate in tutorial sessions. The world of ChatGPT and Excel is vibrant and constantly evolving. By seeking knowledge beyond these pages, you empower yourself to navigate the ever-changing landscape of AI-driven data solutions.

Points to remember

- **Clear and Specific Prompts**: Craft precise prompts with specific instructions, using action verbs and detailing the desired outcome. Clarity in your queries ensures accurate and relevant responses from ChatGPT.
- **Provide Context**: Clearly define the context of your Excel analysis, specifying the type of data and the scope of your task. Contextual information helps ChatGPT tailor its responses to your specific data needs.
- **Engage in Dialogue**: Treat ChatGPT as a collaborative partner. Ask follow-up questions and seek clarification if the initial response is not exact. Iterative conversations guide ChatGPT toward the precise solution you're looking for.
- **Verify and Learn**: Always verify ChatGPT's responses by cross-referencing with reliable sources and conducting additional analyses in Excel. Human oversight is crucial for accuracy. Treat ChatGPT's suggestions as a starting point for your own exploration and learning.

Multiple choice questions

1. What is the significance of clear and specific prompts when using ChatGPT in Excel tasks?

    a. Clear prompts enhance ChatGPT's vocabulary

    b. Specific prompts ensure accurate and relevant responses

    c. Clear prompts are essential for ChatGPT to function offline

    d. Specific prompts are only necessary for complex Excel tasks

2. Why is providing context crucial when interacting with ChatGPT for Excel analyses?

    a. Context enhances ChatGPT's general knowledge

    b. Contextual information helps ChatGPT tailor responses to specific data needs

    c. Providing context increases ChatGPT's processing speed

    d. Context is irrelevant when using ChatGPT for Excel tasks

3. How should you approach ChatGPT's responses if they are not precisely what you need?

    a. Ignore the response and rephrase the same question

    b. Treat ChatGPT's responses as definitive answers

    c. Engage in a dialogue, ask follow-up questions, and seek clarifications

    d. Discontinue the conversation and start a new one

4. What role does human oversight play in the interaction with ChatGPT for data analysis in Excel?

    a. Human oversight is unnecessary; ChatGPT is always accurate

    b. Human oversight ensures ChatGPT's ethical behavior

    c. Human oversight is indispensable for verifying ChatGPT's responses and ensuring accuracy

    d. Human oversight only applies to beginners, not experienced users

5. Which of the following best describes the relationship between ChatGPT and the user in Excel tasks?

    a. ChatGPT is a standalone solution, requiring no user input

    b. ChatGPT's responses should be accepted without verification

    c. ChatGPT and the user engage in a collaborative partnership, with the user providing clear prompts and oversight

    d. ChatGPT can handle Excel tasks independently; user input is optional

Answers

1	b
2	b
3	c
4	c
5	c

Index

A

absolute cell reference 13, 14
advanced ChatGPT usage
  skills 202, 203
advanced filter items
  avoiding, in list 88, 89
  using, in list 87, 88
AGGREGATE function
  using, to lookup numeric data 98, 99
  working 99
AI addon
  installing, to Excel 203, 204
AI Excel Bot
  about 203
  reference link 203
AI tools
  about 203
  AI addon, installing to Excel 203, 204
  AI Excel Bot 203
  Bing Chat 203
  Formula Bot 203
AND function 10
approximate lookup 169-174
approximate match lookup
  in array 80
  working 81
array
  approximate match lookup 80

B

Bing Chat
  about 203
  reference link 203
bottom n values lookup
  about 69, 71
  working 70, 71

C

cell addresses lookup
  about 105
  working 105, 106
cell reference
  returning 122, 123
cells range reference 12
ChatGPT for optimal results
  setting up 196, 197
ChatGPT prompt
  context 198
  exemplar 199
  mastering 198
  persona 199
  task 198
ChatGPT prompt accuracy
  about 200
  crisp and concise 200, 201
  limitations 201, 202
  self-critic 200
  self-prompt 201
column deletion 117
column insertion 116, 117

D

database functions
  using, to lookup numeric data 93-95
data from bottom up lookup 118-120
data horizontally lookup 118
data to left lookup 115
data to right lookup 115
data vertically lookup 118
duplicate lookup values
  returning 131
  working 131, 132

E

exact lookup
  about 162
  implementing 163-168

exact match default 111, 112
Excel
  advanced skills 2-6
  learning 2
  used, for installing AI addon 203, 204
Excel cell referencing
  about 11
  types 12
Excel formulas 6, 7
Excel functions
  about 6, 7
  accessibility 8
  arguments 8
  built-in 8
  compatible 8
  composition 7
  results 8
Excel intersection operator
  using, for two-way lookup 89-92
Excel tables
  about 14
  creating 15, 16
  usage 16, 17, 18

F

FILTER function
  AND/OR logics, using 140-142
  bottom n item lookup 144, 145
  common item list lookup 155
  data lookup, with wildcard 146, 147
  end-of-the-month date item, returning 156, 157
  holiday data lookup, excluding 148, 149
  month data lookup 153-155
  multiple columns and rows, returning 136, 137
  multiple criteria lookup, using 140-142

multiple non-adjacent columns
    and rows, returning 138, 139
  odd/even numbers lookup 149
  repeated n items lookup 150, 151
  time value lookup 152
  top n item lookup 144, 145
  uncommon item list lookup 155
  week data lookup 153-155
  weekday data lookup 147, 148
  weekend data lookup 147, 148
  weekend data lookup,
    excluding 148, 149
  X item lookup 142-146
  year data lookup 153-155
  Y item lookup 142-146
Formula Bot
  about 203
  reference link 203
full column reference 12
full row reference 12
Fuzzy lookup 190-192

H

horizontal lookup 60

I

images look up 101-104
INDEX lookup 48-50
inner join 174

L

last blank cell lookup
  about 77
  working 78
last/first non-empty cell
  returning 129
last match lookup
  with criterion 74-76
  working 77
last negative number lookup 78, 79
last negative text lookup 78, 79

left anti-join 174
list function lookup
  using 179, 180
  working 180-182
list item lookup
  about 66
  unique value lookup 68, 69
  working 66-68
lookup functions
  classification 19
  need for 18, 19

M

MATCH lookup 50, 51
MAX function
  using, to lookup numeric
    data 99, 101
  working 100
mixed cell reference 13, 14
MONTH function 10
multiple adjacent columns
  returning 113
multiple columns
  returning 59
multiple criteria lookup 57-59
multiple non-adjacent columns
  returning 114

N

named range reference 13
nesting functions
  about 9
  complexity, resolving 10, 11
  rules 11
  working 10
no match values
  returning 124
non-adjacent columns
  returning 126, 128
  working 127

non-contiguous array lookup
  about 60, 61, 130
  working 62, 130
numeric data lookup
  with AGGREGATE function 98, 99
  with MAX function 101
  with SUMIFS function 95, 96
  with SUMPRODUCT function 97, 98

P

pivot table
  using, to lookup unique item list 106-108
Power Query
  date without holiday lookup 184, 185
  end-of-month date item, returning 188-190
  multiple columns, returning 168, 169
  multiple results, returning 168, 169
  repeated n item lookup 185-188
  weekday data lookup 182, 183
  weekend data lookup 182, 183
Power Query add-in
  installing, for Excel 2010 161
  installing, for Excel 2013 162

R

relative cell reference 13, 14
repeated item lookup
  about 81
  working 81-83
reverse-lookup multiple results
  about 55
  working 55-57
reverse-lookup single result
  about 53, 55
  working 54

S

Spill Range 113
SUMIFS function
  using, to lookup numeric data 95, 96

SUMPRODUCT function
  using, to lookup numeric data 97, 98

T

table joins lookup
  inner join 174
  left anti-join 174
  using 174-176
text length lookup
  about 64, 65
  working 65
three-way lookup
  about 52, 53, 124
  working 125, 126
top/bottom n item lookup 177-179
two-way lookup 48
types, Excel cell referencing
  absolute cell reference 13, 14
  cells range reference 12
  full column reference 12
  full row reference 12
  mixed cell reference 13, 14
  named range reference 13
  relative cell reference 13, 14

U

unique item list lookup
  with pivot table 106-108
unique value lookup
  about 68, 69
  working 69

V

VLOOKUP
  about 22
  approximate match 23, 24
VLOOKUP myths
  about 25
  case-sensitive lookup, avoiding 33, 34
  case-sensitive partial match lookup, avoiding 32, 33

columns deletion lookup,
   avoiding 28
columns insertion lookup,
   avoiding 28
horizontal lookup, avoiding 41-43
last to first search lookup,
   avoiding 36, 37
left lookup, avoiding 25
multiple criteria lookup,
   avoiding 26, 27
multiple non-contiguous arrays
   lookup, avoiding 44, 45
partial match lookup,
   avoiding 30-32
return multiple columns lookup,
   avoiding 26
return multiple non-contiguous
   columns lookup, avoiding 43, 44
return multiple results lookup,
   avoiding 34, 35
reverse lookup, avoiding 39-41
top or bottom N values lookup,
   avoiding 37-39
two-way lookup, avoiding 29

W

wildcard lookup
   integrating 120, 121
wildcards lookup
   characters 63
   using 62
   working 63, 64

X

XLOOKUP function
   working 118

Made in the USA
Monee, IL
04 June 2025